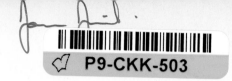
POLITICAL COMMUNICATION

POLITICAL COMMUNICATION

Craig Allen Smith
*The University of North Carolina
at Chapel Hill*

Harcourt Brace Jovanovich, Publishers
San Diego   New York   Chicago   Austin   Washington, D.C.
London   Sydney   Tokyo   Toronto

ISBN: 0-15-570709-4
Library of Congress Catalog Card Number: 89-84242

Printed in the United States of America

To Stephie,
my most vocal constituent,
as she heads
for kindergarten.

PREFACE

"Politics is talk," they say, and "they" are largely correct. Somewhere along the way our ancestors discovered how to resolve their disagreements through the use of words rather than with clubs. Gradually these ancestors moved from head-bashing to club-waving, then to verbal threats that evoked memories of the club, and, in just the last few centuries, to verbal agreements.

Without communication, politics would have no legitimate authorities, no laws, no collective identities, no legislative deliberations, no judicial interpretations, no sense of historic precedent, no diplomacy, no projected budgets, no bureaucracies, no political advertising, no speeches, no nominating conventions, no news, no public affairs programs, no press conferences, no promises, and no deceptions. Otherwise, politics would be largely the same.

How then shall we define politics, communication, and political communication? *Politics* is the process of orienting a community by reconciling diverse interests and power relationships. *Communication* is the process of negotiating understanding through interpretation and characterization of the symbolic world. *Political communication* is the process of negotiating a community orientation through the interpretation and characterization of interests, of power relationships, and of the community's role in the world. *Things get done through politics, and politics gets done through communication.*

As a field of study, political communication is a sapling; but the sapling has deep roots. Aristotle thought it necessary to write both the *Politics* and the *Rhetoric* to explain the nature of community. Centuries later, Machiavelli advised *The Prince* about power and communication. In this century, political scientist Harold Lasswell defined the study of "politics" and "communication" as necessarily interdependent: the political question "Who gets what, when, and how" implicitly demands consideration of "Who says what in which channel to whom with what effect?" (Lasswell 1948, 1958)

This book offers a framework for understanding political communication. The framework is illustrated with historical examples; but, it is not a survey of "Great Moments in Political Talk" for reasons that will become clear. A theory of political communication is advanced in Part One and subsequently employed in Part Two to explain such political phenomena as political journalism, social movements, election campaigns, congressional deliberation, the presidency, the judiciary, and foreign policy rhetoric. An Appendix covers quantitative and qualitative research methods appropriate for studying political communication so that serious students can undertake term projects that go beyond the usual library searches.

The theoretical framework advanced here emphasizes the interpretive processes through which each of us makes sense of the political world and the political communities we create to help enlighten ourselves and everyone else. It is not a book about political oratory, commercials, or debates, or about elites manipulating the minds of the helpless masses. Rather, it is a book about people who, in the course of their otherwise busy lives try to govern one of the most powerful and influential nations the world has ever seen.

Our political leaders are chosen by us and their records reflect our priorities. They try to deliver what we say we want, even if we do not really like it when we get it; and they justify what they do in terms of our requests. Only when political officials believe that their constituents can both judge complex policy questions and see through smokescreens will the quality of political communication improve. The framers of the Constitution created a system of separate national institutions with shared powers. This system is balanced against an assortment of state governments whose powers are similarly shared. And, all of this is bound together with the notion of popular sovereignty. This book was written to improve the nature of political communication in America by sharpening our faculties for understanding it.

There are four underlying theoretical propositions to this book:

1. Each of us understands the world through our *personal interpretive processes*, which include motivating, symbolizing, preferencing, and reasoning.
2. Our appraisals of the world lead us toward relationships with others. Among these relationships are political communities built on *social interpretive structures*. These social structures evolve as a result of the following: shared motivating processes

produce power, shared symbolizing produces language, shared preferencing produces ideology, and shared reasoning produces logic.

3. Each political community struggles for the right to define the world for others, and that temporarily dominant groups define and distribute resources and sanctions.

4. Clues to the evolutionary political processes, their communities, and their progress can be found in political messages and in the differential reactions of audiences.

These theoretical propositions are grounded in twentieth-century American social science literature. There will be time to synthesize individual research reports later. The pressing need right now, I believe, is for a theoretical framework that synthesizes the ideas of pioneers like Abraham Maslow, Milton Rokeach, Kenneth Burke, Paul Lazarsfeld, William Schutz, James MacGregor Burns, Victor Turner, Marshall McLuhan, and Richard Neustadt with those of people like Ernest Bormann, Charles Stewart, Dan Nimmo, David Zarefsky, Roderick Hart, Theodore Windt, Jeffrey Tulis, Kathleen Jamieson, and many others.

The book's orientation toward interpreted reality means that it will draw upon the political lessons of our culture. This includes, of course, both purposefully political acts like the Civil War, the Nixon–Kennedy Debates, and the 1988 presidential campaign, as well as unintentionally political acts like the Three Mile Island nuclear accident. But it also includes political lessons from the popular culture at large, including fictional depictions of history, heroes, values, political processes, and our adversaries. This is critically important in contemporary America when our accepted realities are a composite of real and fictional depictions, as when viewers watched "real" Democratic presidential candidate Bruce Babbitt and a "fictional" HBO candidate called Tanner stroll through a Washington park comparing their 1988 presidential campaigns. Politics *is* talk, but is talk communication? That will be the subject of Part One.

References

Lasswell, Harold Dwight. 1948. The act of communication. In *The communication of ideas*, ed. by Lyman Bryson. New York: Institute for Religious and Social Studies, pp. 37–51.

——. 1958. *Politics: Who gets what, when, how.* New York: Meridian Books.

Machiavelli, Niccolo. 1935. *The Prince*, trans. by Luigi Ricci. New York: World Literature, New American Library.

Acknowledgments

Someone once said that many of Jimmy Carter's troubles as president stemmed from his tendency to thank the people whose advice he actually took. Undaunted by his example, I will do the same.

First, there were the professors whose thinking and teaching influenced the mind behind this book: Roderick Hart, Charles Redding, Hank Ewbank and, most particularly, Charles J. Stewart. The positions developed in this book could not have been developed without the influence of these people.

Second, there were the students and faculty who comprised the Department of Speech-Communication at the University of North Carolina during the 1980s. It has been an honor and a privilege to work side by side with the likes of Lawrence Rosenfeld, Beverly Whitaker Long and all the rest. Students like Amy Kittner, JoLee Credle, Angela Watkins, Darren Carrino, Wayne Goodwin, and Stephanie Sedberry have made teaching fun and exciting on the good days and better than it might have been on the others.

Third, there were the people who worked to bring this particular project to fruition. Ted Windt of the University of Pittsburgh, and Kathie Turner of Tulane University provided the kind of helpful criticism that requires and enhances enduring friendships and mutual respect. Robert Ivie of Texas A&M University and Cathy Hennen of Auburn University contributed important suggestions. Ron Grant compiled the index quickly and thoroughly. Most important, though, is Marlane Agriesti Miriello who materialized on my office doorstep one morning, ready to talk about this project. Without her interest and professionalism, this book would not have been written.

Finally, I would like to thank my patient family. Stephie and Debbie put up with postponed activities, some abridged book readings, and an unnecessarily terse rebuke or two. And Kathy, though she need not have done so, curtailed her other activities to provide me with writing time. She also pretended that my daily assurance that "the next chapter will be quicker" was a reasonable fantasy.

TABLE OF CONTENTS

POLITICAL COMMUNICATION

Part 1
A THEORY OF POLITICAL COMMUNICATION

You communicate to cope with the world. Through communication you establish your personal identity, establish relationships, influence behavior, and interpret things and actions. In a world of people, you could neither manage nor monitor influence in your social relationships without communication.

Politicians spend so much time "talking" rather than "acting," precisely because *talk is action*. Especially in the political realm, we communicate with others to cope better with them, with our differences, and with the world around us. Murray Edelman suggested that politics is essentially a spectator sport in which you root for "your side" even if you lack a direct interest in the contest or a clear grasp of the teams (1964). In a similar vein, Dan Nimmo and James Combs noted the melodramatic quality of political news as continuing episodes of moral conflict (1983).

Political communication is not only government communication. When you watch the news, read a political bumper sticker, laugh at a political wisecrack, reflect on conflicting political arguments, or denounce something as unfair, you engage in political communication. To understand why this is so, you first need to understand the nature of human communication. Only then can you knowledgeably turn to the uses of communication in political activity.

Paradigms in Communication

People have been trying to understand human communication for centuries, with varying results. We have used, and largely discarded,

1

three views of communication. Each view, or *paradigm*, framed theorizing and research for many years and, therefore, influenced conceptions of political communication (Kuhn 1970).

Many people assumed that human communication worked like a machine. This *mechanistic paradigm* relied on a simple stimulus-response notion of cause. It assumed that when A spoke, B understood and agreed (Fisher 1978). This paradigm was sometimes called the "bullet model" (or "hypodermic model") because it assumed that speakers shot messages at targets or injected information into their listeners' minds. This paradigm provided a warehouse of misleading metaphors: sender, receiver, encoding and decoding, channel, communication breakdowns, the "same wavelength," feedback, target audience, and message. Although this paradigm works intuitively, it could never adequately explain why different individuals respond differently to the same message.

Theorists first modified the mechanistic paradigm to account for *individual differences*, such as personality, beliefs, values, and attitudes. If we could psychoanalyze an audience, they theorized, communication could still be studied mechanistically. This revision produced both an escape clause for mechanistic theory (experiments failed because of undiscovered differences among listeners) and an avalanche of psychological attitude-change studies.

Indeed, the psychological research led some theorists to conclude that the mechanistic assumptions were unnecessary. If mechanistic theory required knowledge of countless psychological variables, they reasoned, it would be better to conceive of communication as individuals creating meaning from the available stimuli. The *intrapersonal paradigm* held that communication was an intrapersonal process; whether people heard news from source A, B, or C, or experienced it firsthand, they would filter it through their personality type, values, knowledge, beliefs, and attitudes to render it meaningful (Fisher 1978).

The intrapersonal paradigm required the development of attitude surveys and statistical techniques to measure people's thoughts. But it assumed that (1) questionnaire responses accurately reflect thoughts and feelings and that (2) thoughts and feelings are consistent across time, situations, and relationships. Communication studies employing these techniques therefore proved problematic.

One problem with both the mechanistic and intrapersonal paradigms surfaced in a 1940 election survey in Erie County, Pennsylvania. Columbia University researchers found midway through the campaign that people conversed with their neighbors and coworkers. *The People's Choice* (Lazarsfeld, Berelson, and Gaudet 1948) suggested that information might pass from the mass media to opinion leaders and from them to other citizens. This two-step flow of communication undercut the mechanistic sender/receiver paradigm apart from intrapersonal factors. The mechanistic and intrapersonal paradigms were challenged by a *social paradigm*, in which group affiliation and patterns of association seemed to affect communication. Unfortunately, research testing the two-step flow proved inconclusive, and researchers were compelled to suggest a four-step flow and later an "n-step flow" (Katz and Lazarsfeld 1955). They had discovered that group affiliation is related to communication, but they were able neither to predict nor to control those influences.

In short, these three paradigms contributed significantly but imperfectly to our understanding of communication. The mechanistic paradigm saw interdependent humans, but it underestimated individual differences and reference groups. The intrapersonal paradigm highlighted the role of individuality, but it underestimated both group affiliation and the interdependence of communicators. Finally, the social paradigm emphasized the role of group norms and aspirations, but it undervalued the factors leading individuals to create and sustain those groups in the first place.

Note that each paradigm reflected the state of available knowledge and research tools and stimulated the very research that eventually undermined its own assumptions. That is the nature of scientific inquiry (Kuhn 1970). Without these early studies, communication theory and research could not have advanced. The need to test our ideas should highlight the importance of conducting theoretically based research. Two related paradigms currently in vogue enable us to pull together the more useful elements of the three early paradigms.

The *Symbolic interactionist paradigm*—traced to George Herbert Mead's lectures at the University of Chicago (1934)—assumes that your behavior depends on your interpretation of your environment. That interpretation need not be "correct," it need only seem reasonable to you at the moment of action. Your interpretation of the environment evolves through communication in accordance with your access to depictions of the environment and your perception of related experiences. Throughout this process, *communication simultaneously guides, and is guided by, your interpretations of self, role, situation, other, and culture* (Wood 1984).

Because interdependent individuals anticipate and influence one another, messages are merely tokens in the negotiation of understanding. Indeed, communication simultaneously conveys relational information along with substance. Their interactions lead people to behave differently in different situations and relationships. In short, symbolic interaction holds that you use symbols and relationships to comprehend the world and your roles in it.

Systems theory is more than most people infer from the everyday use of the word "system." *Systems* are goal-seeking entities comprised of interdependent components engaging in *processes* that transform inputs into outputs. The existence and behavior of any system is profoundly influenced by its *subsystems'* performance of assigned *functions* and by its own functional role in the *suprasystem* of which it is a part. But input does not equal output because the processes actively transform their inputs. Systems are governed by the natural tendency toward disorder, known as *entropy*, and they require maintenance. As the system fights entropy and pursues its goals, it evolves into new phases; but it can evolve in any direction at any pace (a principle called *equifinality*).

Relationships are the systemic structures that shape, and are shaped by, communication processes. Unlike machines, persons are ever-changing. You establish relationships to meet your needs and, when the resulting process changes your needs, you adapt your processes and relationships. Buckminster Fuller spoke for each of us when he said, "I seem to be a verb."

Symbolic interaction and systems theory mesh rather nicely. Taken together, they suggest that goal-seeking individuals use cognitive and relational processes to interpret the world and to cope with it. Symbols, relationships, culture, role, and communication are functional necessities if the individual is to transform environmental stimuli into behavioral responses, and groups of people develop shared symbolic patterns even as shared symbolic patterns define social groups. It is only through the process of human interaction that we can form the relationships and associations that create systems. And it is in relational contexts that we engage in the process of communication to fulfill our personal and social needs. Let us now try to synthesize what we know of human communication into a theoretical framework.

Chapter 1 will explain the personal interpretive processes of motivating, symbolizing, preferencing, and reasoning. Chapter 2 will examine the process by which diverse interpreting persons create political communities and shared interpretive structures, while Chapter 3 will describe the process by which these communities compete for the right to interpret life for the others. Chapter 4 will elaborate the important adaptive function performed by rhetoric.

References

Edelman, Murray. *The Symbolic Uses of Politics*. Urbana, IL: University of Illinois Press, 1964.

Fisher, B. Aubrey. *Perspectives on Human Communication*. New York: Macmillan, 1978.

Katz, Elihu, and Paul F. Lazarsfeld. *Personal Influence: The Part Played by People in the Flow of Mass Communications*. Glencoe, IL: Free Press, 1955.

Kuhn, Thomas S. *The Structure of Scientific Revolution*. Chicago: University of Chicago Press, 1970.

Lazarsfeld, Paul F., Bernard Berelson, and Hazel Gaudet. *The People's Choice*. New York: Columbia University Press, 1948.

Mead, George Herbert. *Mind, Self, and Society*. Chicago: University of Chicago Press, 1934.

Nimmo, Dan, and James E. Combs. *Mediated Political Realities*. New York: Longman, 1983.

Wood, Julia T. *Human Communication: A Symbolic Interactionist Perspective*. New York: Holt, Rinehart and Winston, 1984.

Chapter 1
PERSONAL INTERPRETIVE PROCESSES

Each individual ultimately understands what is "real" in private, by interpreting bits and pieces of life. Political scientists Dan Nimmo and James Combs observe that

> whether a real world exists or not, the only way we can know it, grasp it, make sense of it, is through communication. Even when we are directly involved in things, we do not apprehend them directly. Instead, media of communication intervene, media in the form of language, customs, symbols, stories, and so forth. That very intervention is a process that creates and recreates (constructs and reconstructs) our realities of the moment and over the proverbial long haul. Communication does more than report, describe, explain—it creates. In this sense all realities—even those emerging out of direct firsthand experience with things—are mediated. (1983, 4)

But how do individuals create or interpret reality?

Everyone has four interdependent processes which influence their communication in very personal ways. We will refer to these as the motivating, symbolizing, preferencing, and reasoning processes. Because these processes are personal, you can serve as your own best example.

The Motivating Process

All systems seek goals, and the *motivating process* is the process through which individuals formulate their needs and goals. Let us consider psychological needs and the psychological functions of political attitudes and talk.

Basic Needs

Psychologist Abraham Maslow theorized that all humans experience five types of needs that are ordered in a pyramidlike hierarchy (1943). Most fundamental are *physiological* and survival needs, followed by the needs for *safety* and *security*, the needs for *love* and *belonging* to a significant other, and the needs for *respect* and *esteem*. At the top of Maslow's pyramid is the need for *self-actualization*—your need for personal fulfillment. Maslow's theory contends that you need to meet the most basic needs first. When deprived of a fundamental need, you immediately attempt to satisfy it, often projecting your frustrations from one sphere into another. Many psychobiographies, for example, explain political behavior through displaced personal needs (Lasswell 1948; Greenstein 1975).

William Schutz theorized that we all need *inclusion* in relationships, *control* over relationships, and *affection* (1958). The ideally social person is comfortable alone or with people, while oversocial and undersocial persons are comfortable in only one setting. The democrat is comfortable controlling or being controlled as circumstances warrant, while autocrats need to control, and abdicrats need to be controlled. The personal individual is capable of developing relationships and of sharing affection, while underpersonal people avoid affection, and overpersonal individuals go to extremes to be liked.

The personal need for social control has self-evident political implications, but the other two are less obvious. Social and oversocial people are likely to work with others in civic and political groups, in campaigns, and in government. But undersocials are unlikely to participate in political efforts and may even feel alienated from the political community and its symbols. Personal and overpersonal individuals may find in political life an arena for winning affection, while underpersonals may avoid the fracas even though they have much to contribute. The balance between your personal and interpersonal needs undergirds your political opinions and affects your political behavior.

The Functions of Political Views

What is the connection between personal and interpersonal needs and political communication? Put bluntly, you listen for what you need to hear and you hear what you need to believe. You avoid people and ideas that complicate your needs, and you engage in communication to satisfy your needs. In this sense political views perform psychological functions.

Psychologists Smith, Bruner, and White found that opinions about Russia, for example, served four psychological functions (1956). Consider how mistrust of the Soviet Union during arms control negotiations can perform four distinct psychological functions for four hypothetical citizens. One might use the Soviets to establish a unique personal identity by arguing against prevailing enthusiasm (the *expressive function*). Another person might mistrust the Russians because, mistrusting her husband, she needs a consistent rationale for trusting the previously untrustworthy (the *object appraisal function*). A third person might use mistrust of the Soviet Union to create and sustain relationships with significant others, including our first two hypothetical citizens (the *social adjustment function*). Finally, a fourth person might use mistrust to resolve inner conflicts about his own toughness, trustworthiness, or awareness of world affairs (the *externalization function*).

Notice that the point here is not whether the Russians are trustworthy or untrustworthy; decide that question for yourself. The point is, rather, that you will decide the question (1) when you are motivated to decide it and (2) on the basis of your need structure at the moment of decision.

Prior to Smith, Bruner and White's landmark research, most people had assumed that political opinions were fundamentally rational; that votes reflected an informed policy preference. But their book not only explained how you sometimes act on the basis of logically inconsistent beliefs, it explained why you often *need* to do so. Nevertheless, their research emphasized individual opinions, and their approach proved more useful for explaining known opinions than for predicting unknown positions.

Social Judgment and Ego Involvement

The *social judgment* theory of attitudes maintains that you interpret new information in terms of your existing beliefs and your personal involvement in the topic. You first decide how far the new information is from your interpretive system, and then you place it within that system—you do not coolly appraise each new bit of information and then revolutionize your world around it (Sherif, Sherif, and Nebergall 1965). Your behavior, therefore, entails not just a single anchor attitude, like "I oppose candidate Hogwash's foreign policy position," but a range of attitudes around an *anchor*.

Some attitudes fall within a *latitude of acceptance*, some within a *latitude of rejection*, and some within a *latitude of noncommitment*. Sometimes you assimilate a neutral or opposing statement within your latitude of acceptance and other times you contrast it by pushing a supportive or neutral comment off to the latitude of rejection. Indeed, you are more likely to exhibit assimilation and contrast effects when *ego-involved*—that is, when your sense of identity is deeply involved with the issue. Woodrow Wilson was unable to accept compromises that would have strengthened *his* League of Nations;

Franklin Roosevelt tried to pack the Supreme Court with supporters after they ruled portions of *his* New Deal unconstitutional; and both Lyndon Johnson and Richard Nixon took personally the opposition to *their* Vietnam War policies (a self-fulfilling prophecy). Ronald Reagan's involvement in the SDI/"Star Wars" defense system and aid to the Nicaraguan Contras also suggest the difficulty of subtle judgments when one's self-image is on the line. Similarly, your abstract and impersonal attitudes about unemployment, abortion, mandatory drug testing, hostage deals, and tax increases can change dramatically when they suddenly affect your family and friends.

In short, you approach the political world with a set of personal and relational needs. Political opinions and activities fulfill psychological functions, enabling you to restructure your needs. Fundamentally, you tend to believe what you need to believe.

The Symbolizing Process

Humans are prepared to communicate in several ways, the most fundamental being our peculiar ability to use *symbols*, or representations. These symbolic representations include words, numbers, phrases ("right to life"), myths ("The good guys always win"), images ("Honest Abe"), and rituals (nominating conventions).

Using Symbols

Kenneth Burke has observed that only humans use symbols (1966). Any animal learns that thunder signals the approach of rain, but it takes human symbolizing to understand the probability of precipitation.

It is critically important to understand that there is no inherent connection between a symbol and your meaning for it. The relationship between meaning and symbol develops through use, as you infer patterns in people's symbol usage and adopt a new word to describe a new *referent*. Routine patterns of symbol use tempt you to forget that (1) some aspects of a referent must be overlooked if you are to capture any of it in a symbol and that (2) differently motivated people will overlook different aspects of the referent, thereby (3) creating personalized symbol-referent-meaning combinations.

Your ability to use symbols is profoundly significant. First, representation enables you to conceive of absent people and things, like George Washington and World War II. This enables you to transcend the limits of time and place and, thereby, provides you with a sense of history and tradition. Second, symbolic representation enables you to share experiences with others. This sharing of experiences includes the sharing of different perspectives on the same experience, since no two people ever experience precisely the same phenomenon in precisely the same way. Third, symbolic representation allows you to identify and to label both intangible and tangible phenomena. Without symbolic representation, we could not conceive of abstractions like "freedom," "patriotism," "government," and "fairness." Fourthly, the ability to symbolize and your consequent sense of shared vicarious experience and tradition foster the development of a *culture* among those who share your symbols. This sense of culture creates a present out of the shared history and prescribes a future based on the past and present. Finally, your ability to symbolize leads you to develop *cognitive processes* for organizing and using your symbols. These cognitive and perceptual processes, in turn, enable you to identify similarities and differences among phenomena, people, objectives, and motives. Let us, therefore, consider the personal subsystems through which you use these symbols.

Constructivism

A school of thought known as *constructivism* maintains that you deal with the world through *interpretive schemes* that channel your symbolizing and through *strategies* for converting your symbols into behavior.

Constructivists argue that the key to understanding how humans interpret their environment is the *personal construct system* (Delia, O'Keefe, and O'Keefe 1982). Simply, a *personal construct* is any bipolar dimension that you use to interpret, to evaluate, or to predict. For example, you might use honesty/dishonesty and liberal/conservative as constructs for interpreting, evaluating, and predicting the behavior of politicians. But even people who employ the same personal constructs can value them differently, as one prefers the conservative pole and another the liberal. Moreover, people who employ identical constructs identically valued will *integrate* or structure them differently; as one person emphasizes integrity over ideology, and another emphasizes ideology over integrity.

Personal construct systems vary in *differentiation*, as the raw number of constructs in the system increase the potential for subtle distinctions. A Democrat/Republican construct system, for example, is less differentiated than one that identifies liberal, moderate, and conservative types of Democrats and Republicans. Finally, your personal construct system may be more *articulated* than another's in the sense that its constructs are carefully refined and usefully abstract.

Presidents Ford and Carter tried to deal with the aftermath of Vietnam by refining the constructs associated with draft evaders into "pardons," "earned pardons," and "amnesty."

Your personal construct systems, then, provide you with the means to interpret, to evaluate, and to predict the flow of events. It is through these personal constructs that you make your experiences meaningful. William E. Connolly, following philospher Martin Heidegger's ideas on language, writes that

> for things to be, they must be brought into a web of articulations which gives them boundaries, specificity, complexity; but any particular web of discourse fixes things in particular ways and closes out other possible modes of being. (Connolly 1987, 145)

Your vocabulary permits understanding, in part, by closing off some avenues toward understanding. You may remember, for example, how reporters struggled to find a label for the "sale of American arms through Israel to Iran in exchange for the release of hostages with the profits diverted to the Nicaraguan Contras." Bizarre possibilities like "Irangate," "Contragate," and "Iranloo" were symbolic tags that would have filed the event under "-gate" for political scandal or "-loo" for disastrous defeat. The public generally chose to file it as the Iran/Contra "affair" and move ahead. Might a catchier scandal label have heightened public concern? Might heightened concern have rendered one of the scandal labels more popular? The interdependence of needs and symbolic categories suggests the possibility.

Election studies by David Swanson and his colleagues suggest the importance of the constructivists' contribution. Their studies of voters suggest a difference between *political specialists*—who differentiate among candidates on the basis of specifically political constructs like issues, record, party, and campaign style—and *political nonspecialists*—who differentiate among candidates on the basis of very general, nonpolitical constructs like attractiveness, sincerity, and empathy. They also discovered differences between *politically complex perceivers*, whose highly differentiated interpretive systems permit them to draw subtle distinctions, and *politically noncomplex perceivers*, who draw on a few rudimentary constructs to reach gross judgments (Swanson 1981). Since there is as yet no evidence linking political specialism with political complexity, it seems that campaigns are perceived by at least four types of interpretive systems: complex and politically specialized, noncomplex but specialized, noncomplex and politically nonspecialized, and complex but nonspecialized. Clearly, these four types of people can be expected to interpret differently the same political message in ways unrelated to their partisanship, interest, or issue orientation.

Whatever their content or structure, personal construct systems are highly functional. You need your construct system to order the wealth of symbols available to you, and you use your individual construct system as long as it works for you. Moreover, your personal and social needs motivate you to revise or to protect your construct systems from challenge.

Beliefs and Perceptions

The symbolizing process structures and interprets the world, producing a set of *perceptions.* You draw on memories from childhood as well as your dreams. You may be utterly confident in these images and *believe* them, or you may recognize them as ideals. In either case, you use these images as points of comparison and evaluation, as when some people complained that Presidents Ford and Carter did not "seem like presidents."

Increasingly complex symbolic systems permit increasingly complex beliefs since both permit careful shadings. Likewise, the more complex your beliefs are, the greater your need is for a similarly complex vocabulary. Thus, your need to verbalize complex beliefs creates either the need for an appropriate vocabulary or the need to simplify your beliefs. Somehow you must choose between these conflicting needs.

The Preferencing Process

Let us coin the term *preferencing* to refer to the process of establishing priorities among needs, beliefs, reasons, and behavior. Preferencing encompasses not only the process of preferring one talk show over another, for example, but the creation of your personal basis for preferring. Notice that you have preferences among both your likes and your dislikes. For example, an election simply measures your preference among the nominees; it neither measures the intensity nor the direction of that preference.

You draw on three sorts of needs and beliefs to establish your preferences: values, authorities, and derivations. Each of these emerges from, and influences, your motivating and symbolizing processes.

Values

Values are enduring standards by which you evaluate specific beliefs, conditions, and phenomena (Rokeach 1969, 1973). Two questions demand attention when studying values: What do you value? and How do you value it? The "what" refers to your selection of standards such as morality, patriotism, beauty, and material comfort. "How" you value requires comparative analysis. Generally, you probably value morality, peace, and patriotism but find few policies that simultaneously satisfy all three values. Instead, you find trade-offs: policy A is moral but risks war, while policy B is patriotic but morally indefensible. You therefore develop *value priorities* to answer the question "Do I prefer value A or value B?" Your complex arrangement of value priorities is referred to as your *value system.*

Since they are embedded in your motivating and symbolizing processes, your individual value system is stable but not static. You see some values as especially pertinent in particular situations or relationships. This is particularly relevant when you borrow values from personal relationships to evaluate public behavior. President Reagan nurtured support for his early economic policies by describing government spending in terms of the household budget, thereby tapping into a different set of value priorities.

The notion of value systems has been challenged by some writers who argue that it overestimates your rational consideration of the thousands of choices you face every day. Our perspective acknowledges routine, virtually reflexive choices. The point here is that your needs and symbols affect your value priorities which affect those preferences that *are* considered rationally and that then spill over to affect your routines, habits, and, therefore, less considered choices. One such shortcut to preferencing is your choice of preferred authorities.

Authorities

The world is too complex for you to personally verify every bit of information. Sooner or later you must accept or reject information because of its source. Your *authorities* are the information sources that you incorporate into your personal preferencing and the bases of their authority.

Psychologists have found that your personality governs your general reliance on authorities. *Authoritarianism* refers to a high score on the California F (for Fascism) Test: right-wing authoritarians score high; left-wing authoritarians (like communists) score low; and nonauthoritarians score in the middle (Adorno 1950). Authoritarianism is not, nor was it ever intended to be, a content-free measure of your dependence on authorities.

Milton Rokeach developed the D (for Dogmatism) Scale as a content-free measure of people's reliance on authority, defined as your ability to differentiate between information and its source (1960). A high score on the D Scale indicates a personality that cannot consider information apart from its source and, thus, suggests a heavy reliance on authorities; while a low score suggests a personality type that habitually considers the source and message as independent.

Authoritarianism and dogmatism directly relate to both politics and communication. *Authority-reliant* people are likely to accept uncritically information and direction from authorities, even when those authorities are misguided. *Authority-resistant* people are likely to ignore authoritative information and direction, even when it is wise and prudent. Moreover, authority-reliants may have difficulty persuading people who balk at an initial command (and authority-resistants will balk), while authority-resistants may have difficulty exercising necessary and legitimate authority (and authority-reliants will require its exercise). You fall somewhere on a continuum that ranges from authority-reliant to authority-resistant. Because most people fall somewhere in between, you should beware of the medical student's tendency to see symptoms in everyone.

Whatever your personal authority dependence, you cast as your authorities those sources that fit your value priorities, and you cast them along a continuum. Although we tend to think of "good" authorities, most Americans have regularly used detested authorities such as Adolf Hitler, Karl Marx, Ayatollah Khomeini, and the Ku Klux Klan. They serve you as authorities because they are sources of information whose reputations influence your acceptance or rejection of specific information.

Consider a few examples of political authority. Which news media articulate and apply your personal value priorities regarding political news: the *Daily Worker*, the *New York Daily News*, the *New York Times*, the *Chicago Tribune*, the *Atlanta Constitution*, the *Wall Street Journal*, *USA Today*, C-Span, CNN, CBS, NBC, ABC, the *National Enquirer*, the *Thunderbolt*, or perhaps your local newspaper? Which politicians articulate your personal value priorities regarding political leadership: Jesse Helms, Ronald Reagan, George Bush, Robert Dole, Elizabeth Dole, Sam Nunn, Andrew Young, Al Gore, Richard Gephardt, Michael Dukakis, Geraldine Ferraro, Gary Hart, or perhaps a local person? Which clerics articulate and apply your value priorities regarding politics and moral considerations: the Ayatollah Khomeini, Jerry Falwell, Billy Graham, Jesse Jackson, Daniel Berrigan, Meier Kahane, or your local clergy? These questions and choices merely scratch the surface for purposes of illustration. The odds are that you found in each list a set of heroes, a set of villians, and a set of unknowns or nonauthorities. Your choice of authorities assimilated and contrasted your perceptions of the various names to match your needs, your available symbolic framework, and your value priorities.

Derivations

Derivations are the preferences and the bases for preferring that hinge on your authorities. Do you like President Bush because of his "flexible freeze" approach to spending? Do you like the "flexible freeze" because President Bush supports it? Or does your support of President Bush and his policies hinge on the judgment of other authorities (Evans and Novak perhaps, or the op-ed page of the *New York Times*)?

Political preferences are fluid, and you can think of your political views as drops of water that instantly combine to create a body of water that is indivisible into its original drops. Values are the depths, authorities the steady currents, and derivations are much of the rest. Against the background environmental processes of evaporation and precipitation we can try to shape and structure the body of water ourselves. But every contact with the water or its container creates ripples that further change it.

Rippling characterizes the preferencing process. A change in your values ripples through your authorities and derivations in ways that depend on the structure you created. A change in your authorities splashes back to your underlying values and ripples through your derivations. And a change in your derivations ripples through your authorities and values. The extent of the rippling depends on the extent of the change and its functional importance: Few ripples reach the deep values. Derivations flow into the currents left by changed values and authorities. Changing your derivations (1) protects your values and authorities from change and, thereby, (2) keeps your rippling from splashing over into your other preferencing waters.

The preferencing process consists of both your set of preferences and your personal framework for preferring: your values, your authorities, and your derived preferences. Your preferences are fluid, and changes constantly ripple through them. Somehow, you must make sense of all this rippling, and that leads us to the reasoning process.

The Reasoning Process

The reasoning process is your personal method for reconciling symbols, preferences, and motives into a personally meaningful conception of reality. It is the unavoidable practice of "making sense" of things. You try to be rational and consistent when you pause to think, but only rarely do you truly pause. Most of the time you muddle through, relying on habit and routine as your guides along the path of least resistance.

Making Sense

Every choice makes sense to the chooser at the moment of decision. For example, let us say you made a decision. Your decision may not have made sense to observers, and, later, it may not have even made sense to you. But if anything else had seemed more reasonable at the moment of choice, you would have chosen it. This is not to say that your choice was wise, logical, or prudent, but it "made sense" to you given your particular complex of needs, symbols, and preferences and a particular range of alternatives.

Many seemingly unwise decisions make sense to the chooser at the moment of choice. Why would President Wilson not compromise with Senate moderates so that we could join his League of Nations? Why would President Hoover not admit the necessity of a temporary safety net during the Great Depression? Why would President Carter attempt a military rescue of the hostages after repeatedly denouncing such a mission as unwise? How could Colonel Oliver North consider the Iran-Contra plan a "neat idea" long after it had undermined the Reagan administration? How could Gary Hart invite reporters to monitor his personal life? Somehow, each choice made sense to the person at the time of choice.

The key to understanding political behavior is understanding the reasoning through which a behavioral choice makes sense. At this level, we need to cut through concerns about how people *should* reason and concentrate on how they *do* reason.

Aristotle observed that people reason mostly through a logical form he called the *enthymeme*. An enthymeme is (1) built on probability rather than certainty and (2) requires audience completion. For example, the statement "My opponent is a politician, and that's reason enough to oppose her" requires the audience to fill in the general premise that politicians are crooked or tricky. The enthymeme, therefore, joins the speaker and audience in a cooperative reasoning endeavor. People with similar motivating, symbolizing, and preferencing processes can complete each other's logical puzzles more easily than can people with dissimilar processes.

Stephen Toulmin developed a view of argument that advanced Aristotle's conception of the enthymeme (1964). Toulmin's model begins with the argument's *claim*—its point or conclusion. If the claim is challenged, the arguer supports it with *data*, which are themselves subject to challenge. The connection between data and claim is called the *warrant*, and it is supported by *backing*. The listener may accept or challenge any element: claim, data, warrant, or backing. Toulmin also identified *qualifiers* like "usually" and *reservations* about the claim like "except when" or "unless."

The thrust of Toulmin's theory is that reasoning is based on proof sufficient for the reasoner. Of course, your acceptance or rejection of claim, warrant, or data will ripple through past and future arguments. You may accept an inaccurate, invalid argument compatible with your motivating, symbolizing, and preferencing processes and you may reject an accurate and valid argument incompatible with those processes. The key to reasoning is therefore your ability to supply the data, warrant, and backing necessary for you to process the claim and its ripples.

Narrative Rationality

Historian David Carr writes that, "Human existence and action . . . consist not in overcoming time, not in escaping or arresting its flow, but in shaping and forming it" (1986). People experience time through narrative, or stories. Carr maintains that you live in a present that embodies your remembered past and that you act in expectation of a future that is a projection of your past and present. In short, you cast yourself in an unfolding story and act it out. But because you choose the appropriate story and your role in it, you can switch stories whenever your motivating, symbolizing, and preferencing processes require.

Philosopher Howard Kamler explains that stories perform five important psychological functions that help you to know and protect what you know from counterargument. Stories let you believe what you need to believe by defining what constitutes relevant evidence and what does not. Stories cover gaps in your understanding by explaining the otherwise unexplainable. Stories give structure to your life by contextualizing ambiguous episodes. Stories protect your beliefs with implicit defense mechanisms that spare the story and its evidence when it grows irrelevant. And finally, Kamler writes, stories enable you to communicate, because you project your private stories onto public events and you adopt public stories like history and cultural myths (Kamler 1983).

You search for understanding by imposing narrative structure on events. From a motivational perspective, you need to believe that life makes sense. Life is difficult enough without believing that every act or event occurs at random. This leads you to adopt story lines that explain events in ways compatible with your motivating, symbolizing, and preferencing processes. Each narrative structures the past, present, and future and prescribes a preferred course of conduct from a particular vantage point. Each narrative has an author, a narrator, a protagonist, and an audience; and you strive to narrate your own life, although authority-reliants may strive to find a good narrator.

The narrator's vantage point—in time, intellect, wisdom, values, and character—positions the narrative for the audience. *Reader-narrator identification* is central. When you identify with a narrator you step into her story, enact it, and retain the experience. Stories inviting identification encourage you to assimilate the narrator's data and warrants, thereby encouraging agreement. Stories discouraging identification encourage you to contrast the narrator's data and warrants, thereby encouraging disagreement—a process known as *polarization.*

The narrator's image and appeal are important to narrative logic, because an ill-defined or unconvincing narrator can be ignored, and a repelled audience may use the story for its opposite lesson. Thus, identification overpowers logical rigor (Fisher 1987). Consider the following reconstruction of a postspeech exchange between columnist George Will and a questioner:

> QUESTIONER: With the American people spending sixty cents of every dollar on defense . . .
>
> WILL (*softly*): Your figure is wildly erroneous.
>
> QUESTIONER: No it isn't. You'd better check your figures.
>
> WILL: Oh, I check that one frequently and it is nothing like sixty percent.
>
> QUESTIONER: Well, I don't want to argue about figures . . .
>
> WILL: Oh, but I do. They are important. (Will 1988)

The questioner wanted to use data as a springboard toward credibility and a presumably disarming question. By challenging the figure, Will transformed it from data to claim and undermined the questioner's credibility. Then he trumped the questioner's implied warrant that "Your time is valuable" with an explicit warrant presumably shared by those attending his lecture at the National Archives: "[Figures] are important." Signs of audience identification with Will rippled through the audience, and when the question finally surfaced, it was but a harmless interruption by a careless and ill-informed person. Notice that all of this transpired before anyone could check the actual figure!

Charles Dickens's *Christmas Carol* illustrates both the form and the force of narrative logic. Dickens devised a narrative in which a despicable protagonist is haunted by Christmas spirits who reacquaint him with his past, present, and future. The spirits help Scrooge to see a happier past, an unseen present, and an unwanted future. He avoids the unwanted future by reweaving threads from his forgotten past with the opportunities of the unseen present. But you are not led to identify with Scrooge lest you rationalize his behavior. Instead, you view Scrooge's transformation from the perspective of his nice, loving, forgiving, and all-around Christmassy nephew—the very perspective you are intended to adopt as a universal guide to life.

Fisher writes that each narrative enacts a set of values and that these enacted values govern the narrative's audience appeal. You judge each narrative by its *narrative coherence* (Does the story work as a story?) and by its *narrative fidelity* (Does the story fit your motivating, symbolizing, and preferencing processes?). Fisher argues that you look for *good reasons*—stories that are (1) true and consistent with what you know and what you value, (2) appropriate to whatever decision is pending, (3) promising in effects for yourself and others, and (4) consistent with what you believe is an ideal basis for conduct (1987).

This view of communication hinges less on the rules of formal logic that prove claims than on the psychological power of the motivating process to steer you toward the acceptance of safe and familiar claims. Reasoning is the integration of information into a coherent, relevant, compatible, promising, and proper narrative form.

The demands of narrative logic frequently require you to borrow familiar story lines to make sense of unfamiliar events. Like "fungible assets" that can be transferred from one budget category to another, "fungible narratives" can be transferred to new settings. Candidates borrow the narratives of war, crusade, and sport to describe their campaigns as fierce contests of high moral purpose; while journalists prefer soap opera, vaudeville, or theater of the absurd narratives to capture the tawdry triviality of campaign hoopla.

Nimmo and Combs argue that you get your accounts of political realities from mass media organizations that live and breathe according to the *melodramatic imperative* that moral justice is at the core of every story (1983). It is a narrative logic that provokes anxiety and suspense as good guys fight bad guys day after day with otherwise incredible plot twists. Through the kind of logic that enabled Bobby Ewing to simply show up alive after being dead for 26 episodes, a vice presidential candidate is publicly disgraced for serving in the National Guard.

On matters of importance, like politics, you try to use the rules of inductive and deductive logic, but it takes a concerted effort to do so. Narrative logic coordinates your needs, your symbolic categories and perceptions, and your values and authorities so that you can, literally, "make sense" from all sensory stimuli.

Summary

Your world is more than a molecular or physical habitat. The molecular world matters, of course. But thanks to your human ability to reason symbolically, you rarely need to experience the physical world's dangers to modify your behavior. You prepare for the forecasted weather to avoid frostbite and you slow down for warning signs to avoid accidents.

You are able to experience the world both directly and vicariously because you symbolize. Your personal needs for survival, security, belonging, esteem, and fulfillment and for inclusion, affection, and control influence your unique symbolic world. In accordance with your needs, you develop a unique symbolic inventory by creating categories, by cataloging perceptions, and by establishing values, authorities, preferences, and narrative forms for sorting them all out. Your personal interpretive processing consists of four discernible subprocesses: motivating, symbolizing, preferencing, and reasoning.

You cope with life by interpreting new developments through your personal interpretive process. It is the essence of you, as a unique person. So, whenever possible, you interpret the world through your existing interpretive system. You trust the adequacy of your motives, your symbolic categories and beliefs, your preferences, and your reasoning rather than their challengers. New things make sense to you when they fit your familiar interpretive processes.

But sometimes your familiar categories and logic disappoint you. You are disoriented until you can adapt your personal interpretive processes to the new world out there. You may reexamine your needs, reconstitute your symbolic inventory, revise your preferences, or borrow a new narrative logic. You then approach the world armed with a new and improved interpretive process.

This chapter dealt with political communication at the personal level. It should be clear by now that studying political communication by focusing only on political messages overlooks the process by which those messages become meaningful to you. With this personal interpretive process in mind, let us now consider how multiple individuals engage each other to create political communities.

References

Adorno, Theodor W., Else Frenkel-Brunswick, Daniel J. Levinson, and R. Nevitt Sanford. *The Authoritarian Personality*. New York: W. W. Norton, 1950.

Aristotle. *Rhetoric.* Translated by W. Rhys Roberts. New York: Oxford University Press, 1924.

Burke, Kenneth. *Language as Symbolic Action.* Berkeley: University of California Press, 1966.

Carr, David. *Time, Narrative, and History.* Bloomington: Indiana University Press, 1986.

Connolly, William E. *Politics and Ambiguity.* Madison, WI: University of Wisconsin Press, 1987.

Delia, Jesse G., Barbara O'Keefe, and Daniel J. O'Keefe. The Constructivist Approach to Communication." *In Human Communication Theory: Comparative Essays,* edited by Frank E. X. Dance. New York: Harper and Row, 1982.

Fisher, Walter R. *Human Communication as Narration: Toward a Philosophy of Reason, Values, and Action.* Columbia: University of South Carolina Press, 1987.

Greenstein, Fred I. *Personality and Politics: Problems of Evidence, Inference, and Conceptualization.* New York: W. W. Norton, 1975.

Kamler, Howard. *Communication: Sharing Our Stories of Experience.* Seattle: Psychological Press, 1983.

Lasswell, Harold Dwight. *Power and Personality.* New York: W. W. Norton, 1948.

Maslow, Abraham. "A Theory of Human Motivation. *Psychological Review* 50 (July 1943): 370–96.

Nimmo, Dan, and James E. Combs. *Mediated Political Realities.* New York: Longman, 1983.

Rokeach, Milton. *Beliefs, Attitudes, and Values: A Theory of Organization and Change.* San Francisco: Jossey-Bass, 1969.

———. *The Nature of Human Values.* New York: Free Press, 1973.

———. *The Open- and Closed-Mind.* New York: Basic Books, 1960.

Schutz, William. *FIRO: A Three Dimensional Theory of Interpersonal Behavior.* New York: Rinehart, 1958.

Sherif, Muzafer, Carolyn Sherif, and Roger Nebergall. *Attitude and Attitude Change: The Social Judgment-Ego Involvement Approach.* Philadelphia: W. B. Saunders, 1965.

Smith, M. Brewster, Jerome S. Bruner, and Robert W. White. *Opinions and Personality.* New York: John Wiley and Sons, 1956.

Swanson, David L. "Constructivist Approach." In *Handbook of Political Communication,* edited by Dan D. Nimmo and Keith R. Sanders. Beverly Hills: Sage Publications, 1981.

Toulmin, Stephen. *The Uses of Argument.* Cambridge: Cambridge University Press, 1964.

Will, George. Address at the National Archives. Televised by C-SPAN. Washington, D.C., 1988.

Chapter 2
POLITICAL COMMUNITY AND SHARED INTERPRETIVE STRUCTURES

Communication occurs when two or more persons (as described in Chapter 1) try to make sense of one another's behavior through their respective personal interpretive processes. Personal motivating processes move each to engage (or ignore) the other; personal symbolizing processes enable each to categorize and to interpret the other; personal preferencing processes enable each to embrace (or refute) claims of similarity; and personal reasoning processes provide each with a recipe for coherence. We try to make sense of others' behavior while self-consciously managing our own image.

When two such persons feel a momentary sense of recognition, unity, consubstantiality, or "usness," they experience what anthropologist Victor Turner calls *communitas,* which can progress through three stages. At first there is *spontaneous communitas*, when compatible people

> obtain a flash of lucid mutual understanding . . . when they feel that all problems, not just their problems, could be resolved, whether emotional or cognitive, if only the group (which is felt in the first person) as "essentially us" could sustain [itself]. (Turner 1982, 48)

The experience of communitas is so rewarding that we try to extend it as a shared existence by developing *ideological communitas* of shared language and culture. Then, we may try to make the feeling permanent by institutionalizing status, roles, rules, rituals, and other structures of *normative communitas.* But because the rewarding, almost magical, moment of communitas is a spontaneous feeling it cannot be fully preserved through structure, and, eventually, a moment of spontaneous communitas occurs with a different person.

Thus, communities develop and decay through communication in search of communitas.

Clearly, coordination is central to meaningful communication, and the coordination of ever-changing persons is no easy task. We tend to save for future use the logistical plans that effectively coordinate a set of persons in a given situation. These become our *social interpretive structures*, and we use them to manage our relational systems by easing the process of coordination. In the political sphere, we create *political communities* that embody our shared motivating, symbolizing, preferencing, and reasoning.

This chapter will examine the social interpretive structures we create to ease our political communication. As we coordinate our motivating processes we create *power.* As we coordinate our symbolizing we construct a shared *language.* As we coordinate our preferencing we construct a shared *ideology.* And as we coordinate our reasoning we construct a shared *logic.* Power, language, ideology, and logic interact to create a *political subculture*, and the people who share that subculture—that is, the people who interpret their worlds through shared power, shared language, shared ideology, and shared logic—constitute an interpretive community, even if they do not personally know one another.

An interpretive community that similarly interprets political events constitutes a *political community*. Democrats and Republicans, blacks and whites, rich and poor, women and men, young and old are all examples of political communities. But groups of elected representatives, police officers, veterans, legal professionals, diplomats, campaign consultants, journalists, and criminals constitute individual political communities because each has, at varying levels of differentiation and integration, shared needs, shared symbols, shared preferences, and shared stories. This chapter will explain how political communities create, and are created by, their political subcultures.

Power

Few people would disagree with the statement that politics revolves around power. But what is power, and how is it related to communication? James MacGregor Burns considers *power* a relational process

> in which power holders (P), possessing certain motives and goals, have the capacity to secure changes in the behavior of a respondent (R), human or animal, and in the environment, by utilizing resources in their power base, including factors of skill, relative to the targets of their power-wielding and necessary to secure such changes. (Burns 1978, 13)

Burns's conception of power therefore emphasizes "the motives and resources of power holders, the motives and resources of power recipients, and the relationship among all these."

The *power base* consists of individuals' means to fulfill or frustrate the needs of their fellows. But power recipients cannot experience power unless they interpret it as power. Power recipients reflect on their needs, their perceptions of the resources and needs, their preferences, and impose a narrative past-present-future structure on their alternatives. In short, power occurs through communication.

Relationships: Needs versus Risks

You engage other persons in communication when they seem likely to fulfill your needs. This is not quite so crass as it sounds. Remember that your motivating process consists of the balance among your personal needs for physical survival, safety and security, love and belonging, esteem, and self-actualization; interpersonal needs for more or less inclusion, affection, and control; and the resulting expressive, object appraisal, social adjustment, and externalization functions. Appearances and situational factors provide important data for our initial interpretative processes.

But communication poses risks, because a person's ability to satisfy your needs is part and parcel of that person's ability to frustrate those same needs. Your estimate of their need-fulfilling potential is balanced against your estimate of the perceived risks. In short, you engage in communication with those persons whose ability to fulfill your needs seems sufficient to warrant the risk.

Thibaut and Kelley theorized that the key to managing relational risks is your *comparison level of alternatives* (1959). You remain isolated or in an old relationship until an alternative (including solitude) seems more promising. Most people therefore minimize these risks by preferring regular communication with people whose interpretive processes resemble their own.

Relational continuity mainly happens because communication with people who interpret things much as you do is relatively easy. But regular communication also homogenizes differences between personal interpretive processes as the individuals develop shared interpretive structures. Moreover, regular communication with people who share your basic interpretive processes reinforces the importance and usefulness of your motives, symbols, preferences, and reasons.

But because relationships meet needs that are relative and fluid, you eventually reach a point where one or more of the following occurs: (1) you decide that the other is incapable of meeting your need, (2) the other fulfills your original need but is unable to meet your newly evolving needs, (3) the risks of association outweigh the potential benefits, or (4) an alternative relationship offers a more promising fulfillment-risk balance. In short, your needs and reasoning influence your relational preferences.

Notice that our relational continuity hinges on our impressions of one another, our respective needs, our assessments of each other's ability to fulfill our needs, our appraisal of the risks implicit in the old and new relationships, and the alternative relationships thought to be available to each of us. Each of these impressions emerges from our personal interpretive systems. Each of these impressions influences the power base.

In politics, this process fosters the tension between stability and change, between stable coalitions and the courting of short-term collaborators, and between apathy and political activism. Individuals in pursuit of complementary personal need-fulfillment create a shared motivational structure, or power base. In one interpretive community, the need for productive work is coupled with physical survival; in another, with social esteem; and in a third, with a sense of personal fulfillment. Members of the community exercise power over one another by granting or withholding the fulfillment of other members' needs.

From Individual Needs to Group Membership

Power → needs

Whether attained at great risk or simply accepted because it came cheaply, membership in a power relationship fits into the members' motivating processes. Each member sees the relationship from a personal perspective. This is not to say that group members have similar motives. On the contrary, unique needs and circumstances led them to the same group for different reasons.

Any group or community, therefore, provides for its members a cafeteria of appeals. You will find something of whatever you need through membership, but your comparison of alternatives may lead you to prefer membership in a group that only partially satisfies your important needs because it seems the best choice overall.

The process whereby differentially motivated individuals combine to create a group with its own needs is called the *assembly effect.* Member satisfaction with a group depends less on the composition of the group than on the interaction among its members. Any political community is a set of differentially motivated persons reaping personal gratifications from membership in exchange for acceptance of the risks imposed by the relationship.

Since relationships synthesize individuals into units, we can compare social groups in terms of their syntality and synergy. *Syntality* refers to a group's characteristic tendencies. We shall see later that the House of Representatives and the Senate have different syntalities. Syntality also enables us to distinguish between individual and group behaviors, like the AFL-CIO's endorsement of the Carter-Mondale ticket and members' landslide vote for Reagan-Bush.

The energy that members expend to sustain their groupness is called *synergy*. Synergy highlights the fact that individuals tend to wander away from relationships unless attention is devoted to maintenance. Urban political machines built their power through attention to the personal needs of immigrants, the poor, and others who later repaid that attention with votes. We will see later that social movement organizations require considerably more synergy than do institutionalized groups like the Bureau of the Census.

Consider the example of the John Birch Society, which was founded in 1958 for the express purpose of *recapturing* America from communist control under the dynamic personal leadership of Robert Welch. By 1964, the Birch Society was a force to be reckoned with, contributing mightily to the Republicans' nomination of Barry Goldwater for president. But by 1966, their membership virtually evaporated. Despite their politically extreme views, Birch members were unusually likely to have grown up in small-town America, to have attended college, to hold white-collar jobs, to earn more than $10,000, and to support the Republican party. Why would such upscale individuals join an active, extreme, autocratic organization?

Of the members surveyed, 62 percent reported joining the John Birch Society for ideological support, while 8 percent joined to fulfill their needs for political commitment. The fulfillment/risk principle is evident in the sharp membership decline, when only one in three fulfilled his or her needs for ideological support and four times as many people found political commitment as sought it (Grupp 1969). In short, individuals joined the John Birch Society in search of ideological support, invested considerable commitment and synergy without finding that support, and withdrew from the group because they judged membership dysfunctional.

This section discussed the relationship between individual motives and power. It stressed that differently motivated individuals negotiate a shared power structure through which they are capable of fulfilling and frustrating one another's needs.

Language

If two symbolizing persons are to satisfy one another's needs, they need to coordinate their symbolizing. Toward the notion of "strong national defense," for example, they might (1) share feelings toward a shared definition, (2) share feelings toward unique definitions, (3) conflict over a shared definition, or (4) conflict over personalized definitions (Elder and Cobb 1983). To coordinate their symbolizing, people construct languages.

A *language* is a shared symbolic structure consisting of a vocabulary and a grammar by which to arrange the words. The key to language is the tacit agreement by individuals to abide by the language's rules. To say that we "speak English" is to contract to use words as they appear in the dictionary and to arrange them in accordance with proper grammar. We further agree that any breach of this contract can result in misunderstanding.

Our agreement to share in the vocabulary and rules of a common language has several important political implications, for, as David Green has observed,

> whoever shapes public understanding of the labels thereby shapes the nature of political discourse. The history of political language is a history of struggles to shape the publicly accepted meanings of these key terms. (Green 1987, ix)

One political implication of shared symbolizing is that fluency in a community's language is a criterion for membership. English-speaking and French-speaking Canadians have experienced the tension between cultural diversity and national unity for many years, and now Castilian Spanish is being challenged by several traditional regional dialects that had been outlawed by the Franco regime. Here in America, we have witnessed similar bilingualism controversies over the teaching of "Black English" and Spanish in public schools.

A community's language defines its perceptions. Language enables its users to classify and to interpret elements of their environment. Haig Bosmajian suggests that people in power define and that they invariably define things to the further disadvantage of the less powerful. This tendency is subtle when "nonwhite" implicitly reinforces "white" as the standard or when a "woman lawyer" is singled out for attention. But labeling was brutal when Nazi depictions of Jews as vermin facilitated the annihilation of millions of human beings (Bosmajian 1974; Bytwerk 1983). It is also difficult to find either opponents of "SDI" or supporters of "Star Wars," as the position and vocabulary intertwine.

Only people with a shared language can develop a shared identity. Just as individuals could not know anything other than the sensory present without symbols, communities cannot develop common narratives without language. When we discuss fantasy and rhetorical vision, it will be important to remember that such visions exist in a shared language.

Fluency in several languages is necessary for political survival. Murray Edelman identified four kinds of language that perform particular political functions (1964). *Hortatory language* encourages mass support for the political regime through emotionally charged abstractions like "New Deal," "New Frontier," and "standing tall," which mean different positive things to different individuals.

The *legal language* of contracts and court decisions intimidates nonexperts and permits experts greater interpretive leeway. When "the party of the second part agrees to waive all remedies expressed or implied except as stipulated under applicable statutes," the second party retains an attorney to interpret their legal rights.

Administrative language assumes compliance, generally without using arguments, to bolster the user's authority. It is a language grounded in institutionalized power relationships that victimizes the person who wanders into the administrative clutches. Administrative language presumes the legitimacy of the administrative process and of those who administer it, arguably because the administrator's claim to legitimacy is the most derivative, and therefore, the least secure.

Finally, *bargaining language* "offers a deal, not an appeal," so that motivated persons with incompatible values can reach agreement. Legal language can anesthetize us to contractual risks; bargaining language can seem callous in a public address; and emotional exhortations are awkward around the conference table.

Unfortunately, few of our neighbors are sufficiently fluent in legal, administrative, and bargaining languages to adequately represent their interests before commissioners at public hearings about schools, utilities, and zoning. Most of us are all too susceptible to hortatory language that seeks generalized support for the leadership of a political community, whether it is a union's toughness, a party's nominee, or a demographic group's demand for recognition.

Only when a political community develops a language does it acquire a voice, and without a voice it cannot interact with other political communities. With a voice it can articulate its preferences and develop a shared ideology. But because language arises from the sharing of personal symbols, our personal meanings for a shared symbol differ. Every symbol, therefore, evokes conflicting positive images among members of the community. These conflicts are submerged behind the shared meaning until policy failures or adversaries exploit them. The result is either a new label for an old policy or a new policy under the old label (Green 1987).

Ideology

As individuals communicate, their preferencing processes intertwine to create an ideology. *Ideology* refers to a set of socially shared preferences about the nature of life, built on shared value priorities, shared authorities, and/or shared derivations. Whatever a community collectively believes or imagines is its ideology.

[handwritten margin note: neutral]

Ideological Conviction

Precisely because an ideology is a construction of preferences, it is not subject to exact verification. Sociologist John Wilson anticipated Walter Fisher's position on narrative logic when he explained that ideology entails a meaningful expression of order:

> Consistency with [its overarching] principle is the governing criterion for the acceptance or rejection of an idea or event. The appeal of the ideology therefore lies not in its rational validity but in the conviction with which the heterogeneous events of the social world are integrated. Once an ideology has been fully absorbed there is no such thing as counterevidence (1973, 94)

[handwritten margin note: ideology vs. worldview]

It matters little to the believer whether an ideology is factually accurate or logically consistent, it matters only that it is believed and preferred. Belief makes it accurate and consistent.

In ideologies, faith and conviction override observational proof. Observations that can be used to confirm an ideology are cherished, even—perhaps especially—when a blatantly unrepresentative observation can be used to refute a host of observational proofs. But when observation and belief conflict, belief wins.

[handwritten margin note: but this part of def isn't neutral]

Since our preferences are personal and a product of our personal needs, symbolizations, and reasonings, they are more likely to be felt than understood. The social-judgment literature suggests that people consider the amount of attitude change asked of them before considering the appeal (Sherif, Sherif, and Nebergall 1965). If this is so, we decide first and then make sense of the decision.

There are many times when we coolly study opposing arguments and supporting evidence before rendering a decision. Try to recall an occasion when you sorted out the important issues on which a political decision should hinge, found appropriate facts, figures, and testimony, and then, only then, reached a decision. Surely people reason that way. But the fact that you can recall specific instances of such decision making indicates just how exceptional they are. We can, and do, reason that carefully—sometimes. The rest of the time we look for preferencing shortcuts.

Ideology provides us with shortcuts by suggesting the values, authorities, and derivations that should be employed. This shortcutting is psychologically functional because it increases the likelihood that your choices will be met with social approval: love and belonging, esteem, inclusion, affect, and control. Develop a personal preferencing style, and your peers will question your judgment.

If reasons tag along after a decision in most cases, we welcome their tardy arrival with a passionate embrace and a hearty "Thank goodness you're here, I was beginning to worry about you." *We* know that we are rational people who would not engage in snap political judgments; and because we need to believe that about ourselves, we embrace the reason however tardy, pay tribute to its importance, and defend it from sceptics. Ideology is a ready source of tardy reasons, and ideologues rely on conviction and commitment to demonstrate their wisdom.

Components of Ideology

As a shared preferencing structure, ideology consists of community values, shared authorities, and derived preferences.

Community Values

A community's fundamental values can be assessed in two ways. Rokeach used a value survey to identify people's rankings of the 36 *instrumental and terminal values* across social communities (1973). His results indicate his respondents' ranking of value abstractions but do so in a way that treats "freedom" as though it means the same thing to each respondent.

A second approach maps the recurrent values underlying a community's talk. A study of presidential addresses to the nation (1963–1984), for example, identified three levels of American cultural values (Smith and Smith 1985). The core values of morality, peace, patriotism, effort and optimism, and progress and change pervaded all 105 addresses. When diverse presidents all frame their divergent policies with the same values, it suggests a concordant reading of the American pulse. Taken together, the two approaches to community values suggest the deep foundations of the ideology.

Shared Authorities

At the community level, authority figures are of two general types: practical and symbolic. *Practical authorities* are actual people exercising influence within a community's social structure. These include police officers, legislators, soldiers, teachers, doctors, and everyone else whose influence stems from their work.

Of greater ideological significance are the community's *symbolic authorities*—those people, real or imagined, who exercise influence because they "mean something" to members of the community (Klapp 1964). Their influence can be unrelated to their practical influence, as when an ineffective congressman skips committee meetings to be seen regularly on C-SPAN. This category includes purely fictional characters like the Huxtables and Bunkers, who influence our beliefs about the American family. It includes people like Charlton Heston, Al Pacino, Jane Fonda, Jimmy Stewart, and John Wayne, whose portrayals of meaningful characters make them meaningful characters. It also includes many practical authorities like George Washington, Abraham Lincoln, Susan B. Anthony, Martin Luther King Jr., and General George Patton, whose practical influence made them meaningful symbols.

The 1980 and 1984 nominating conventions featured battles for the right to quote Franklin Roosevelt. Ronald Reagan claimed that Democrats had betrayed the beliefs that Roosevelt, Reagan, and mainstream America shared. Actually, Roosevelt's practical authority infuriated Republicans of his day and contributed to his role as a potent symbolic authority for Democrats. By invoking Roosevelt's symbolic authority, Reagan (1) appealed to the traditional Democrats' preferencing process, (2) enabled Republicans to prefer Roosevelt's leadership to Herbert Hoover's passivity, and (3) undermined the usefulness of Roosevelt's symbolic authority as an anti-Republican weapon. Small wonder that Walter Mondale and Ted Kennedy objected to Reagan's Republicanization of Roosevelt.

The relationship between ideology and shared authorities extends into matters of information as well. Members of the conservative community are inclined to accept authoritatively the opinions of Paul Harvey, Evans and Novak, and Patrick Buchanan; whereas members of the liberal community are inclined to prefer information from Sam Donaldson and Mark Shields. These voices gain authority by providing information and perspective that can be readily digested through audience interpretive systems. The corollary to the example is that conservatives find Donaldson and Shields—and liberals find Harvey, Buchanan, Evans, and Novak—utterly insufferable.

A step up from journalists are the "think tanks," or research institutes, relied on by practical authorities for background studies and policy alternatives. The Rand Corporation and the Brookings Institution have felt the emergence of the more conservative American Enterprise Institute and the Hoover Institute during the 1980s. Think tanks are organizational systems that embody a set of preferences in their hiring, investigating, and advisory practices.

Derived Preferences

At the fringe of an ideology are shared preferences based on values, authorities, and still other derivations. President Reagan's authority grew largely out of his commitments to bold leadership, self-evident morality, and straightforward simplicity. But the Iran-Contra scandal of 1986–87 raised questions about the wisdom of his boldness, the legality and unconsidered morality of his policies, and his oversimplification of complex issues. As his personal credibility faltered, so did support for derivative policies like aid for the Nicaraguan Contras.

Does a community believe in a policy such as the Strategic Defense Initiative because it directly embodies their shared values, because it is supported by a shared symbolic authority, or because it is integrated with other shared derivations? Your preference is ideological to the extent that it hinges on your belief in a community's shared preferences rather than upon your independent personal preferencing.

Because ideology is based on belief rather than proof, and because the social sharing of preferences provides important social support, ideology is largely resistant to counterpersuasion. But if believers find their ideology dysfunctional, they tend to make sweeping changes in it. For years, the Praise the Lord ministry of Jim and Tammy Faye Bakker transformed *Charlotte Observer* exposés into successful fund-raising campaigns with references to martyrs, tests of faith, and the determination of heathens to disrupt the Lord's work. But allegations of Reverend Bakker's lewd liaisons with church secretary Jessica Hahn and even a male employee of the PTL community severely undermined his ideological authority in his community and indirectly undermined the political authority of television ministries in general. We use and protect our community's ideology as long as it functions for us, but when it becomes dysfunctional, the comparison level of alternatives invites us to join a new community and to adopt its set of shared preferences.

Types of Ideologies

Ideologies can be classified along three dimensions: differentiation, specificity, and openness (Wilson 1973). Ideologies, like personal construct systems, are *differentiated* with respect to the number of elements they contain. An ideology based on conflict between capitalists and the proletariat is less differentiated than one that considers the economic and social implications of corporate and proprietary forms of ownership on relations with skilled and un-skilled workers in trades, industries, and services.

Ideological *specificity* refers to the tendency of one community to identify particular heroes, villains, and complaints, while others refer to an ambiguous "them" or an unstaffed conspiracy.

Finally, *openness* is an ideology's ability to incorporate or to tolerate outside beliefs, as when one political lobby refuses to support a candidate because of a single dispute, while another supports that same candidate despite several differences. The Birch Society's Robert Welch insulated his closed ideology with the *principle of reversal*: Everything is the opposite of its appearance (Welch 1958).

Ideologies are functional in three ways. Your personal needs render you more or less susceptible to ideology types. You may need a shared preferencing system that is simple, general, and closed as a way to simplify politics so that you can devote your energies to your other needs. Or you might need a highly differentiated, specific, and open ideology to account for conflicting needs, resources, and relationships. A major difference between the two is flexibility. Complex ideologies are relatively elastic and endure through confusing situations, while simple ideologies may snap under strain.

But we should note that your personal needs may not directly match your ideology. For example, your needs for inclusion, affection, and control could conceivably lead to a satisfying membership in a community whose ideology is less than fully satisfying. If this were to happen, the community might "help" you to embrace the ideology, you might modify the ideology, or you might find membership too costly. It is this complex interaction that produces in-group disagreements and factions. If group affiliations were purely ideological, there would be little need for discussion: either believe or leave. But all of us periodically have reservations about the conduct of communities to which we have strong emotional bonds.

The types of ideologies offer varying appeals. A general, simple ideology allows diverse members to "fill in the blanks" through their personal interpretive processes. Many Americans believe that President Kennedy's assassination resulted from a conspiracy, but there is little agreement among them as to the identity of the conspirators. Whether the conspirators were Cubans, Russians, Mafia, FBI, right-wingers, left-wingers, or crazed fans of Marilyn Monroe depends on the personal and social demonologies of the people completing the enthymeme.

Conspiracy theorists constitute an interpretive community by virtue of their belief in conspiracy. Writers like Lyndon LaRouche, Robert Welch, and John Stormer took the general theme of conspiracy and fleshed it out by specifying conspiratorial forces and insulating their arguments from counterargument. In a general sense, it may be that simple and general ideologies are useful for recruiting believers, but that complex ideologies better mobilize members for action.

An ideology is common ground on which diverse individuals can meet because they believe, perceive, and imagine roughly the same things. A populist ideology, for example, holds that "we the common people" are badly treated by the special interests, even though we each personally interpret "we," "common," and "interests." For example, the late millionaire Governor Nelson Rockefeller of New York is reputed to have favored a tax break "for the little guy making less than $200,000." At the other extreme, elitist ideology holds that the wisdom, talent, taste, and judgment of the best people are being diluted by the pedestrian influence of the mass. Historically, people granted admission to society have quickly begun to wonder about the wisdom of admitting those who come next. An elitist ideology therefore includes union workers who opposed civil rights and blacks who opposed women's rights, as well as the stereotypical "Harvard/Yankee" elitism.

Logic

When we reason together, we create a system of *logic* that enables us collectively to move from cause to effect, from past to future, and from data to claim. When narrative logic moves from the individual to the social level, it becomes a shared vision. Recall that reasoning is the process through which individuals arrange facts, beliefs, values, images, and perceptions into a coherent and familiar narrative that explains the world. At the social level, the community attempts to make sense of the world for its members by interpreting events in terms of its language, ideology, and power. Through this process, members work toward a shared reality.

Rhetorical Visions

Small group research by Robert Bales revealed that individuals develop shared identities by *fantasizing* (1970). The verbalizing, expressing, or dramatizing of a fantasy orients listeners to the present by drawing on past and future. Sometimes these fantasies fall flat. But when listeners recognize the fantasy as one of their own, they respond emotionally as well as cognitively. They hitchhike on the original comment and extend the fantasy by polishing the image, adding examples, and extending it. Then a third person recognizes the fantasy and joins the fun. Soon individuals have drawn on their individual pasts and futures to create a shared present.

Community members actively negotiate a common orientation to their present, and they are bound to one another by the shared vision and by the process of creating it. This process is called *chaining*, as in "they created an elaborate fantasy chain" or "the fantasy chained out to the entire group" (Bormann 1972).

Informal group fantasizing about political matters occurs daily. Consider the following example:

A: There sure are a lot of crazies around these days, like Moammar Khaddafi.

B: Yeah, those terrorist bombings are awful. Our archaeology seminar cancelled our trip to the Pyramids because of them.

C: Well, I certainly think that Khaddafi and the other terrorists are wrong; but what about the people who are bombing abortion clinics here in America?

A: Sure, but how often does that happen, really? You're making a mountain out of a molehill.

B: That's probably true. There's lots more danger from drunk drivers and regular crime than from mad bombers.

C: Yeah, there sure are a lot of crazies out there!

B: Really!

Three individuals build on A's observation that "There are a lot of crazies around these days" and ultimately accept it as a group vision. They do this, despite moving from Moammar Khaddafi to abortion bombers, to drunk drivers and criminals. Put differently, this community kept supporting the central claim even though they changed the data. Each person embraced a different argument in support of the claim, but together they accepted the same claim. That is, they saw the same vision.

Ernest Bormann extended Bales's work by suggesting that group fantasizing occurs in public as well as private communication settings (1972). He theorizes that people in society engage in the same kind of fantasizing as the people in our hypothetical group. Sometimes the shared fantasies of many people coalesce into an overarching *rhetorical vision*, which serves as a shared logic. The vision enables those who share it to reason together. This process was evident in the 1978 debate over ratification of the Panama Canal Treaties.

After 14 years of negotiations, the Senate ratified two new treaties regarding the Panama Canal in 1978. Ronald Reagan had attacked President Ford's support of the "giveaway" of "our canal" during the 1976 North Carolina primary, and voter response indicated that the fantasy had begun to chain. Richard Viguerie and other leaders of the emergent New Right used the "giveaway fantasy" to mobilize conservatives, to solicit contributions, and to develop electoral hit lists for the 1978 elections.

President Jimmy Carter and Republican Congressman Philip Crane from Illinois were the primary advocates for and against— respectively—the new treaties, and each relied on a rhetorical vision. Carter said that the original treaty had not been signed by any Panamanians and was unfair to Panama, while Crane considered it an example of shrewd diplomacy. Carter said that the existing treaty only granted America the use of the canal *as though* we had sovereignty over it, while Crane claimed American sovereignty over the canal. Carter said that the existing treaty fostered resentment among our hemispheric neighbors, while Crane saw neighbors wrongfully trespassing on our property. Carter said that the new treaty would strengthen our claim to the canal by stipulating that America could militarily intervene in Panama if they closed the canal, while Crane argued that we needed no country's permission to defend what is already ours.

Notice that treaty ratification was imperative in Carter's vision and that rejection was imperative in Crane's. The Senate ratified the treaties without resolving the struggle between visions. Opponents of the treaties used it as a 1978 campaign issue, and the seizure of hostages in Iran in 1979 seemed to confirm Crane's vision, despite the fact that the Iranians were not connected to Panama or Central America. Jimmy Carter preferred facts and moral principles to visions, and he was unable to defend the vision within which his policies made sense. But Ronald Reagan preferred visions to detailed legal arguments, and he effectively established the Reagan-Crane vision of world affairs during the 1980s.

Examples of rhetorical visions abound in political communication. The nineteenth century witnessed struggles between the slave-holding and abolitionist visions, between secession and unity, and between elitism and populism. More recently, we have seen struggles between rugged individualism and social responsibility visions, between integrationist and segregationist visions, between feminist and chauvinist visions, between internationalist and isolationist visions, and between pro-life and pro-choice visions, to name only a few.

Every political community has a rhetorical vision, and many of those visions conflict. But policy usually can be framed in the dominant vision. Political advocates can either try to establish their logic as the dominant rhetorical vision or they can frame their policies in the dominant vision. People usually try to employ the generally accepted logic of their community.

reason/warrant

Abraham Lincoln's "Emancipation Proclamation" freed the slaves *not* because slavery was morally reprehensible (as the abolitionists had argued and as most of us learned in school) but on military grounds to induce Confederate surrender. The effect of Lincoln's choice was to achieve the abolitionists' goal without establishing their vision as dominant. When southern whites reclaimed political power in the wake of Reconstruction, their move toward legal segregation was unhindered by dominant moral arguments. The antebellum vision had not only remained dominant in the Confederate states, it chained further as perceptions of corruption, defeat, exploitation, and economic ruin merged with the fantasy of racial superiority to energize the white supremacist vision.

Since fantasies need to chain out among individuals, it is not possible for one person alone to establish a vision. A rhetorical vision is a community product. A speaker or author can try to make a proposal appealing, but factors discussed previously (needs, symbols, beliefs, language, ideology, and power relations) influence response to the fantasy. Despite ample evidence and urgings by Presidents Nixon, Ford, and Carter, Americans resisted the energy crisis of the 1970s. Perhaps we did so because it conflicted with our long-standing vision of abundance. Indeed, today's defenders of Nixon's 55-miles-per-hour speed limit stress its life-saving benefits and ignore the logic of energy conservation.

Although rhetorical visions are a group product, an ability to articulate a rhetorical vision powerfully can establish any person as an ideational leader for a political community. Examples abound. Huey Long built a powerful movement among the poor and disenfranchised with his "Share Our Wealth" vision (which was more accurately "Share *Their* Wealth"). At about the same time, Detroit's Father Charles Coughlin addressed his vision of "social justice" to a nationwide radio audience. More recent examples include Governor George Wallace's defense of segregation, Reverend Martin Luther King, Jr.'s "dream" of racial justice, Gloria Steinem's exposition of feminism, New York Congressman Jack Kemp's advocacy of "supply-side economics," and Reverend Jerry Falwell's leadership of the Moral Majority. Many of these visionaries became symbolic leaders for their communities.

Some poor ideas blossom and some good ones die on the vine. Rhetorical visions provide a framework for making sense of the world. We seem to demand that the vision make sense and trust it to be accurate and valid. Popularity is no guarantee of either accuracy or validity, and unpopularity is no measure of stupidity. Free speech enables us to test ideas and fantasies for the purposes of refining our visions and discarding those that are flawed.

Conclusions

Chapter 1 dealt with the personal interpretive processes that prepare us to communicate. This chapter examined community structures/created when we engage one another in communication. Our needs and our appraisal of costs and benefits enable us to decide which relationships to further and which to terminate.

When we form relationships and communities with other people, the interaction changes us. Our personal construct systems become a shared vocabulary that shapes, and is shaped by, our experiences. Our preferencing processes grow into an ideology that shapes, and is shaped by, our social concerns. Our shared personal needs define the community's power relationships. And personal reasoning grows into shared rhetorical visions that shape, and are shaped by, unfolding events.

By now it should be clear that communities will arise around competing powers, languages, ideologies, and logics. The process through which they struggle for leadership is the subject of Chapter 3.

References

Bales, Robert F. *Personality and Interpersonal Behavior.* New York: Holt, Rinehart, 1970.

Bormann, Ernest G. "Fantasy and Rhetorical Vision: The Rhetorical Criticism of Social Reality." *Quarterly Journal of Speech* 58 (December 1972): 396–407.

Bosmajian, Haig. *The Language of Oppression.* Washington, D.C.: Public Affairs Press, 1974.

Burns, James MacGregor. *Leadership.* New York: Harper and Row, Colophon Books, 1978.

Bytwerk, Randall. *Julius Streicher: The Man Who Persuaded a Nation to Hate Jews.* New York: Stein and Day, 1983.

Cronen, Vernon E., W. Barnett Pearce, and Linda M. Harris. "The Coordinated Management of Meaning: A Theory of Communication." In *Human Communication Theory: Comparative Essays,* edited by Frank E. X. Dance. New York: Harper and Row, 1982.

Edelman, Murray. *The Symbolic Uses of Politics.* Urbana: University of Illinois press, 1964.

Elder, Charles D., and Roger W. Cobb. *The Political Uses of Symbols.* New York: Longman, 1983.

Green, David. *Shaping Political Consciousness: The Language of Politics in America from McKinley to Reagan.* Ithaca, NY: Cornell University Press, 1987.

Grupp, Fred W., Jr. "The Political Perspectives of Birch Society Members." In *The American Right Wing,* edited by Robert A. Schoenberger. Atlanta: Holt, Rinehart, and Winston, 1969.

Klapp, Orrin. *Symbolic Leaders: Public Dramas and Public Men.* Chicago: Aldine, 1964.

Rokeach, Milton. *The Nature of Human Values.* New York: Free Press, 1973.

Schutz, William. *FIRO: A Three-Dimensional Theory of Interpersonal Behavior.* New York: Rinehart, 1958.

Sherif, Muzafer, Carolyn Sherif, and Roger Nebergall. *Attitude and Attitude Change: The Social-Judgment Ego-Involvement Approach.* Philadelphia: W. B. Saunders, 1965.

Smith, Craig Allen, and Kathy B. Smith. "Presidential Values and Public Priorities: Recurrent Patterns in Presidential Addresses to the Nation, 1963–1984." *Presidential Studies Quarterly* 15 (Fall 1985): 743–53.

Thibaut, John. W., and Harold H. Kelley. *The Social Psychology of Groups.* New York: John Wiley and Sons, 1959.

Turner, Victor. *From Ritual to Theatre: The Human Seriousness of Play.* New York: Performing Arts Journal Publications, 1982.

Welch Robert. *The Blue Book of the John Birch Society.* Belmont, MA: Western Islands, 1958.

Wilson, John. *Introduction to Social Movements.* New York: Basic Books, 1973.

Chapter 3

INCONGRUENT COMMUNITIES AND THE STRUGGLE FOR LEADERSHIP

So far we have seen that individuals interpret their worlds through their interpretive processes and that they communicate with similarly oriented others to create interpretive communities. This leads to a society in which communities of individuals—many of whom never meet one another—think, feel, and behave along similar lines. Since each of these communities believes it properly understands the world, each believes that most of the other interpretive communities are wrong and, in many cases, even dangerous.

Consequently, incongruent interpretive communities compete for the right to interpret the world for everybody else. This chapter will examine the kinds of interpretive control over which these diverse communities struggle, a "wishbone model" of their competition, and the nature of leadership.

The Sources of Dominance

The struggle for dominance is central to political communication. Each of the following dimensions is important, and particular communities try to maximize one or more of them. Each affects, and is affected by, communication among community members and among communities.

Power

As discussed in Chapter 2, every community has a power base through which it fulfills and frustrates members' needs. Communities contend for power in society along three dimensions: distribution, scope, and domain. The *power distribution* concerns who holds how much of which powers. The *scope of power* is the range of issues or policy areas over which they exercise power, whereas the *domain of power* is the range of persons over whom they exercise it (Dahl 1968). Up until his death, the Ayatollah Khomeini apparently held most of the distributed power over a wide scope of issues for much of the Islamic domain. By contrast, North Carolina distributed its power so that the governor lacks veto power and influential legislators are able to wield personal power over their issues and people. Iran and North Carolina exemplify two distinct approaches to community power, and if they seem odd to you, it is because you are employing your community's interpretive framework rather than theirs. What are the resources that are distributed in the community?

Power in a community consists of authority and influence. *Authority* is a structural or role-based power resource. In pursuit of Turner's "normative communitas" (1982), members of the community create a role structure in which the resources needed to fulfill and frustrate their needs are vested in a role or office, with that authority flowing from one officeholder to the next. Authority may be either institutionalized through constitutions and laws or recognized informally, as when Coretta Scott King delivers her annual civil rights "State of the Dream" address.

Meager authority can sometimes be parlayed into a power base if superiors are unable or unwilling to exercise their authority. President Reagan's managerial style delegated an unusual amount of authority, leading to the misadventures of Admiral John Poindexter, Colonel Oliver North, and many others; whereas President Carter delegated little authority, and he was consequently held personally accountable for the nation's disappointments.

Influence occurs when individuals inspire changes because of personal qualities valued by members of the community. John Kennedy and Ronald Reagan each demonstrated a range of qualities valued by enough Americans to enhance the basic presidential authority they shared with Gerald Ford and Jimmy Carter. Personal influence is also important in legislatures, especially in the Senate, where 100 senators spend six or more years building 51 vote majorities with relatively few positional resources. Especially important to personal influence is the notion of credibility and its components of trustworthiness and expertise, which we will later discuss in detail. One who betrays a trust or reveals weaknesses will lose some measure of personal influence in the community, often leading to a loss of positional authority as well.

The Constitution dispersed governmental power in America. First, it acknowledged the scope and domain of each state's distributed authority. Second, it distributed national authority among three branches; then it halved legislative authority by creating a bicameral legislature. Each institution was vested with a particular scope of positional authority—executive authority in the president, legislative authority in the Congress, and judicial authority in the Court. But the authority vested in each institution was only partial, so that none of these institutions could function independently. Constitutional checks and balances were a safeguard against any institution accumulating excessive power. The result, as political scientist Richard Neustadt observed, was a system of separated institutions sharing powers (1980).

The dispersal of government authority among so many institutions created the possibility of stalemate. Governmental leaders relying solely on their positional authority to achieve their goals would run smack into other domains holding the remaining authority. It was therefore inevitable that influence would become critical in American government. Influence alone could break the logjams of stalemated authority, and it was the personal influence of people like Presidents George Washington, Andrew Jackson, and Abraham Lincoln; Senators Daniel Webster, Henry Clay, and John C. Calhoun; and Justices John Marshall and Oliver Wendell Holmes and the social influence of abolitionists, populists, laborites, progressives, and suffragettes that shaped, and were shaped by, the distribution of authority in America.

In short, political communication negotiates the scope and domain of the authority and influence distributed among members of a community. Influence can lead to grants of authority, as when the new Chrysler Corporation granted a seat on its board of directors to the president of the United Autoworkers Union or when Americans elected such military heroes as General Dwight Eisenhower or General Ulysses S. Grant to political office. Conversely, authority can enhance personal influence, as when a retired public official becomes an elder statesman.

A society comprises a multitude of overlapping communities. As you interpret your world, you acquire membership in an assortment of interpretive communities, any of which can be applied to a political issue: a political party, an ethnic community, a gender-based community, a religious community, an economic class, a geographic region, a professional community, a community oriented around a particular celebrity-leader, or any number of special interest communities, to suggest only a few possibilitites. Since each of us can take on any number of identities, a society as large as the U.S. includes a universe of political communities, many of them vying for position in the minds of individual members.

Consider the example of abortion. Is abortion a religious, ethical, political, legal, medical, social, psychological, racial, feminist, or power issue? The abortion question entails all these dimensions, and more. But each of us decides how best to interpret the question so that an appropriate set of preferences and reasons can guide us. The pro-life community categorizes abortion as murder; the pro-choice community categorizes it as "pregnancy termination." The pro-life ideology grounds its preferences in the value of God-given life and, consequently, in the transcendent authority of fundamental moral laws; the pro-choice ideology begins with humans' God-given abilities to reason, to prefer, and to influence their own lives. The pro-life vision wants to bring human laws into conformity with God's Laws; the pro-choice vision wants to protect God's thinking, choosing people from a coercive, collective conscience that could compel individuals to violate their own consciences. The two communities differ with respect to their languages, ideology, and logic, not to mention their needs and power relationships.

Clearly, the pro-life and pro-choice subcultures are incompatible, and the members of each community feel the need to espouse and to defend their interpretive structures. Two other points are perhaps less clear. First, the abortion issue cuts through derivations and authorities to involve our most basic values, symbols, preferences, and logic. If you grant the existence of a God, which is more important, God's laws or God's people? What is "life," and does it begin at biological conception or at birth? If you do not grant the existence of a God, then on what basis do you suggest resolving moral and ethical questions, especially when the answers apply to people who decide such questions in relation to a God in which you do not believe? Who best decides moral and ethical questions: the government, communities, or individuals? The ripples from arguments about these beliefs and preferences create ideological tidal waves.

The second point regarding the abortion conflict is that the two communities are struggling for the interpretive power to define the issue for the society. The Supreme Court in *Roe v. Wade* (1973) empowered the pro-choice community and disempowered the pro-life community by granting to prospective parents a restricted right to prefer abortion. Pro-choice now argues that choice is the only policy that preserves individual conscience and the law of the land. Pro-life argues that the God-given right to life from the instant of conception transcends matters of individual conscience and renders any exception unconscionable (Stewart, Smith, and Denton 1989). *A community winning its struggle to frame an issue empowers its language, ideology, and logic for the society*. But that empowerment is temporary. For example, in its 1989 decision in *Webster V. Reproductive Health Services*, the U.S. Supreme Court transformed abortion from a judicial question to a legislative one, and moved debate from Washington to the states.

Legitimacy

Contenders for power, in either the community or the society, must establish their *legitimate, or rightful, claim to power*. First, they must convince themselves of their duty and ability to lead. Once over that hurdle, they must convince potential followers and competing advocates. Potential followers occasionally identify signs of legitimacy and draft a leader (the Mario Cuomo-for-President rumors persist even into the Bush administration), but such drafts are rarely sustained without the draftee's cooperation.

One path to legitimate power—entailing both authority and influence—is the *mythic feat*. Like young King Arthur, who casually pulled the sword from the stone, some leaders arise through the performance of legendary feats. George Washington's leadership during the Revolution, Ulysses S. Grant's victory at Appomattox, and Dwight Eisenhower's leadership of the Allied Forces in World War II all legitimized presidential fitness; but the military careers of General Douglas MacArthur and, to date, Colonel Oliver North did not. Charles Lindbergh's heroic trans-Atlantic flight legitimized his advocacy of isolationism in the 1930s. Most leaders develop a lore of mythic anecdotes—like those about Washington's cherry tree, Lincoln's fireside reading, and Kennedy's war record—often *after* they attain power.

The film of Mr. Bush's World War II heroism and Mr. Reagan's films of World War II heroism enhanced the mythic stature of each. But there are fewer opportunities to accomplish truly mythic feats than there are positions for legitimate power holders. With due respect for the "Massachusetts miracle" and the Bush and Dole war records, the 1988 presidential aspirants demonstrated that mythic feats are not the main avenue toward legitimate power in America. Indeed, supporters tried to legitimize Senator Dan Quayle for the vice presidency by establishing that he had written a law—a feat, rather less than mythic, that suggests the depths to which potential leaders may need to dig for mythic legitimacy.

A second source of legitimacy is, for lack of a better term, *likability*, an important source of influence. People may be so drawn to the warmth of a Ronald Reagan, the sincerity of an Oliver North, or the dynamism of a John Kennedy that they follow that person despite disliking the advice. Gerry Ford began his Presidency making the family pancakes, playing golf, smiling, puffing on his pipe, and petting his golden retriever, Liberty. Advised to "act presidential," he scowled more, banned casual photographs, and lost the election to a smiling Jimmy Carter. But it was hard for Carter to keep smiling through news of hostages, gas lines, soaring interest rates, and Soviet aggression; and when word spread that Carter was "nasty," he lost legitimacy to the homespun one-liners of Ronald Reagan. Certainly, other factors were at work as well. But it is hard to refute the claim that *we prefer political leaders whom we can like as people.*

A third source of legitimate positional authority is the *role*, or structure. The doctrine of the Divine Right of Kings held that a monarch ruled at God's will, rendering opposition as both treason and heresy, regardless of the monarch's likability. Challengers needed to establish that God meant for someone else to rule until the Magna Charta redistributed some of the king's authority to Parliament.

The Constitution, as amended, spells out the structural bases of authority in America. One who wins a fair election and who takes an oath of office has authority, others do not. When President Ferdinand Marcos of the Philippines defeated Corazon Aquino in a blatantly corrupt election, the Reagan administration persuaded Marcos to abdicate and recognized the Aquino government. But significantly, President Aquino had not won a Philippine election, and her claim to legitimate authority has been repeatedly challenged by supporters of Marcos, who was both elected and inaugurated before resigning. To affirm democratic process as the source of legitimate authority in the Philippines, America might better have supported new, well-monitored elections. Because President Aquino's legitimate authority is her American—not electoral—support, her adversaries must oppose American influence as well as her administration. By removing President Marcos, prohibiting his attempted coups, and subjecting Mrs. Marcos to public scorn for her extravagance, America unwittingly set the stage for the eventual death of a disgraced national leader. American policy, therefore, paved the way for a possible coalition that was otherwise unthinkable—a coalition, under the symbolic leadership of a martyred Marcos, of anti-Aquino communists and pro-Marcos property holders against Aquino and American colonialism. Whom one supports is, in terms of legitimacy, less important than the source of the legitimacy.

A fourth kind of legitimacy comes from the possession of necessary *resources* from the power base. Typically, the kid with the football plays quarterback. In the novel *The Lord of the Flies*, the conch shell becomes the symbol of power because it is the only resource by which to summon followers. One reason for Benjamin Franklin's early importance was his ownership of printing presses by which to disseminate radical ideas. Lyndon Johnson built his initial power in the Senate by shrewdly chairing a previously unnoticed committee that distributed office equipment and supplies to appreciative senators. J. Edgar Hoover consolidated and maintained his position as FBI Director by keeping extensive files on anyone capable of challenging him. Television ministers Jerry Falwell and Pat Robertson acquired political influence largely because they controlled personal television networks and mailing lists beyond the reach of most other ministers.

A fifth kind of legitimacy is *ideological*, as contenders gain legitimacy from their ability to apply the community's shared interpretive system. There is a prophet dimension here, as advocates claim to be the source of truth. Robert Welch founded the John Birch Society in 1958 to take America back from the communists by alarming and informing people. He was quite clear that the Birch Society would tolerate no divergence from his views, and he even published an annual scorecard of the percentage of communist influence in every nation of the world, based on his own personal insights. The economic leadership of Ronald Reagan and Jack Kemp in the early 1980s was based on the idea that cutting taxes would stimulate the economy to outgrow the deficit. Anyone who argued against their plan was, by definition, a "tax-and-spend liberal" unable to reach their higher economic consciousness. Faith in this higher economic consciousness and the ability to apply and to defend it became a source of ideological legitimacy.

We have discussed five sources of political legitimacy that can be nurtured by aspirants to political leadership. These five sources provide a shifting foundation. A mythic feat may propel one to prominence, but continuing support for nasty or fanatically wrong heroes is rare. Leaders need to conserve their legitimacy by using available opportunities to shore up their vulnerabilities, as did oil tycoon John D. Rockefeller when he had himself photographed giving nickels to children.

Procedures

A political community can frequently control the procedures by which the society arrives at legitimate decisions. Procedures in politics are like the home-field advantage in athletics, where familiarity with subtleties provides an advantage.

First, procedures *determine the criterion for victory.* Who wins an election? It's not always the person with the most votes. Presidential elections are won with a majority of the electoral votes; and the national popular vote, the winning margin, the number of states won, the number of demographic categories won, and the regional emphases simply do not count. In some multicandidate elections, a candidate with 49.99 percent of the votes must face a runoff election, while in others, the top vote-getter wins regardless of the size of the field. Legislators know whether a bill requires majority or two-thirds support; they can reroute it to committees where those votes are more (or less) probable, or they can make it a rider to an indispensable bill. Political communities argue about the criteria for victory because they constitute the societal framework in which the communities' competing power, language, ideology, and logic will be decided.

Second, procedures *control access to the decision-making process.* Both political parties have toyed with their formulas for nominating candidates since the 1968 demonstrations. First, an affirmative effort was made to find delegates other than white male protestants over 50. Then, winner-take-all primaries were replaced with proportional representation. Then, state primaries became the norm, ultimately clustering into Super Tuesday to produce overnight multistate delegations. We may soon see the end of the runoff primaries so common in the South.

No procedural change is neutral, since some communities benefit from it and others suffer. The Democratic party has suffered from its changes far more than the Republicans have because the Democrats functionally replaced state political parties with a proliferation of minority caucuses. The result is 50 organized Republican parties, each capable of mobilizing a state campaign, and a rainbow of independent national caucuses unable to effectively mobilize Democratic presidential votes in multiple states. In short, the Democratic representational reforms have proven functionally inappropriate. But there is little prospect of the Democrats returning to organization by state parties now that women and blacks constitute the backbone of the party's electoral support.

Third, procedures *control the agenda.* The ability to decide which ideas will be voted on and in what order is fundamental in representative government. William Riker coined the term *heresthetics* to describe this art of "structuring the world so you can win" (1986, ix). He argues that it is a lost art, comparable to rhetoric, grammar, and politics. Should the legislature pass the budget and then vote on proposed programs or vote on the programs and then consider the resulting budget? Heresthetics affect the agenda when choices are structured pragmatically to align the preferences of a majority on each vote with the ideology of the rule-making community.

Aspirants to political power should pay close attention to procedures and to the authority and influence that shape them. Failure to play by the accepted rules can be construed as amateurism or anarchy, neither of which enhances political credibility. But playing by the ("house rules") always works to the advantage of the rule makers. The dilemma is best solved by learning the existing rules to minimize advantage. Demonstrated competence with the house rules may earn the challenger an opportunity to amend them, but flaunting the rules will not. Sometimes the conflict is so fundamental that groups are willing to work outside the established decision-making procedures. These political movements constitute an exception that merits separate discussion in a subsequent chapter.

The congressional pay raise fiasco of 1989 exemplifies the political importance of procedural rules. Concerned by the distracting and potentially corrupting influence of fund-raising and outside income, a coalition of legislators drafted a bill to (1) eliminate outside income for senators and representatives and (2) provide a 50 percent pay increase to compensate for the lost income, that would (3) become effective unless voted down. Legislators traditionally pass pay raises that affect only the next legislature. Presidents Reagan and Bush endorsed the plan, perhaps recognizing that the new arrangement would reduce congressional distractions and increase the incentive for legislative effectiveness, and it would do all of this immediately. But opponents of the bill portrayed it as a back-room maneuver to steal a ridiculous amount of money. The press recognized the familiar narrative and passed it on to a public ready and willing—after a sleazy presidential campaign—to assume the worst. The press and public largely ignored the proposal to eliminate outside income and demanded a vote on the bill. With the choice now under the watchful eye of a suspicious press and public and framed as a vote either for or against a secret raise scheme, the bill was handily defeated. The 50 percent raise was dead; but the distractions of outside income continue, and the incentives for legislative success are still diluted. In this case, procedures affected the outcome, and the outcome was not quite what the general public expected.

Political communities struggle for a favorable share of legitimately distributed power (positional authority and personal influence) through which to negotiate procedures favorable to their shared needs and preferences. They compete for these sources in order to orient the society toward the "proper" means and ends.

Competing Groups and the "Wishbone Model"

How, then, do groups compete for control? The process can be illustrated by thinking of society as a wishbone. The top of the wishbone is the established order—the political community temporarily institutionalized as the source of legitimate political control. The two sides of the wishbone can be thought of, respectively, as *communities pressuring for innovation and reversal*, although there will rarely be only two sources of pressure. The established order must accommodate the pressures applied to the two branches to maintain a larger sense of community and to retain its authority. A degree of openness enables the established order to distribute its resources in a way that fulfills and frustrates the needs of individuals and communities sufficient to balance pressures for stability and change. But some leaders try to exercise arbitrary power, denying both the demand and the worth of a community to the society. This can lead to increased pressure, such that the wishbone breaks and a new community establishes a new order. In the Netherlands, for example, government opposition to illegal, but popular, commercial television led first to a naval attack on a "pirate" station and then to a new government and system of broadcast regulation.

It is the purpose of government to resolve disputes among communities within legitimate decision-making arenas, thereby preserving and enhancing the legitimacy of the system and its procedures. People rarely take to the streets when established authorities have been responsive to changing communities' needs. In this sense, extremists play a tragically important role in the process of social change. Let us consider two illustrative cases: the movements for American labor and civil rights.

In the mid-nineteenth century, unions and strikes were illegal and opposed even by many labor leaders. But experience demonstrated that management never negotiated without pressure. The American Federation of Labor emerged as the most important union, but not by itself. Its major gains came when the Industrial Workers of the World relied on violent strikes, kidnappings, and bombings to challenge what they called "wage slavery." Faced with the revolutionary IWW, most companies preferred to grant higher wages to the less extreme AF of L workers. But the IWW opposed American entry into World War I, and any hint of legitimacy or public support vanished. Suddenly, the AF of L had become the most radical labor group on the scene and it fell on hard times. Then in 1935, John L. Lewis led a large, impatient faction out of the AF of L and created the Congress of Industrial Organizations. The CIO struck whole industries (like automobiles and steel) rather than individual trades like (welders or brakemen), quickly establishing itself as the most radical labor group of its day. Once again the AF of L benefitted from the contrast effect. Since they merged into the AFL-CIO in the 1950s, labor has lost much of its political power. Only when radical voices were heard from the wings did the established order negotiate seriously with the blue-collar community.

The civil rights movement followed a similar pattern. There was little institutional support for civil rights reform as long as Reverend Martin Luther King, Jr., was regarded as the most radical voice in America. But by the mid-1960s, two things had happened. First, Dr. King framed his call for civil rights in the dominant logic and values of the American tradition. For example, King's "I Have a Dream" speech, perhaps the greatest speech of the twentieth century, used language and ideology familiar to middle-class white America—morality, patriotism, fair play, and money—to position himself as a responsible voice of America's conscience. Second, the tendency of segregationists to violently challenge the laws and procedures of the established order undercut the legitimacy of segregation. By 1964, King's mainstream rhetoric of change and the segregationists' violent rhetoric of stability combined to impel America toward civil rights legislation. The alternative would have required middle-class white America to endorse one community's brutally violent suppression of citizens who sought nonviolently equal participation in the power, language, ideology, and logic of their society. Visible governmental efforts to improve the lot of black Americans ended in the late 1960s, when the segregationist violence and rhetoric cooled, when the urban riots stopped, and when the struggle lost Dr. King's narrative voice. When in the 1970s a white Californian took his charge of "reverse discrimination" to the Supreme Court, and when white parents protested school busing, the pressure for change shifted to the other branch of the wishbone.

The wishbone model offers a sobering view of social change in America. If we look our history squarely in the eye, we see that our established leadership has largely ignored "responsible pressures" for social change until a violent, quasi-revolutionary wing has made negotiation with moderates prudent. Extremists rarely get what they want; they are usually harassed, jailed, beaten, deported, and even killed, and they are usually despised by moderates in their own communities. But without these extremists, mainstream communities do not seem to hear the needs and demands of responsible moderates. Indeed, the seemingly unending dilemma about terrorists and hostages—to deal or not to deal—bothers us precisely because our political culture has so often negotiated only when confronted by extremists. The underlying logic seems to be, We will not deal with extremists nor will we deal with anyone seeking far-reaching change, unless compelled to choose between the two.

The wishbone model is not a prescription for extremism but a warning not to foster it by isolating responsible communities. Franklin Roosevelt provides a considerably more upbeat example. Roosevelt's presidency began in a climate of rampant frustration in a society of radical communities. Over five years, Roosevelt effectively co-opted members from each community by incorporating diluted versions of their prescriptions into his "New Deal." Revolutionary workers were guaranteed the right to organize and to bargain collectively, supporters of Huey Long's plan to redistribute the wealth were given the progressive income tax, supporters of Townsend's guaranteed pension plan were given the Social Security Act, and on it went. By co-opting these diluted demands, Roosevelt gave to members of each community a vested interest in his community, thereby ending the radical threat. The conservative community thinks Roosevelt gave away too much, and the radical community thinks he undermined a necessary revolution; but for more than 50 years, most American communities have found stable growth because of the established order's eventual responsiveness to the needs of diverse communities.

Leadership as Relational Orientation

Leaders and followers are interconnected systemically, and neither role exists without the other. A systems analysis of leadership, therefore, asks not "What constitutes leadership?" but "Why do some people follow other people?" "There are two reasons," answered Barbara Kellerman. "Leaders satisfy certain individual needs, and leaders satisfy certain group needs" (1984, 79). *Leadership* is the process of mobilizing resources (positional authority, personal influence, language, ideology, and logic) to fulfill/frustrate followers' personal and/or community needs to realize their purposes (adapted from Burns 1978, 18). Leadership mobilizes communities to affect the social wishbone.

Styles of Leadership

James MacGregor Burns (1978) has described two basic ways in which some people mobilize others for a common purpose. He calls these styles transactional and transformational leadership, and they deserve our attention.

Transactional Leadership

Transactional leadership trades power resources for support: I fulfill your needs so that you will fulfill mine, and vice versa. Political machines—like those of Boss Tweed of New York, Huey Long of Louisiana, and Richard Daly, Sr., of Chicago—emerged where disoriented people in need were willing to trade their loyal political support for food, shelter, protection, a Thanksgiving turkey, and, sometimes, a job. Periodically, these political bosses abused their power. But by satisfying their constituents' most basic needs, they motivated community rationalizations of their abuses: "All politicians are crooked, at least these help me" and "They have made this a better place for people like me, and they deserve a little something for doing it" exemplify the logic. Of course, the emerging style of leadership tends to produce a community of grabby people who expect government to resolve their personal and social conflicts.

Transactional leadership is also apparent in legislative communication. Legislators representing diverse interpretive communities support and oppose any bill for a host of reasons, yet they must somehow develop a majority coalition. Through positional authority or personal influence, a few members of the legislature who feel strongly about passage talk with members for whom the bill is noncritical. The pursuit of community interests and self-interests frequently leads to a transaction: I consider the vital needs of your community on matters peripheral to mine if you consider the vital needs of my community on matters peripheral to yours. Of course, "vital" and "peripheral" are subject to interpretation, and opposition candidates can be relied on to offer competing interpretations. But at this level the legislative process works transactionally.

Transactional leadership is perhaps less obvious when political candidates make promises to induce our support. Candidates who promise "economic opportunity" and "no new taxes" are trading language to communities of motives for electoral support. Not unlike the poor immigrants with their turkeys, we congratulate ourselves on our rational evaluation of the candidates and prefer one over the other, concluding that: "neither candidate is great, but this guy will take care of people like us." The candidate gets the vote, and we get the promise. The uneducated, poor immigrants got turkeys. In many ways, the process is the same.

Transactional leadership entails bargains, not manipulation. Dan Hahn captured the essential dilemma:

> If I want you to like me and I know you will if I do X, does that mean that if I do X I am manipulating you? Or have you manipulated me? (1987, 262)

Behavioral psychologist B. F. Skinner reportedly manipulated pigeons to turn in circles simply by offerring them birdseed, but one wonders if the pigeons might report manipulating psychologists into feeding them by merely turning in circles! Did Ronald Reagan manipulate us to vote for him by promising tax cuts, or did we manipulate him into promising tax cuts? The best answer is "yes"—to both parts. The point is that *community leadership is interdependent: Leaders cannot lead without followers any more than followers can follow without a leader.*

A leader can manipulate language and logic to induce favorable interpretation by followers, but the interpretive processes of those potential followers constrain the leader's options. If followers later feel tricked, their aggravation ripples through their interpretive systems undermining their respect for their leader. Recall both the public outrage when the Iranian rescue mission contradicted Carter's repeated denunciations of force and the outcry over the hostage deals after Reagan vowed repeatedly not to deal with terrorists.

The transactional leader uses community logic, ideology, and language to legitimately distribute the power resources. Leadership of the society, therefore, requires either the mobilization of a community sufficiently large and powerful to carry the polity (*majority politics*) or the use of multiple power bases, multiple languages, multiple ideologies, and multiple logics in order to mobilize multiple minority communities into a sufficiently large and powerful alliance (*coalition politics*). Majority politics evidences clear, consistent, and relatively concrete language, ideology, and logic because it emerges from a single community; whereas coalition politics provides abstract, ambiguous, even contradictory language, ideology, and logic because it needs to simultaneously satisfy the needs of diverse and potentially conflicting communities. Whether these groupings occur before elections, as in America, or after elections, as in France, a nation's diverse interests coalesce eventually into clusters. Leadership facilitates the clustering process.

Society-level transactional leadership is often viewed with suspicion by the communities. It is here that we find murmurings of "It's all politics," as a community's purposes are compromised to attain part of its program. Transactional followers who invest power in their leader in exchange for need fulfillment are disappointed by anything less.

But to distribute those resources, the transactional leader must deal with rival communities and their leaders. A majority leader is in a good position to fulfill constituent needs, except that constant favoritism to the majority community may encourage the mobilization of disparate minorities into an opposition coalition. A transactional leader of a minority community can probably win resources for that community only by joining a coalition or by acquiescing to the majority community on other questions; either way, need fulfillment is only partial. A transactional leader of a coalition serves as a *broker* of minority needs, building bank accounts of needs and resources. It is not surprising that transactional followers frequently feel betrayed.

It is imperative for transactional leaders to be able to create power resources suited to their community. The followers' demands for responsiveness and the leadership's need for legitimacy combine to create a spiral toward insatiability that can deplete the leadership's warehouse of resources. Successful transactional leadership, therefore, requires a resource factory; and language, ideology, and logic are its raw materials. Transactional leaders can give speeches to one community and new streets to another; they can proclaim holidays to honor the symbolic leader of one community and appoint judges from another; they can denounce drug trafficking and cut funds for drug enforcement; and they can hold press conferences without revealing anything of substance. In these ways and others, transactional leaders create extra resources for distribution among their competing domains. Through this process, transactional leaders who hold power can generate more resources, as when an urban machine accommodates newly emerging communities. But the process is demanding and risky precisely because it is generally unsatisfying to transactional followers.

Transformational Leadership

Transactional leadership is prevalent, but it fails to account for all effective leadership. Would a true transactional leader ever risk community disfavor? If not, where is the leadership? It is at this point that personal preferencing enters the picture.

Every leader will sense periodically that the community has misunderstood its symbols, inverted its priorities, legitimized unworthy authorities, or applied inappropriate narrative forms. At some of these times, the leader's personal preferences run toward principle rather than power. *Transformational leadership* occurs when a leader transcends existing needs and seeks to satisfy higher needs, moving leader and the led to "higher levels of motivation and morality" (Burns 1978, 20).

It is through transformational leadership that power, language, ideology, and logic evolve. This is not to say that government or other established communities exercise it; rather various members of various communities take it on themselves to revise the language, ideology, and logic to better satisfy the needs of members. The doctrine of supply-side economics propounded in the early 1980s by Ronald Reagan and Jack Kemp illustrates the process.

Conservatives and Republicans argued for 50 years that (1) government programs undermine individual initiative, (2) government spending causes inflation, and (3) taxation hurts economic growth. Everyone dislikes taxes, but a broad coalition of interpretive communities accepted taxation by subordinating their economic wants to the needs of society. The doctrine of supply-side economics modified familar constructs, reordered preferences, and interpreted economic trends through a new narrative form. Supply-side economics proposed tax reductions and cuts in federal domestic spending to stimulate economic growth, which would generate additional revenue that would enable us to simply outgrow the massive deficit. When opponents argued that tax reductions would widen the deficit, supply-siders generally responded that they had failed to move to the higher plane of economic consciousness. The taxes and spending were cut, and the deficit grew and grew.

But the supply-side doctrine was nevertheless embraced and justified in many communities because it legitimized the fulfillment of several needs unrelated to, but more basic than, the deficit. In supply-side economics, the needs of society required us to accept more take-home pay and to provide less support to marginal minority communities. The argument worked nearly as well as the policy failed.

Supply-side economics transformed the way members of several communities judged economic policy and thereby altered the leadership of the nation. Reagan and Kemp moved their audiences to a higher moral plane by showing them their moral obligation—not to pay taxes that underwrite social programs but to stimulate economic growth by spending their own money, thereby providing the dependent an opportunity to improve themselves. Notice that this argument stakes out high moral ground by transcending the liberal and Democratic doctrine of collective responsibility for the disadvantaged; it is also considerably higher ground than the old conservative argument that government has no right to interfere in free enterprise.

Burns is right to observe that transformational leadership uniquely offers the potential to inspire, to exhort, and to uplift a community of followers. We see ample evidence of that in the leadership of Jesus Christ, Mohandas Gandhi, Abraham Lincoln, Woodrow Wilson, and Reverend Martin Luther King, Jr. But Burns is perhaps naive if he believes that transformational leadership necessarily lifts leaders and followers to a higher moral plane.

The career of Adolf Hitler may indicate the potential danger of transformational leadership, since a Nazi analyzing Hitler in 1942 would probably have stressed his exemplary transformation of German consciousness. The problem here is that the loftiness of moral standards is judged within an interpretive community: we regard Gandhi, King, and Jesus Christ as morally uplifting leaders because they refined and extended dimly lit values. This is not to say that all beliefs and values are equally lofty, nor is it to equate in any way the morals of Hitler, Gandhi, and Jesus; it is to say that the ways in which these moral values are understood and used by human beings occur within personal and community interpretive processes. It seems safer to discuss transformational leadership not as a move to a higher moral plane but as a move from one interpretive framework to another. This captures the potential for uplifting leadership without requiring it.

Unlike transactional leadership, transformational leadership must demonstrate the inadequacy of existing interpretive frameworks and the adequacy of the proposed needs, symbols, preferences, and reasons. Transformation requires that members admit shortcomings in their interpretive systems. This is less straightforward than it sounds. We rely on our interpretive frameworks to make sense of the world, and we are unlikely to abandon a framework that works for us. Indeed, authority-reliant persons often respond to an interpretive challenge by clinging even more tightly to their interpretive frameworks (Rokeach 1960).

The key is the comparison level of alternatives between the old and new interpretive systems. Given the believers' facility with the old power relationships, language, ideology, and logic, we can expect them to require (1) a distinct loss of confidence in their old interpretive system, (2) a new interpretive system that is exceptionally promising, or (3) a balance between the two. The outside challenge is likely merely to frighten believers into increased reliance on their interpretive authorities. Recall how the *Charlotte Observer*'s allegations of PTL Club corruption encouraged contributions for its defense, whereas allegations from within PTL's community quickly toppled the Bakkers. A more politically significant transformation centered around the Panama Canal Treaties of 1978.

The U.S. and Panama began renegotiating the canal treaties in 1964. The Carter administration concluded two treaties (1) affirming Panamanian sovereignty over the canal, (2) guaranteeing America preferential use of the canal, and (3) granting America the right to intervene militarily if the canal were ever closed. The treaties were supported by most military and congressional leaders. But several conservatives saw in the Panama Canal potent images of Teddy

Roosevelt's Rough Riders and they used the canal treaties to challenge the prevailing logic of American foreign policy.

The New Right talked about the "giveaway" and "surrender" of the canal as a sign of American weakness. President Carter was left to explain how America had tricked Panama into the original treaty, that Panama already owned it, and that America lacked legitimate authority to defend it—a narrative unlikely to inspire confidence. Although the treaties were approved as expected, the New Right had established a new interpretive framework, and they had generated mailing lists of people who shared it. The mailing lists and contributions from the Panama campaign helped them to mobilize the New Right community and to unseat several vulnerable Democrats in 1978. The election of 1980 empowered this community, which demonstrated its military muscle in Grenada, Nicaragua, Lebanon, Libya, and the Straits of Hormuz. When the "good neighbor" moved out and "Rambo" moved in, a new interpretive community began to exercise leadership (Smith 1986).

The Panama Canal controversy is one of many interpretive transformations in American history. Consider some of our other watershed shifts in prevailing assumptions. In 1787, we shifted from the Articles of Confederation's 13 separate states to the Constitution's 13 states with a central government. In 1862, we shifted from the assumption that white people could own black people to the assumption that slavery was unthinkable. In the early twentieth century, we shifted from the assumption of appointed senators to popularly elected senators. In the 1930s, we shifted from the assumption of rugged individualism to the assumption of a safety net for the unfortunate. These and other changes rippled through American society and transformed many communities.

Transformational leadership entails several important processes. Because reorientation must account for history, it requires a reinterpretation of events that would otherwise complicate belief. Revisionists elevate otherwise obscure figures and events or challenge the importance of familiar ones. They construct "conspiracy arguments" that allege secret transactions between the current leadership and enemies of the community (Hofstadter 1965). But most often they find the "real lesson" in history by subordinating the familiar lesson and elevating a new one (Zarefsky 1980). With our anchor in the past moved, the straight line of history runs from the revised past through the present to a different future—one inviting the new interpretive system.

Reorientation must also provide an internally consistent logic. The principles by which people interpret the world must be sufficiently consistent for them to do so. But there are variations on the process. Remember that authority-reliant and authority-dependent members have divergent needs for leadership. An ideology and logic may be difficult for followers to apply precisely because its central premise is the need for authoritative leadership. Once again, the John Birch Society illustrates the possibilities.

John Birch Society doctrine created many confusing points. If President Kennedy helped the communists, why was he shot by a Cuban sympathizer? And if the Vietnam War was a communist plan to waste our military and economic resources, why was it opposed by leftist demonstrators? But precisely because Birch Society derivations and logic frequently conflicted, followers turned to Robert Welch for his authoritative answers. The need for leadership and followership was nurtured by a confusing ideological logic.

Leadership versus Power

Leadership and power are not the same. Leadership uses the resources of power to achieve goals shared by many in the community. Coercion uses the resources of power to achieve goals opposed by the community, whereas persuasion induces members of the community to take on and to value shared needs, shared symbols, shared preferences, and shared reasoning. Persuasion fosters a sense of community; coercion undermines community.

Coercion usually comes into play when there is a failure of leadership. Those who can neither manage their authority and influence to sustain transactional leadership nor transform community standards are often tempted to overwhelm their opposition. This happens when leaders are more impressed by their resources than are their followers. Short-term coercive victories often become long-term losses.

Conclusions

This chapter discussed the processes by which interpretive communities compete for the means to interpret the world for others. This competition is fundamentally sincere, as people try to save other people from mistaken ways; but in the heat of conflict, it can become self-serving and ignoble.

Communities strive for a favorable distribution of legitimate power so that they can influence the procedures by which conflicts are resolved. The wishbone model of social change illustrated the role played by challenging groups and extremists, as communities mobilize to influence the established order. Leadership mobilizes communities into majorities or coalitions by transacting within the interpretive structure or by transforming the community's interpretive structure. Their mobilizations confront the established order with a constellation of often conflicting needs and resources, which are dealt with transactionally or transformationally using the society's language, ideology, and logic.

The primary theme of this chapter was that political leadership involves the orientation and reorientation of followers by competing groups. But no group has the public ear all to itself. A compelling argument may go unnoticed, or a momentary celebrity may steal the spotlight for a trivial issue. Moreover, it is the individual's willingness to doubt his or her own interpretive system that leads to reorientation. This orientation is accomplished through basic rhetorical techniques, and they are the subject of Chapter 4.

References

Burns, James MacGregor. *Leadership*. New York: Harper and Row, 1978.

Dahl, Robert A. "Power." In *International Encyclopedia of the Social Sciences*, 12, 407–08. New York: Macmillan and Free Press, 1968.

Hahn, Dan F. "The Media and the Presidency: Ten Propositions." *Communication Quarterly* 35 (Summer 1987): 254–66.

Hofstadter, Richard. "The Paranoid Style in American Politics." In *The Paranoid Style in American Politics and Other Essays*, 3–40. New York: Alfred A. Knopf, 1965.

Kellerman, Barbara. "Leadership as a Political Act." In *Leadership: Multidisciplinary Perspectives*, edited by Barbara Kellerman, 63–90. Englewood Cliffs, NJ: Prentice-Hall, 1984.

Neustadt, Richard E. *Presidential Power: The Politics of Leadership from FDR to Carter*. New York: John Wiley and Sons, 1980.

Riker, William H. *The Art of Political Manipulation*. New Haven: Yale University Press, 1986.

Rokeach, Milton. *The Open- and Closed-Mind*. New York: Basic Books, 1960.

Smith, Craig Allen. "Leadership, Orientation, and Rhetorical Vision: Jimmy Carter, the 'New Right,' and the Panama Canal." *Presidential Studies Quarterly*, 16 (Spring 1986): 317–28.

Stewart, Charles J., Craig Allen Smith, and Robert E. Denton, Jr. *Persuasion and Social Movements*. 2d ed. Prospect Heights, IL: Waveland Press, 1989.

Turner, Victor. *From Ritual to Theatre: The Human Seriousness of Play*. New York: Performing Arts Journal Publications, 1982.

Zarefsky, David. "Lyndon Johnson Redefines 'Equal Opportunity': The Beginnings of Affirmative Action. *Central States Speech Journal*, 31 (Summer 1980): 85–94.

Chapter 4
RHETORIC IN POLITICAL COMMUNICATION

The axiom that "You cannot not communicate" reminds us that we cannot control the ways in which others attend, interpret, construe, or react to our behavior. Communication is not what a speaker says but how speakers and listeners and writers and readers cooperatively interpret their realities to find—to coin Turner's term, (1982)—"communitas." But even if you cannot not communicate, it is entirely possible to communicate badly.

What Is "Rhetoric"?

Because others make sense of your behavior through their interpretive systems and not yours, it is prudent to adapt. *To adapt your communicative behavior to their interpretive systems is to engage in rhetoric.*

Aristotle defined rhetoric as "the faculty of discovering, in a given situation, the available means of persuasion" (1924). For Donald C. Bryant, rhetoric was the "rationale of the informative and suasory in discourse" (1953). Bowers and Ochs defined it even more inclusively as the "rationale of instrumental symbolic action" (1971).

Today, students of rhetoric are conceiving of it in increasingly inclusive ways, such that it has become, for many, the study of culture. The danger in defining rhetoric or anything else too broadly is that the label, or concept, becomes less and less useful. Without denying others the right to use the term "rhetoric" broadly, we will use it in a more traditional, restricted sense.

Rhetoric here refers to *the process of consciously adjusting ideas to people and people to ideas* (adapted from Bryant 1953). Put differently, rhetoric is the process of thinking consciously about the best way to mesh your needs, symbols, preferences, and reasons with others' needs, symbols, preferences, and reasons. It is the strategic aspect of communication through which you decide how best to help your partner(s) share your interpretation.

Notice that this definition of rhetoric is restricted neither to public speeches nor even to discourse, because you adapt to others' interpretive processes in even the most intimate dialogues. Notice also that rhetoric is not corrupt. As Plato argued in *The Gorgias*, people who complain about the abuses of rhetoric could not make their complaints understood without it. Rhetoric is a necessary and desirable process if you wish to be understood by anyone other than your identical twin. This chapter will examine the functions of rhetoric in political communication.

The Governmental Functions of Rhetoric

If individuals and communities are to endure as a united society, they need to develop and sustain a sense of community. We find in the writings of ancients like Isocrates and Aristotle the theme that the community creates and is created by communication. Rhetoric, as the process of consciously adapting to one's partner(s) in communication, contributes to the performance of five functions necessary for governance: rhetoric helps to unify, to legitimize, to orient, to resolve conflicts, and to implement policies.

Rhetoric functions to *unify* a society by nurturing the sense of inclusion and participation among its diverse communities with their varied people, languages, ideologies, logics, and traditions. The basic act of communicating with another person establishes a sense of relationship, which may provide that magical moment of "communitas" discussed in Chapter 3. Beyond that, what is said blends a variety of symbols, myths, values, and reasons that evoke recognition and identification among those in the audience.

Rhetoric serves to *legitimize* by justifying the distribution of power in society as people use language to explain to one another who should defer to whom. The distribution is legitimized by grounding it in a community ideology, like divine right or popular sovereignty, or in a community narrative, like social Darwinism's survival of the fittest. Powerholders, aspirants to political power, and followers alike justify their behavior in a legitimation rhetoric appropriate to the community.

Rhetoric helps to *orient* society by framing goals and problems in a coherent narrative familiar to the community. American presidents tend to frame policies in terms of warfare—the war on poverty, the war on inflation, the war on drugs—a metaphor that encourages dependence on their leadership and discourages dissent. The depicted political landscape frames political reality for the citizenry and undermines the search for alternative frameworks.

Rhetoric can *resolve conflicts* in several ways. Abstractions enable people to lose their differences in their support of "freedom," "a strong national defense," and "help for the truly needy." Rhetoric also can draw new distinctions to create a middle ground. President Ford, for example, allowed Vietnam-era draft evaders to earn pardons, thereby allowing their return from Canada without condoning their behavior. It is also through rhetoric that facts are challenged, arguments are advanced, and decisions are announced.

Finally, rhetoric serves to *implement policies* by mobilizing or by narcoticizing constituents. Mobilizing involves activation and organization, as when the Reagans encouraged us to "Just say no!" to drugs or when the Nixon administration urged us to turn our thermostats down to 68 degrees in winter to save energy. Narcoticizing involves pacification and distraction, as when terms such as "user fees" and "revenue enhancement" substitute for "tax increases" or when an official profusely praises the advisors whose advice she rejected. Normally, rhetoric mobilizes supporters and narcoticizes opponents. But it is possible to mobilize the opposition and to narcoticize supporters.

Theoretically, rhetoric can be separated from governance. In tribal days, for example, the person with the heaviest club performed all five functions until deposed. There was no need for rhetoric then. The governance of a few Neanderthals was uncomplicated, as force legitimized itself and survival needs oriented the tribe. Conflicts were resolved and solutions implemented by virtue of the heaviest club. But the turnover rate was high, and the transitions from headbasher to headbasher were problematic. Eventually, they began to hit each other with words and threats. Still later, they constructed roles, responsibilities, sanctions, procedures, and institutions to stabilize their governance.

Some people would argue even today that rhetoric is only marginally related to governance, that those with authority and a monopoly on the resources need not be concerned about adapting to their subjects. But rhetoric is the process through which new transactional resources are created and by which community standards are transformed.

Functional Rhetoric as Situational

At least since Aristotle's time, rhetoric has been viewed situationally. Lloyd Bitzer's interest in rhetoric as a functional adjustment to situational problems led to his model of the "rhetorical situation"

(1968). Central to each rhetorical situation is an *exigence*—an imperfection marked by a degree of urgency. Some exigences, a tornado for example, cannot be affected directly by communication; so exigences that can be influenced by communication create *rhetorical situations*. The rhetor sees the exigence and realizes that it can be influenced through communication with an appropriate *audience*. But the rhetor's attempt to enlist the audience's assistance is subject to a variety of situational *constraints*: the audience may distrust the rhetor; they may accept neither the imperfection nor its urgency; they may fail to recognize their power; the rhetor may be unskilled; or discussion of the exigence may worsen it. *The rhetor's goal is to respond appropriately to the situational exigence, audience, and constraints.*

Although each persuasive effort is unique, exigencies and constraints often recur. We refer to recurrent rhetorical situations—like election campaigns, inaugural addresses, and accusation and defenses—as genres of rhetoric, and we often study the genre for advice about specific situations. An international crisis is an exigence for a president; a newscast is an exigence for the station's news department; and an election is an exigence for a candidate. But exigences are interpreted, and no two people will attribute identical imperfection or urgency to the same difficulty.

"The Rhetorical Situation" (Bitzer 1968) provoked several responses. The major criticism was that the exigence, audience, constraints, and their interconnectedness are themselves established through rhetoric. Richard Vatz argued that rhetors define or redefine the situations rather than merely react to predetermined structures (1973).

Vatz's argument is compelling, but it overstates the case. Rhetors often *try* to redefine exigences, constraints, and identities, but their audiences work within their own personal and social interpretive systems. This means that most audiences need familiar explanations and arguments, because new ones traumatize their interpretive systems. Consequently, most political rhetors frequently build on prevailing audience motives, symbols, beliefs, and narratives. Bitzer revised his model in light of the comments by Vatz and others. Although Bitzer's revision (1980) greatly enhances his model by responding to the criticism, too many people still focus on the original 1968 essay.

Rhetorical situations evolve through four stages (Bitzer 1980). The first stage entails the *origin and development of constituent parts*, as exigence, audience, and constraints are defined through rhetoric. The situation reaches *maturity* in the second stage, as the elements align so that an audience capable of influencing the exigence is susceptible to influence by a prepared rhetor working within the constraints. But this moment is transient, and many meetings adjourn without reaching decisions. During stage three the situation *deteriorates*, as the audience disbands, the deadline is missed, or the constraints change. The rhetor must attempt to restructure the situation lest it *disintegrate* (stage four) to the point that the audience or constraints no longer exist or that the exigence can no longer be modified through talk.

Throughout the evolutionary process, the rhetor's goal is a *fitting response*, which either resolves the exigence (a *terminal response*) or moves the situation toward maturity and the possibility of terminal resolution (*instrumental response*). Perhaps the most troublesome rhetorical situations confront a highly constrained rhetor with an undefined but urgent exigence that is, by virtue of its fluidity, not susceptible to resolution by any known audience. Consider the case of Legionnaires' Disease.

An American Legion convention at a prominent Philadelphia hotel found several of its members suddenly dying for no apparent reason. Unexplainable deaths constitute urgent imperfections in most interpretive frameworks. The exigence invited some kind of verbal response, but what kind: outrage, warnings, reassurance, blame? And without knowing the cause of the exigence, to whom should the verbal response be addressed? Information about the crisis quickly reached everyone through news coverage, such that people everywhere watched for unexplained deaths. It was soon apparent that the problem affected only those legionnaires in that hotel. Should they be sent home or quarantined? By this time, the exigence of unexplained death had invited investigation by medical personnel, who eventually defined the causal exigence as a defect in the air-conditioning system. That exigence could then be remedied by trained technicians.

Definition of the exigence as environmental rather than, say, biological warfare against our veterans or some form of divine retribution was an important instrumental response, without which the exigence could not have been terminally resolved. But that instrumental definition created a tremendous public relations exigence for the hotel. Indeed, the hotel was so closely associated with this frightening episode that people became reluctant to stay there, and eventually it closed. Might a name change have helped to save the hotel by instrumentally disassociating the safe hotel from the dangerous hotel?

Bitzer's revised model of rhetorical situations thus accounts for the definition and redefinition of situational elements as well as responses to situational givens. In political contexts, we are especially likely to find institutionalized exigences, audiences, and constraints; for example, a candidate wins election only by garnering a legally predetermined portion of votes cast by registered voters under prescribed procedures on a certain day. Jesse Jackson drew more votes than Al Gore in the 1988 Georgia primary, but because delegates were won at the district level, Gore emerged with more convention delegates. This is the exigence-based resolution, regardless of any rhetor's efforts to redefine the situation. For this reason, Bitzer's model is especially applicable to the study of political rhetoric, even if other kinds of persuasion afford persuaders greater flexibility. As Oliver North should have learned by now, situational constraints should not be ignored.

Political Relationships and Rhetorical Situations

Rhetorical exigencies are resolved through the cooperative efforts of the rhetor and his or her appropriate audience, that is, through relationships. We contact our elected officials; we march on the capitol; the president asks our cooperation—all of these are relationships comprising political roles. This leads us to consider the ways in which people consciously adjust their relationships to resolve situational exigencies.

Adherence

Before it can be said that a rhetor has influenced another, there must come a moment when that other person *adheres* to the rhetor's position as preferable to his or her alternatives, including those previously preferred by the other person. Chaim Perelman's pivotal study of argumentation shed important light on this process.

Perelman approached the study of argument by differentiating between *demonstration*, or formal logic, which impersonally calculates conclusions, and *argumentation*, which seeks to win adherence to the claims that it presents. Unlike demonstration, argumentation is audience centered and arises from the audience's interpretations. But audiences, for Perelman, are neither listeners seated in an auditorium nor households gathered around their televisions; they are "the ensemble of those whom the speaker wishes to influence by his argumentation" (Perelman and Olbrechts-Tyteca 1968, 19), whether directly or indirectly.

A rhetor creates arguments to win the adherence of a *particular audience*. A presidential candidate advances somewhat different arguments to win the adherence of voters in Iowa, New Hampshire, Texas, New York, and Kansas, for example. But Perelman argues that each rhetor is also guided by a personal conception of a *universal audience* that is both competent and reasonable—the audience we address when debating with ourselves about the wisdom of buying a car or voting for a candidate. The universal audience need not be universal in size; whenever you believe that you alone exercise common sense, you have the adherence of your universal audience in your quest for the adherence of a particular audience.

Argumentation moves from rhetor-audience agreement about premises to agreement about a conclusion. It starts with universally accepted *facts* and the *truths* that link them (from religious doctrine to scientific method) and *presumptions* about the nature of reality. Any statement loses its status as fact, truth, or presumption when it loses its universal acceptance; that is, when it is challenged. A rhetor must therefore begin the process of arguing with an assessment of the particular audience's adherence both to universal facts, truths, and presumptions and to those facts, truths, and presumptions accepted as universal aspects of reality by members of the particular audience. These alone are the rhetor's starting points for argument.

From matters of reality, Perelman's rhetor moves to matters of preference. As discussed in the first three chapters, individuals develop preferences and communities coalesce around shared preferences. Perelman's particular audiences develop around their shared conceptions of *the preferable*. A particular audience's conception of the preferable is based on its *values*, the *hierarchies* of values it constructs, and its *loci*. We have discussed already the nature of values, but loci require elaboration.

The term *loci* is the plural of the Latin *locus* and refers to the "places" or "topics" around which preferences are constructed. We can imagine two persons who agree about facts, truths, presumptions, values, and hierarchies but, nevertheless, disagree about a government policy. The place at which their disagreement about the preferable occurs might be the *locus of quality* or the *locus* of *quantity* or one of the other loci suggested by Perelman. Or it might be between *general loci*, which apply to all of the particular audience's relationships and situations, or *special loci*, which govern limited circumstances. The particular audience is defined in terms of its adherence to a particular set of values, hierarchies, and loci and not by any other characteristics. One need not be female to adhere to feminist arguments about equal pay for equal work, nor need everyone with female chromosomes adhere to neo-Marxist arguments about dominance and exploitation. Even more pointedly, civil rights reforms in America would never have been possible unless portions of the majority had accepted the minority's conception of the preferable.

Because the rhetor wants the particular audience's adherence to the conclusion, not merely the premises, she must choose which premises to highlight. The rhetor's choice of premises heightens their *presence*, or salience, in the audience's conception of the conclusion by bringing those premises forward from the mind's dim recesses. Sometimes the rhetor introduces new facts that go unchallenged or uses facts and presumptions to introduce new general or special loci for the audience. Sometimes the rhetor works toward *communion* with the audience so that they accept the rhetor as a prophet of the preferable. But in any case, the rhetor works to alter the audience's adherence to a new conclusion based on its preferred reality. This is accomplished with the techniques of liaison and dissociation.

Techniques of liaison transform audience adherence to the premises into adherence to the conclusion by joining them together in new ways. *Quasi-logical arguments* resemble formal calculations but require audience acceptance. Some arguments *establish the structure of reality*, while others are *based on the structure of reality*. *Techniques of dissociation* split an audience's existing preference into paired terms of appearance (term 1) and reality (term 2). By separating the two for the audience, the rhetor makes term 2 acceptable for the audience by reconciling conflicts about the meaning of term 1. The techniques of liaison and dissociation are illustrated in President Ford's first address to the Veterans of Foreign Wars.

Gerald Ford assumed the presidency, pledging to heal America from the scars of Watergate and Vietnam. Among the problems were some 50,000 people who had evaded the draft or deserted. The VFW's premises should have been self-evident, but many citizens judged the war a mistake and believed the draft-dodgers had been vindicated. Unelected President Ford had to bring them together, and he began to do so in an address to the VFW convention (Ford [1974] 1975).

Ford established communion with his membership in several veterans' organizations, his appointment of a new Veterans Administration administrator, his praise of veterans, and his concern for VA hospitals. He built on their reality to pull all veterans, regardless of wars, into one audience—of which Ford himself was commander in chief—and affirmed his view that "unconditional, blanket amnesty for anyone who illegally evaded or fled military service is wrong." The veterans were wildly enthusiastic about their new president, who had yet to transfer their adherence.

Ford began the transfer by metaphorically establishing the structure of the new realities. The task of this new president was "to bind up the nation's wounds," because like the veterans, the draft-dodgers "in a sense, were casualties, still abroad or absent without leave from the real America." This required Ford to dissociate America from real America and blanket amnesty, which was wrong, from earned amnesty, which was right, by invoking universal American truths, presumptions, values, hierarchies, and loci:

> I want them to come home if they want to *work* their way back . . .
> [and] I will act promptly, fairly, and very firmly in the same spirit that
> guided Abraham Lincoln and Harry Truman. As I reject amnesty, so I
> reject revenge. (Ford [1974] 1975)

Quickly Ford returned to his discussion of veterans' issues and problems and the role of America's military role in the world. President Ford gave veterans a rhetorical doughnut of communion filled with the bitter jelly of earned amnesty. They could enthusiastically embrace this president, who was one of them and who shared their premises, or reject him because of his amnesty program. There was some outcry against President Ford's program, but far less than accompanied his pardon of former President Nixon without rhetorical justification some three weeks later. Gerald Ford did what he felt was right and presented it responsibly to the audience most likely to reject it, and they respected him for it. If the VFW did not transfer its adherence to earned amnesty, they, nevertheless, followed their rhetorical commander in chief.

Perelman's conception of argument is important for understanding the human dimension of argument and the interaction between arguments and audiences.

Identification and Polarization

Identification is the process of finding or creating common ground with others to overcome division, and it is the central concept in Kenneth Burke's approach to persuasion (1966, 1969).

Proper identification demands both a strong sense of self and a sensitivity to others. Research on the concept of *rhetorical sensitivity* has found two types of insensitive people (Hart, Eadie, and Carlson, 1980). *Rhetorical reflectors* habitually tell audiences what they want to hear, not what they themselves really think. Reflectors avoid arguments, criticism, and unpleasantness in general. Like the human chameleon in Woody Allen's *Zelig*, reflectors sacrifice self in the pursuit of acceptance. Sadly, others eventually recognize the reflectors' lack of straightforwardness, and they are left with neither self-confidence nor meaningful relationships.

Conversely, *noble selves* habitually speak their minds, no matter whom or how it hurts. Sportscaster Howard Cosell, talk show phenomenon Morton Downey, and most of John Wayne's film characters, for example, bluntly spoke their minds. Columnist and speech writer Patrick Buchanan expresses himself with a biting conviction that has won the enthusiastic loyalty of his fellow conservatives, but his prose on behalf of Presidents Nixon and Reagan compounded their problems by antagonizing liberals and many moderates. When people take offense at their bluntness, noble selves dismiss displeasure as the listeners' problem.

The rhetorical reflector and the noble self are both engaged in perverted identification. Both simplify the communicative act by engaging in only half of it. The reflector adjusts to people but avoids adjusting the people to him. The noble self adjusts people to her but avoids adjusting to people. Proper identification requires a delicate balance. *The rhetorically sensitive person says what she thinks in a way that respects her audience's sense of self, values, and reality.*

Could a Minnesota liberal identify with Louisiana conservatives during intense civil rights conflicts? Before a Louisiana State University audience, Vice President Hubert Humphrey alluded to his largely overlooked days as a pharmacy student on that campus, expressed his pleasure over their recent Sugar Bowl football team, and shared their enthusiasm for mascot "Mike the Tiger." Could the head of the American Nazi party identify with students and faculty at a disproportionately Jewish Ivy League university? George Lincoln Rockwell traded his uniform for a business suit and stressed his alumni status for a Brown University audience, establishing himself as a temperate, rational member of their community rather than a crackpot.

The Humphrey and Rockwell examples illustrate how speakers can create a shared past from audience experiences. Emphasizing the "we" relationship enabled Humphrey and Rockwell to temporarily reduce hostility by redefining the context from politics to alumni affairs. They established themselves as acceptable narrators before beginning their substantive messages. It is difficult to dislike pleasant people who demonstrate that they are related to you. Each speaker tried to ego-involve his audience in a narrative relationship so that it would assimilate, rather than contrast, his message. Was that deceptive? Not at all. Each speaker wanted, and deserved, a fair hearing that he could not otherwise have received. It would have been deceptive for either to fabricate an educational background or to use the same text at a variety of universities. Rockwell's audience nibbled more of his bait than we might have expected before recognizing it and spitting it out; Humphrey's audience found its national government somewhat more reasonable.

The counterpart of identification is *polarization*, which encourages individuals to submerge their differences in the face of a common enemy. Polarization *subverts* the credibility of rival communities and *affirms* the sense of group identity in the face of the enemy (King and Anderson 1971). It creates an in-group out of distaste for an out-group.

There is no better example of polarization in American politics than the career of Richard Nixon. First, he built a coalition of Americans who were anticommunist, anti–Eastern upper class, and anti-Truman. He later won the 1968 presidential nomination by telling conservative delegates that their choice was between the moderate Nixon and the liberal Rockefeller while telling liberal delegates that their choice was between the moderate Nixon and the conservative Reagan. He won the election by highlighting public dissaffection from the Johnson-Humphrey administration and from public fear of George Wallace's extremism. He defended his Vietnam policies by uniting those who disliked protestors into a "great silent majority" of Americans who implicitly supported him. His policy of *détente* threatened the Russians with an American-Chinese alliance while threatening the Chinese with a Soviet-American alliance. He was reelected in 1972 in preference to the perceived extremism of George McGovern. *In all of these significant cases, Nixon mobilized support around people's dislikes and fears.* Perhaps this constant negativism is part of the reason why few people rushed to Nixon's aid when he was himself charged with misconduct; he had provided little ground for identification other than our greater dislike or distrust of others.

The Nixon case illustrates the power of polarizing rhetoric. He, like many others, was able to build coalitions capable of winning elections by playing off dislikes, divisions, and differences. But he nurtured animosity and fueled the prospects for out-group coalition building. Nixon exemplifies both how one can ride the rhetoric of polarization to world leadership and how a steady diet of polarization can endanger one's legitimacy.

Adolf Hitler also demonstrates that people are easily united against something. Throughout post–Reformation Europe, Protestants and Catholics rarely came together unless it was to oppose Jews. In 1932, Hitler took power in a land that in just six decades had unified, become a world power, and suffered humiliating defeat. Hitler emphasized the shared Germanic language and mythology. But with little heritage of national unity, he transcended Protestant and Catholic differences by affirming their similarities in the face of a subverted Jewish community (Bosmajian 1974; Bytwerk 1983).

Polarization may be an easier path than identification sometimes, but it raises serious ethical and practical questions. The mobilization of dislikes and fears can be healthy for society and for individuals, as when we are polarized against organized crime, drugs, drunk driving, and foreign invasion. At other times, the exploitation of dislikes and fears can be unethical and dangerous to individuals and society alike, as in the Hitler example, Joe McCarthy's subversive witch-hunts of the 1950s, the antiestablishment movement of the 1960s, the swine flu scare of 1975, and the antitaxation sentiment of the late 1980s.

In cases of polarization, people united by their fundamental dislike(s) have difficulty uniting around productive alternatives. This means that (1) their existence depends on the continuance of the very thing they despise; (2) their community existence is threatened by argument over positive alternatives; (3) the sense of personal and community identity is constructed from the aggravating, ulcerous venom of hostility, which may (4) turn the essence of community against its leader, because (5) division produces guilt, which requires redemption. As polarizers Nixon and Hitler illustrate, a polarized society will often reunite over the rhetorical corpse of its polarizer.

Identification and polarization are linked, such that every attempt at identification will polarize somebody, and every attempt at polarization will nurture identification among others. But one is usually more evident than the other, and the rhetor's choice creates product and byproduct. The point here is that *it matters, politically and ethically, whether one produces polarization as a byproduct of identification or produces identification as a byproduct of polarization.* Some polarization is bound to occur, but we can avoid throwing gasoline on embers.

If you are to make yourself understood to others, you must find or create common ground. Of the three basic paths to understanding, one—the use of already shared motives, symbols, preferences, and reasons—builds on community. But where the available common ground is insufficient to negotiate understanding, you must either adopt others' interpretive perspectives or enable them to adopt your interpretive perspectives. These ongoing adjustments are generally of a delicate surgical variety, only very rarely are there sweeping conversions.

Depiction
We have said that reality is understood only through communication. Depiction—the description of reality through language, images, and other symbols—is the rest of the process. Whenever we speak, write, draw, or photograph, our choice of symbols and their arrangement depicts reality for others and, not unimportantly, for ourselves. Most of us, most of the time, seem to put our mouths in cruise control. This is unfortunate, because language depicts even when it is used reflexively, and many of us carelessly perpetuate depicted realities that we would otherwise argue against.

Some similarities to Fisher on "narrative"

Depiction serves five important functions in public communication (Osborn 1986). Depiction permits the *presentation* of an idea to an audience, whether presenting your idea in a language familiar to the audience, or using innovative terminology to enlarge its scope of understanding. Depiction also permits the *intensification* of feelings, an *identification* among people who share a community's symbols, and a *reaffirmation* of the community values and identity, often by stressing heroes, martyrs, and ritual. Lastly, depiction guides *implementation* of our values in action. Depictions that perform these functions well for audiences are more likely to be retained than those that do not.

Depiction consists of three adjustive processes. All speakers frame the subject, portray the important points to highlight some elements and marginalize others, and characterize the forces at work. Depiction is the rendering of your interpreted reality in a form that invites interpretation by others.

A speaker *frames* a subject for another by placing it in a context, like "The real issue is _____." This guides an audience toward an appropriate interpretive system, thereby orienting its consideration of arguments. Republican Senator Jesse Helms of North Carolina has framed some issues as moral causes that others (even in his own party) see as mainly practical issues. This framing is significant, because people who disagree with a practical proposal may be incorrect, misguided, stubborn, or stupid; but those who disagree on a moral issue are wrong and, perhaps, evil. Thus, framing facilitates or restricts discussion or compromise.

The opening statements by members of the House and Senate Iran-Contra committees revealed multiple framings of the "real issue": Did the President know of the plan? Had the Constitution been violated? Were taxpayers defrauded? Had the CIA run amok? How was foreign policy formulated? Your choice of framework affects your interpretation of the testimony and, ultimately, your judgment.

Finally, a speaker frames events within a narrative. We draw on familiar narratives to interpret new developments. When the *Miami Herald* reported that blond beauty queen/model/actress Donna Rice had spent the night in candidate Gary Hart's townhouse, Rice and Hart claimed that she had innocently borrowed a book and left, unseen, through the backdoor. Subsequent discussion focused on Hart's "poor judgment," and he withdrew temporarily from the race. The competing frameworks asked the public to believe that the 29-year old beauty queen/model/actress was alone with the handsome senator that night because either (1) she wanted to borrow a book, or (2) they had an affair. Since few of us knew either individual personally, we turned to the warehouse of parallels we had learned from movies, novels, tabloids, and television miniseries, in which nobody borrows books. The incident suggests that "Innocent until proven guilty" is a legal framework that applies only in a court of law. The journalistic framework is, "Where there's smoke, there's fire," and we readers often interpret accusation as proof.

Within the framed reality there must be foreground and background, or figure and ground. But which is which? Depiction adjusts the intensity of perceptions by bringing some elements into the spotlight (*highlighting*) and shunting others into the shadows (*marginalizing*). Two cases of defensive rhetoric illustrate highlighting/marginalizing techniques.

Richard Nixon responded to 1952 charges that he had an illegal secret fund by marginalizing legality and highlighting the higher standard of morality. Certainly, most Americans want their public officials to be both legal and moral. By highlighting morality and marginalizing legality, Nixon's "Checkers" speech effectively described a situation in which his fund seemed less wrong than the alternatives used by his opponents. Unfortunately, he never directly addressed the issue of legality and other features of the speech distracted his accusors (Nixon [1952] (1952); Ryan 1988). In this sense, Nixon resolved the exigence by reframing it.

Similarly, Senator Edward Kennedy's 1969 Chappaquiddick speech coupled his acceptance of personal responsibility for the accident that killed Mary Jo Kopechne with a detailed portrayal of the dark night, the narrow bridge, and the sensation of drowning. Kennedy's speech depicted a scene that explained, perhaps even justified, his otherwise indefensible behavior (Ling, 1970; Benoit 1988).

Characterization is the attribution of personal qualities like motives, reasons, and personality traits to persons, things, and forces. For years, George Bush was dogged by the "wimp factor," which seemed unpresidential. But his famous confrontation with Dan Rather during a live interview and a campaign commercial that reverently admired his heroism, industriousness, and governmental experience effectively recharacterized him as one of the most qualified persons ever to seek the presidency.

All presidents invoke "the American people" and all have probably claimed to represent *all* of the people (McGee 1975). They typically speak of all Americans as male and female, employer and employee, rich and poor, young and old, black and white, and Protestant, Catholic and Jewish. But notice how even this long string of communities leaves many Americans out in the cold—the self-employed and unemployed, Hispanics and Native Americans, and Muslims,

Hindus, Buddhists, agnostics, and atheists, to mention only a few. Second, notice the polarizing nature of these balanced pairs. The politician who claims to represent all the people, rich and poor, for example, is reinforcing the society's rich-poor conflict by raising it for specific attention.

There are also significant subtleties in depicted realities. Consider President Kennedy's landmark call for civil rights for *all* Americans: "It ought to be possible, in short, for every American to enjoy the privileges of being American without regard to *his* race or *his* color" (Kennedy 1963, 468, emphasis added). Kennedy's use of the then-acceptable, generic masculine pronoun implicitly characterized American society as male.

One of President Reagan's major rhetorical contributions was his inclusive characterization of the American people. Reagan's speeches and campaign films present a depiction of America not seen since the Frank Capra films of the 1940s. Ronald Reagan's Americans were the:

> men and women who raise our food, patrol our streets, man our mines and factories, teach our children, keep our homes, and heal us when we're sick. (Reagan 1981, 393)

> autoworkers in Detroit, lumberjacks in the Northwest, steelworkers in Steubenville who are in the unemployment lines . . . black teenagers in Newark and Chicago . . . hard-pressed farmers and small businessmen . . . and millions of everyday Americans who harbor the simple wish of a safe and financially secure future for their children. (Reagan 1982, 76)

Reagan identified with people's lives rather than playing them against one another. Moreover, he portrayed an active society of people busily engaged in meaningful and productive work or the pursuit of it. Our attention is drawn to dynamic activity rather than static labels.

Human qualities can be attributed to countries and groups as well as to individuals, and those qualities can make one group seem reasonable and another implacable. Oddly, President Reagan devoted little attention to the rhetorical rehabilitation of Iran. The man who defeated Jimmy Carter partly on the basis of the Iranian hostage issue and who had numbered Iran among a group of "outlaw states run by the strangest collection of misfits, looney tunes, and squalid criminals since the advent of the Third Reich" (Reagan 1985, 880) sold them weapons to improve relations without preparing Americans for the new era. Since communication requires adjustment to an audience's interpretive system, President Reagan invited problems by working with Iranians, whom his constituents still interpreted as dangerous enemies. Characterizations of "we" and "they" foster identification and polarization and transform the bonds between rhetor and audience in relation to exigencies.

We also employ metaphor to characterize elements of reality, and the metaphors, when extended, prescribe conduct. President Reagan in the early 1980s characterized inflation, unemployment, and high interest rates as "symptoms" of economic "illness" that could be "cured" with "proper care" (namely, his) rather than a "quick fix." If the "medicine" was unpleasant, that simply proved that it was doing something. Others characterized the same economic problems as "structural problems" requiring "fine-tuning" and "adjustments." The chosen metaphors characterized the problem and dictated solutions.

This section discussed several dimensions of depiction that describe our world to ourselves and others. Our conceptions of framing, highlighting and marginalizing, and characterizing may sometimes overlap. But the important point is that *any description of anything entails depiction, and a depiction speaks to others' interpretive systems.* A depiction that cannot be comfortably digested by an audience will likely be rejected or ignored. The persuader is no chemist who can guarantee results, but the depicted reality is an important ingredient in political communication.

Conclusions

In summary, the Constitution created a governmental system that divided responsibility for the shared functions of unifying, legitimizing, orienting, resolving, and implementing among three institutions at three geographic levels. The system was especially dependent on persuasion for its operation because it required approval of office holders, interinstitutional coordination, clarification of ambiguities, adaptation to overlapping and conflicting constituencies, and resolution of middle-range conflicts.

This chapter summarized the role of rhetoric in the communication process. It is the adaptive process that enables one person to speak to another person's interpretive system. This is not a simple matter of translation, because it requires fluency with ideologies, visions, objectives, motives, beliefs, and reasons as well as languages.

Ironically, "rhetoric" is a word with a public relations problem. By rights, any term that refers to the process for minimizing misunderstanding should not itself be misunderstood. Plato admitted that rhetoric could be used to educate and to deceive. But he argued that rhetoric itself was necessary to convince people of the dangers of deception and to combat deception by others. Bryant noted the tendency to associate rhetoric with words like "empty," "deception," and "bombast" in 1953, but we still hear the same associations today.

But rhetoric is the process, neither pure nor evil, of intentionally interacting with another's interpretive system. It is a reasoned planning process that (1) identifies or defines the exigence and constraints, (2) identifies or creates audiences capable of resolving the exigence, (3) infers the audience's interpretive system, (4) translates the rhetor's goal through the audience's interpretive system, and (5) presents the message for optimal acceptance.

Rhetors who choose to operate within situational constraints use the available power relations, symbols, and logic to alter preferences. As noted in Chapter 1, we tend to do this whenever possible. But when we accept other people's definitions, values, authorities, logic, and motivations, we frequently resolve the exigence on their terms, not ours. A second choice is to rely on our own unexplained interpretive system, but this often creates confusion and misunderstanding. The third alternative is to induce others to share your interpretive system and then to apply it to the situation. Because this is a complex and difficult task, we too often avoid it.

References

Aristotle. *Rhetoric.* translated by W. Rhys Roberts. New York: Oxford University Press, 1924.

Benoit, William L. "Senator Edward M. Kennedy and the Chappaquiddick Tragedy." In *Oratorical Encounters: Selected Studies and Sources of Twentieth-Century Political Accusations and Apologies,* edited by Halford Ross Ryan, 187–99. Westport, CT: Greenwood Press, 1988.

Bitzer, Lloyd F. "The Rhetorical Situation." *Philosophy and Rhetoric* 1 (Winter 1968): 1–14.

———. "Functional Communication: A Situational Perspective." In *Rhetoric in Transition: Studies in the Nature and Uses of Rhetoric,* edited by Eugene E. White, 21–38. University Park: Pennsylvania State University Press, 1980.

Bosmajian, Haig. *The Language of Oppression.* Washington, D.C.: Public Affairs Press, 1974.

Bowers, John W., and Donovan J. Ochs. *The Rhetoric of Agitation and Control.* Reading, MA: Addison-Wesley, 1971.

Bryant, Donald C. "Rhetoric: Its Function and Its Scope." *Quarterly Journal of Speech* 39 (December 1953): 401–24.

Burke, Kenneth. *Language as Symbolic Action.* Berkeley: University of California Press, 1966.

———. *A Rhetoric of Motives.* Berkeley: University of California Press, 1969.

Bytwerk, Randall. *Julius Streicher: The Man Who Persuaded a Nation to Hate Jews.* New York: Stein and Day, 1983.

Ford, Gerald R. Remarks to the Veterans of Foreign Wars' annual convention, August 19, 1974. In *Public Papers of the Presidents: Gerald R. Ford*, 22–28. Washington, D.C.: Government Printing Office, 1975.

Hart, Roderick P., Robert E. Carolson and William F. Eadie. "Attitudes toward Communication and the Assessment of Rhetorical Sensitivity. *Communication Monographs*, 47 (March 1980): 1–22.

Kennedy, John F. Radio and television report to the American people on civil rights, June 11, 1963. In *Public Papers of the Presidents: John F. Kennedy*, 468–71. Washington, D.C.: Government Printing Office, 1963.

King, Andrew A., and Floyd Douglas Anderson. "Nixon, Agnew, and 'The Great Silent Majority': A Case Study in the Rhetoric of Polarization." *Western Speech* 35 (Fall 1971): 243–55.

Ling, David. "A Pentadic Analysis of Senator Edward Kennedy's Address to the People of Massachusetts, July 25, 1969." *Central States Speech Journal* 21 (Summer 1970): 81–86.

McGee, Michael C. "In Search of The People: A Rhetorical Alternative." *Quarterly Journal of Speech* 61 (October 1975): 235–49.

Nixon, Richard M. "My Side of the Story." *Vital Speeches of the Day.* (October 15, 1952): 11–15.

Osborn, Michael. "Rhetorical Depiction." In *Form, Genre, and the Study of Political Discourse*, edited by Herbert W. Simons and Aram Aghazarian, 79–107. Columbia: University of South Carolina Press, 1986.

Perelman, Chaim, and Lucie Olbrechts-Tyteca. *The New Rhetoric: A Treatise on Argumentation.* Translated by John Wilkinson and Purcell Weaver. Notre Dame, IN: Notre Dame University Press, 1968.

Reagan, Ronald. "[First] Inaugural Address of President Ronald Reagan," January 20, 1981. In *Weekly Compilation of Presidential Documents.* Vol. 17, 1–5. Washington, D.C.: Government Printing Office, 1981.

———. "The State of the Union," January 26, 1982. In *Weekly Compilation of Presidential Documents.* Vol. 18, 76–83. Washington, D.C.: Government Printing Office, 1982.

———. "Remarks to the Annual Convention of the American Bar Association," July 8, 1985. In *Weekly Compilation of Presidential Documents.* Vol. 21, 894–900. Washington, D.C.: Government Printing Office, 1985.

Riker, William H. *The Art of Political Manipulation.* New Haven: Yale University Press, 1986.

Ryan, Halford R. "Senator Richard M. Nixon's Apology for The Fund." In *Oratorical Encounters: Selected Studies and Sources of Twentieth-Century Political Accusations and Apologies*, edited by Halford Ross Ryan, 99–120. Westport, CT: Greenwood Press, 1988.

Turner, Fictor. *From Ritual to Theatre: The Human Seriousness of Play.* New York: Performing Arts Journal Publications, 1982.

Vatz, Richard E. "The Myth of the Rhetorical Situation." *Philosophy and Rhetoric* 6 (Summer 1973): 154–161.

Part 2
ARENAS
OF POLITICAL
COMMUNICATION

Chapters 1 through 4 explained the general process of political communication. Now we will examine political communication as it occurs in its familiar arenas: the press, election campaigns, congress, the presidency, the courts, foreign policy, and protest movements. In the chapters that follow, political communication will seem like a chameleon. Presidents address the nation on television; legislators work in committee; demonstrators wave placards; diplomats try to match private agreements and public discourse; and judges interpret points of law in written decisions. The nature of the political task and of the professional roles and rules traditionally associated with it influence communication. Marvel at the remarkable flexibility of human communication and at the ingenious ways people have devised to negotiate shared political understandings.

Chapter 5
MASS COMMUNICATION
AND INTERPRETIVE POLITICS

Mention "political communication," and two things usually come to mind: long-winded speakers and mass communication. It was not always so. But political life in contemporary America would be unrecognizable without televised speeches, news reports, and campaign commercials. Mass communication is a version of communication so massive that it has developed its own social system that affects the political process.

This chapter will explore the nature of mass communication to understand the relationship among citizens, officials, and the media. It will discuss American mass communication as an arena, rather than a process, of political communication to understand better the interplay of technological, cultural, economic, interpretive, organizational, and distributive variables that shape news and entertainment as political influences. Our primary focus will be on news and television because they most directly affect our politics.

Mass Communication as a Social System

It is no accident that leaps in widespread political awareness and involvement followed the development of penny newspapers, radio, and television. Each new technology brought the words and actions of political leaders directly to more citizens, including those living in isolated areas, those with little interest in national conflicts, and, now, those who cannot read. Mass communication creates and is created by a society and must be seen in its larger context.

Sociologist Melvin DeFleur's model of mass communication explains how a society develops social subsystems around the functions of message production, message distribution, economic support, and regulation—all of which revolve around the audience(s) (DeFleur 1966; DeFleur and Ball-Rokeach 1982). Let us consider the elements of the model individually before discussing their interactive political implications.

A social system's *culture*—its shared memories and collective wisdom—guides its development of mass communication. The society's shared experience informs its answers to the questions "What do we need to talk about?" and "How shall we go about it?" But because the society comprises multiple interpretive communities with their respective subcultures, "culture" refers more precisely to the dominant subculture. The dominant culture influences the form and content of mass communication in the society, but the form and content of mass communication influence the reach of the various subcultures, thereby influencing the culture.

The community of people engaged in the production of messages for the mass media—whether reporters, directors, actors, singers, or advertisers—constitutes DeFleur's *production subsystem.* The production of a message for mass communication is a complex task. Minimal functions include ideation, scripting, casting, performing, processing, editing, packaging, and technical support. Each medium addresses these functions in its own way, but professionals like writers, composers, and actresses use their skills in a variety of media. They draw their ideas and artistic sense from the premises of univeral and particular audiences in their culture. This subsystem produces the finished message but does not present it to the audience.

The *distribution subsystem* consists of people who get the produced message to an appropriate audience. It includes national distributors like broadcast networks, satellite companies, newspaper syndicates, wire services, and magazine wholesalers, as well as local distributors such as radio and television stations, local newspapers, and newsstands. The distribution function is important, because the producers and audiences who need one another are largely unknown to one another. Distributors try to match a message and an interested audience. In commercial mass communication, distributors use messages to attract audiences for delivery to advertisers.

For several reasons, it is more useful to speak of mass communication "audiences" in the plural. For one thing, each medium has its regular devotees; moviegoers, readers, and television watchers are discernible populations. It is also possible to distinguish among a medium's audiences, like heavy metal, rock, middle-of-the-road, country, easy-listening, classical, and news/talk radio audiences. DeFleur discusses high-brow, middle- brow, and low-brow audiences defined by their tastes. Our socioeconomic structure and culture combine to produce a national audience dominated by low-brow and middle-brow tastes; thus, game shows, soap operas, and rock videos are seen more often than are lectures, Greek tragedies, and ballet. We too rarely remember that *an audience exists for the sole purpose of receiving a message.* Personal needs find sources of fulfillment in mass, as well as interpersonal, communication. Political scandals and movies about corrupt politicians or the "little guy" who takes on "the system" perform personal and social functions for audience members; when they do not, the channel is changed. This leads to the formation of particular interpretive communities based on their commitment to particular kinds of messages. This is easily seen with respect to C-SPAN hearings, financial news, religious services, music videos, and sports.

The *economic subsystem* enters the model for two reasons. First, film, tape, costumes, typewriters, printing presses, and the like cost money, which must be generated somewhere. Although a reader's purchase of a newspaper helps to defray production expenses, it is only a drop in the producer's bucket. The two major forms of economic support in contemporary America are sponsorship and spot participation. *Sponsorship* underwrites production costs in whole or in part, like Hallmark's "Hall of Fame" or the grants acknowledged on PBS programs. *Spot participation* is the sale of message time to people with something to say. Advertisers help the message reach its audience in exchange for a moment with the audience. In a practical sense, sponsorship gives authority for the message to the sponsor, while spot participation gives authority to the distributor who constructs a coalition of advertisers. When the audience desired by sponsors dwindles, the message is in trouble; when the audience desired by the distributor dwindles, the advertising coalition becomes difficult to mobilize, and the distributor is in trouble until changes are made.

The *regulatory subsystem* politically constrains mass communication. It can regulate message production, distribution patterns and practices, audience composition, or funding. The regulatory system comes into play when the free market result dissatisfies a community that is sufficiently powerful politically to activate regulation. In recent years, religious conservatives prevailed on legislators in many states and communities to restrict public access to magazines and videotapes that threaten community standards of morality. In such cases, political power checks the economic power of consumers.

DeFleur's model suggests four broad subsystems that influence mass communication. Let us consider the technological, cultural, organizational, and interpretive influences that shape our political consciousness.

Technological Influences on Mass Communication

Mass communication is the process, and *mass media* are the multiple channels that interconnect people. The term *media* is the plural form of the word *medium*, meaning "in between." A medium, then, is whatever links a speaker with an audience. Public speech is one such medium, although few people refer to it that way. But the development of the medium of print, the medium of radio, and the medium of television caused people to take notice of all communication media.

Most prominent among the medium noticers was the Canadian sociologist Marshall McLuhan. McLuhan argued that each new medium extends our senses, thereby changing the ways in which we sense the world (McLuhan 1964). The printing press increased our visual orientation and linear thinking. Radio invited us to listen, and television combined them to return us to the apparently personal storytelling of tribal life, but now in a global village.

McLuhan's *Understanding Media* (1964) sparked many a discussion during the 1960s. Before long, people began referring to "the mass media" and eventually, and incorrectly, to "the media of television." Worse, discussions of media influence in American life— meaning, to McLuhan, the impact of technology on our sensory and perceptual processes—came to encompass the political biases and profit motives of the people and organizations engaging in mass communication for profit.

People will understand you, or think that they do, if you talk about "media influence." But you should know whether you mean (1) the impact of a technology on our perceptual processes or (2) the choices made by the people and organizations who make mass communication their livelihood. Know which sort of media influence you mean, and ask the same precision from others. For clarity, let us refer to McLuhan's concern as technological influence.

Technological influence concerns the differential aptitudes of various sending and receiving techniques for conveying information. As McLuhan's extensions to the human sensory apparatus, each medium conveys some data and reduces some uncertainties better than others. Print media use words, graphics, and still pictures. Radio uses voice reports and sound. Television uses active visual treatments and voice reports.

The technology of television befriends the political aspirations of people like Gary Hart, Dan Quayle, and the Reverends Jesse Jackson and Pat Robertson, whose messages are enhanced by their personal appearance and presentational style. Could any of them have reached the levels of political influence they attained on the basis of purely written treatises? The technology of television is equally unkind to people like Paul Simon, whose bow tie, glasses, and unfashionable hairdo spoke louder than his policies, and to Robert Dole and Jack Kemp, whose intensity overpowered many viewers. It seems highly unlikely that our greatest presidents—wooden-toothed George Washington, homely Abraham Lincoln, pedantic Woodrow Wilson, and wheelchair-bound Franklin Roosevelt—would have increased their public support with television.

Conversely, Senator Joe McCarthy terrorized much of Washington in the early 1950s because his reckless accusations of communists in government made dramatic, personal, fragmented, normalized copy. He was even reputed to have called a press conference to announce a press conference! Americans, worried about communism in all its forms, inferred from the headlines that McCarthy was doing important work. In the month following Senator Joseph McCarthy's 1950 charge of 205 known communists in the State Department, for example, 85 percent of the stories about McCarthy came from the wire services, 75.5 percent from the Associated Press alone (Bayley 1981, 66). Then in 1954, television caught up with McCarthy. First, a CBS "See It Now" program by Edward R. Murrow and Fred Friendly framed concerns about McCarthy's recklessness and showed him in action. Then, his committee's investigation of the army was televised live. Public support for McCarthy waned when people saw him for themselves. Since no two media convey the same kinds of data, no two media reduce uncertainty in the same way.

The complexity of properly covering expected events with appropriate technology and personnel means that editors need to lean toward routine coverage of the expected at the expense of the unexpected, unless the unexpected is truly dramatic. This often means dramatizing the predictable. It also means that the reporters assigned to cover a story are the least able to truly investigate it, since their role is to report the predictable events developing before their eyes.

Cultural Influences on Mass Communication

Any society makes use of the technologies of mass communication within its cultural experience. Three philosophies have guided media system development around the world (adapted from Siebert, Peterson, and Schramm 1956).

Cultural Approaches to Mass Communication

The *authoritarian approach* developed in monarchies and viewed the press as an additional means toward the mobilization of support. In such cultures there are no legitimate watchdogs. Printing presses could be operated only with a royal license, and disapproval often meant termination of the license and sometimes of the licensee. The goal was neither advocacy nor objectivity but mobilization of support.

The eighteenth century saw the rise of a *libertarian approach* which valued free-market exchange rather than authoritarian control. John Stuart Mill and the other liberal philosophers held that truth and wisdom could best be found through the free exchange of information and views in a marketplace of ideas. It was this libertarian approach that valued a free press and encouraged anyone with an opinion to publish a newspaper. The goal here was neither mobilization nor objectivity but advocacy.

As mass communication grew in this century into a colossal industry, many of the smaller voices were consumed by larger companies. By the 1940s, it had become unreasonable to expect truth and wisdom to emerge from a free and open competition when a few wire services, newspapers, and networks dominated the marketplace. The *social responsibility approach* held that the few loud voices in society had a social responsibility to search out and to verify the truth and to assess and evaluate the wisdom of a decision. The media managers since circa 1940, accepted this responsibility because they realized that the full array of conflicting views was no longer being heard directly from their respective advocates, as in the 1800s. The social responsibility approach sought neither advocacy nor objectivity, but accuracy, and it spawned investigative journalism.

America relied on a libertarian approach well into this century but has now moved toward social responsibility. The Vietnam War, Watergate, the Iran-Contra affair, and the Hart, Biden, and Quayle controversies of 1988 all involved the efforts of mass communicators to energetically, perhaps overzealously, track down, verify, and assess aspects of truth and wisdom. The totalitarian media systems that developed in Nazi Germany and the Soviet Union reflect the cultural philosophies in which they arose. Unfortunately, our mixed tradition sometimes leaves us confused with regard to the kind of media system we want. Consider Spiro T. Agnew's historic moment.

Vice President Spiro Agnew responded to network coverage of President Nixon's Vietnam address of November 3, 1969, with a scathing indictment of television news that blurred all three cultural philosophies (Agnew 1969). Agnew began with a social responsibility

rationale: "Nowhere should there be more conscientious responsibility exercised than by the news media." But he construed that
responsibility as mobilization, as in the authoritarian approach.
Although he said that "right conclusions are more likely to be
gathered out of a multitude of tongues than through any kind of
authoritative selection," he chastised reporters and commentators for
expressing their reservations about the president's address. All three
media philosophies were aired, and the networks failed all three tests,
but for conflicting reasons.

It is understandable when political speakers like Agnew juggle
definitions and philosophies for political advantage. But the rest of us
need to be all the more careful to rationally consider the sort of media
system we want and then to evaluate that system by that ideal. Two
decades later, we have yet to decide what we want from our press. We
want mobilization when we like the government's position. We want
advocacy when we oppose the prevailing wisdom. We want objectivity
when we are undecided and when the prevailing wisdom and policy
seem acceptable. It is little wonder that we are chronically dissatisfied
with our news.

Cultural Preferences in News

Culture also affects the kinds of material produced and distributed
to the audience. Lance Bennett (1988) identified four broad characteristics of American news related to audience demands. These characteristics stem from the fact that news reports occur within the
culture and serve to reinforce it.

American news is *dramatized* to emphasize stories of conflict and
their resolution. Because few people watch or read dull news, journalists spin yarns and heighten action. They speculate about possible
developments and imply that we need to stay tuned for developments.
The melodramatic imperative takes over, and news gravitates toward
dramatic conflicts and their resolution (Nimmo and Combs 1983).

The watchdog role of the press has been used to justify the creation
or heightening of dramatic confrontations. It explains news coverage
of riots and demonstrations as well as the political establishment's
dissatisfaction with that coverage. Dramatic form also heightens the
role of the anchorperson as the narrator and source of truth. But in
any drama, the characters and actors play crucial roles, thereby
increasing the need for interesting personalities.

The second characteristic is that our news is *personalized* by
emphasizing people and their motives and feelings. Fluctuations in

interest rates become stories of the Doe family and their dream of home ownership. Unemployment figures become the story of a steelworker thrown out of work after 30 years on the job. And agricultural policies become tales of the family farm. Matters of policy become human dramas.

Humans of the moment are usually portrayed in familiar, mythic terms. The use of cultural stereotypes serves both to make the drama comprehensible and to reinforce the cultural myth itself. But every so often, an individual so dominates the familiar role that it is redefined. Franklin Roosevelt, for example, so dominated the presidential role that his successors have been uninterested in enacting the presidential role as it used to be known.

Even questions of international relations are reduced to personal stories as though each individual leader is personally able to deliver his or her nation's support. This tendency distracts us from institutional, cultural, sociological, economic, and historical forces and heightens our image of the individuals' importance. It leads us to ignore the systemic forces that simultaneously help and hinder those individuals and to presume that single spokespersons speak unequivocally for whole nations. Personal blame and credit are both exaggerated.

Bennett also notes that our news is *fragmented* into a series of brief stories, none of which tells all that we need to know. Moreover, journalistic formats necessarily provide us with repetitive fragments; headlines predominate and details are lost in the shuffle. Coherence is especially difficult to achieve when people hear a familiar headline and dismiss the story. But in the day-to-day flow of news coverage, coherence comes from the melodramatic form itself (Nimmo and Combs 1983).

Since a bit of data is informative to the extent that it reduces uncertainty, a news report informs to the degree that it reduces audience uncertainty. That becomes problematic on three levels. First, fragmented news is redundant or noninformative when it repeats what is already known. Second, the repetition of familiar news fragments indirectly reinforces their position in the audiences' interpretive systems ("It must be true, I've heard it so often!"). And third, coverage of "what's new" necessarily results in reports that increase uncertainty, undermining our confidence in prevailing interpretive systems and increasing our need for news reports that reduce this newfound uncertainty. Of course, whether news increases or decreases uncertainty depends more on an audience's personal and social interpretive systems than on the news itself.

Finally, American news is *normalized* in the sense that it reflects accepted norms. This is not wholly unreasonable; since American news outlets compete for their audiences, any outlet that is grossly out of step with its particular audience's norms will lose its audience and lose money. Survival and profit both require journalists to be responsive to their audiences' conceptions of reality and the preferable.

Normalization is apparent in the selection of anchorpersons. As narrators of life's dramas, they serve as ultimate arbiters of truth and light (Matusow 1983). They are near-perfect humanoids. They are always suited, never speak with a regional accent, and never smoke or chew gum on the air. They are always serious about the news, even when presenting it in a chummy format. For all they have to say about the day's events, they studiously avoid expressing opinions. They themselves are rarely embroiled in conflict. In short, the prototypical anchorperson is both charismatic and inoffensive.

Like the anchorperson, the news conveyed to us is largely normalized. Much of it concerns middle-aged white men in suits. These suited men understand the dramatic problems faced by the unsuited people of America, and they explain them to the reporter. The reporter then tells us whether the unsuiteds are troublemakers or innocent victims and speculates about tomorrow's developments. The reporter is unlikely to ask why the suited people have the answers; nor will the reporter have the unsuiteds solve the problems faced by the suited people. Indeed, questions like "Why do some people get the suits while others get jeans?" are left to non-normalized reporters like the strident, hirsute, controversial, sometimes disheveled Geraldo Rivera, whose non-normalized reports can be more easily dismissed. Dramatic conflict is inevitably resolved with the reassuring moral that the established system works (Blumler and Gurevitch 1981; Edelman 1988).

As a general rule, these characteristics provide short stories about people and reinforce cultural norms. But problems arise. Since important news is not always dramatic, trivial issues with personable spokespersons get ready coverage at the expense of important issues without celebrities. Perhaps most importantly, the important news that makes us uncomfortable is usually downplayed until it attracts an audience. These biases are apparent in print, radio, and television news.

As an audience, we need to seek out potentially important, undramatic events in the face of dramatic, trivial events to look beyond the interesting people in the story, to look for coherence and understanding, and to seek varied perspectives on the day's news.

Organizational Influences on Mass Communication

The task of mass communication is so immense that it is carried out by organizations rather than individuals. Edward Jay Epstein argues persuasively that most of the characteristics of network news can best be explained as adaptive efforts of these organizations. If news organizations are to avoid operational crises and interference from network executives, they need to follow four kinds of organizational imperatives (Epstein 1973).

First, because networks provide programs to their affiliates many hours of the day and because prime-time programming is their gold mine, they worry about the *audience flow* from one program to the next. Their data show them that national news, unlike local news, is more likely to drive viewers away than to attract them. Lest their news drive viewers away, the networks strive for visually satisfying news—familiar and satisfying images rather than confusing or unsettling images, activity rather than passivity. They cater to the audience's presumed inattention by putting things in motion and by presenting narratives with a beginning, middle, and end and a narrator who, once introduced, is voiced-over the visual.

The assumptions about audience flow suggest several related *economic imperatives*. Since the audience will be small and more likely to tune out than in, news minutes are filled as inexpensively as possible. This leads to stories that come least expensively from cities like New York, Washington, and London, where bureaus can be stationed to report regularly on a relatively small group of active newsmakers.

Network news is subject also to the *national imperative*. There are countless local news outlets but only a handful of national outlets. To avoid tune-outs and to fulfill their function, networks couch stories of importance to particular audiences in universal themes and language—appearance versus reality, little guys versus big guys, good versus evil, efficiency versus inefficiency, the unique versus the routine (Jamieson and Campbell 1983). Local stories usually exemplify or validate some national theme.

Fairness imperatives stem not only from journalists' sense of fairness but from external expectations and regulation. Particularly important was the Federal Communication Commission's Fairness Doctrine, which guided coverage of controversial issues from 1964 until it was rescinded in the 1980s. The FCC stipulated only that "opposing views" be presented, so the networks would customarily find two opposing views and edit them into a dialogue, reducing complicated issues to either-or decisions. Since the networks were required to regard fairness as the unvarnished presentation of opposing views, there was no incentive—in fact there were disincentives—for investigating the truthfulness, accuracy, sincerity, or reasonableness of the opposing views. This promoted demagoguery because community voices could have all manner of outrageous statements aired, and they could defend the otherwise indefensible by charging network bias. The sense that investigative journalism is somehow heroic or unique underscores the fact that it is the exception rather than the rule. The Fairness Doctrine is gone, but two decades of application shaped accepted television procedures.

The organizational perspective also suggests that people working in the production and distribution subsystems to create audience-attracting messages are promoted when they succeed. The ability of a professional to satisfy organizational imperatives is apparent in the career of Roone Arledge. Arledge managed the production of "Monday Night Football" and the Olympics so well that ABC put him in charge of the news. Whether presenting news or sports, Arledge knows that the network needs a multitude of camera angles, personable and knowledgeable anchorpersons, visually appealing graphics, reporters to ferret out the stories behind the story, personalized accounts of the participants, and some kind of eventual winner or loser. Interestingly, Arledge suggested in 1988 that political conventions are hardly worth covering anymore because they have become planned and scripted presentations rather than exciting contests of democracy in action. Whether he realized it fully or not, Arledge was trying to transfer audience adherence to the truths, presumptions, values, hierarchy, and loci of live televised athletic contests to live televised political conventions. When the audience failed to materialize, he faulted the conventions, never considering how the repackaging of an event for mass consumption alters the event in ways that both attract and repel viewers.

Epstein (1973) presents a view of network news as a community of professionals doing their jobs the best they can within their organizational system. Perhaps we would get better news if the imperatives were different—audience flow from news to entertainment, a larger news budget than entertainment budget, a parochial focus rather than a national focus, and incentives to critique public statements. News might be more satisfactory; but those are precisely the imperatives that shape local television news, with dubious results.

This section emphasized organizational aspects of television news because it is the dominant source of news today and because that was the subject of Epstein's important book (1973). But note how the news phenomena of the 1980s—*USA Today* and Ted Turner's two Cable News Network services—mirror the commercial networks. With the exception of half-hour financial and sports reports, the CNN services are 24-hour versions of ABC, CBS, and NBC. Although they could have divided the broadcast day into half-hour stories, they still compact everything into half-hour newscasts. Controversial issues are examined by having liberals and conservatives interrupt one another in shouting contests. For its part, *USA Today* nationalizes the news and substitutes flashy visuals for insightful analysis. The distribution boxes even look like television sets!

News is what it is because it results from organizational decision making. If the message is that the system works, politicians are presented in forms dictated by the news producers' organizational imperatives (Blumler and Gurevitch 1981). Changing the organizational imperatives simply fine-tunes the ways in which the news organizations interpret and depict the news. News organizations and their parent corporations are interpretive communities organized around a constellation of difficult jobs, which they do remarkably well. The movie *Broadcast News* captured many facets of the community's subculture—its motivations and rewards, its symbols and language, its preferences and ideology, its reasoning and logic. We laugh with the movie and foam at the news itself. But we need to find a middle ground from which to consider the fact that all of these news organizations spend all this time and money trying to adapt to *us*. What is our role in the process?

Interpretive Influences on Mass Communication

The dominant theme in most discussions of American mass communication is what "they" tell "us," but we have seen that communication also entails what we do with what they send. Our understanding of the political world is influenced by the news organizations' depicted reality, but it is our personal and social interpretations of that news that inform our political behavior.

Graber's Interpretive Schema

Doris A. Graber explored the ways that people interpret the news they encounter. Relying on extensive interviews with a panel of respondents, Graber discovered people employing a few interpretive schemas: inflation, taxes, unemployment, welfare, Mideast policy, ethical conduct, schools, pollution, and energy policy emerged in her study, but other news could produce other schemas (Graber 1984). Each schema has a cause-and-effect dimension, a person dimension, and an institution dimension, and some also have cultural and human interest dimensions; and each dimension includes frequently heard themes. Graber's schemas are summarized in Table 5-1.

Graber's typical audience engages in *relatedness searches* of the incoming messages for themes related to the dimensions of the audience's schemas. The audience extracts information that affirms its schemas or reduces the schemas' uncertainty. Because its interest in news is relatively low, the audience seeks general understanding rather than factual learning, and few facts are retained. Stories that cannot be related to schemas are generally ignored, and the packaging of a news story—its perceived significance and appeal—strongly affects the scanning process. Let us consider the welfare schemas in Table 5-1 to illustrate the process.

Audience members scanning the news for enhanced understanding of welfare fastened onto all five dimensions of news schemas. Unemployment was cited as the cause and effect of welfare, with inadequate daycare facilities and economic strain noted less often. As for persons, the audience members concluded that recipients and providers of welfare are all greedy and that the recipients cheat. Welfare agencies were judged to be poorly managed, unable to control fraud, and vulnerable to demands for excessive benefits and to provide neither incentives nor assistance for recipients to find work. The audience members concluded that American culture condones cheating, and they pitied welfare recipients for their economic difficulties (Graber 1984, 188).

The audience in Graber's schemas model is not motivated by a need for consistency but by a need for understanding. In the welfare example, for instance, audience members judged all parties to be greedy and pitied recipients even though they cheated. A similar lack of correspondence and outright contradiction can be found between interpretive schemas. Although Ronald Reagan's anecdotes about welfare were proven by his critics to be exceptions, they fit dominant audience schemas for understanding welfare. By contrast, Jesse Jackson's emphasis on subsidized daycare as a solution fit dominant schemas less well than George Bush's plan to reduce welfare with overall economic prosperity to reduce unemployment.

We develop the schemas we use to interpret our news from a number of sources. Education, news, family, and community socialization all play important roles. But we also draw on mass media entertainment for narrative coherence and fidelity.

Table 5-1
Schemas and Themes Used by Viewers of Television News

Themes in Inflation Schemas

In *Cause-and-Effect Dimensions*: High wage demands by unions*; high business profits*; high energy costs*; shortage of goods; excessive consumption; low productivity; strikes; valuation of the dollar.

In *Person Dimensions*: Greedy rich people profit from inflation.

In *Institution Dimensions*: Governments spend wildly*; governments waste money because of inefficiency*; greedy corporations raise prices*; greedy special interest groups extract too much money from the public.

Themes in Taxes Schemas

In *Cause-and-Effect Dimensions*: Expensive social programs*; generally high cost of government.

In *Person Dimensions*: People request too many services from government*; ineligibles collect welfare payments*; taxpayers cheat.

In *Institution Dimensions*: Government spends wildly*; government wastes money because of inefficiency*; government coddles rich taxpayers*; government overpays its workers; government sends too much money abroad.

Themes in Unemployment (Jobs) Schemas

In *Cause-and-Effect Dimensions*: Technological advances*; recession*; weakening of nation's economy; inflation; crime-unemployment link; unemployment-high tax link; excess population; undue automation.

In *Person Dimensions*: People lack skills*; people take advantage of high unemployment benefits*; people are lazy; people have excessive expectations; parents do not instill the work ethic.

In *Institution Dimensions*: Greedy labor unions demand excessive wages*; schools provide insufficient job training; employers practice racial discrimination; government coddles lazy people; government economies produce job losses; government neglects aid to private business; economists make misleading predictions.

In *Human Interest and Empathy Dimensions*: Empathy with Depression type trauma*; fear that unemployed will suffer hunger.

Themes in Welfare Schemas

In *Cause-and-Effect Dimensions*: Unemployment*; lack of daycare facilities; excessive strain on the economy.

In *Person Dimensions*: Recipients cheat*; recipients and providers are greedy.*

In *Institution Dimensions*: Agencies do not control fraud adequately*; agencies have generally poor management practices*; agencies yield to demands for high benefits*; agencies provide no incentives for leaving welfare rolls; agencies do not aid clients in finding work.

Continued on next page

Table 5-1—*Continued*

In *Cultural Dimensions*: American culture condones cheating.
In *Human Interest and Empathy Dimensions*: Pity for economic difficulties of welfare clients.

Themes in Mideast Policy Schemas

In *Cause-and-Effect Dimensions*: Concentration of world oil supplies in Middle East*; danger of war; unrepresentative Middle Eastern governments.
In *Institution Dimensions*: Soviets are expansionist*; U.S. is interventionist*: U.S. State Department performs poorly; Arabs misbehave; Israelis misbehave; U.S. lobbies pressure for advantages.
In *Human Interest and Empathy Dimensions*: Pity for people caught up in hostilities.

Themes in Ethical Conduct Schemas

In *Cause-and-Effect Dimensions*: Insufficient pay.
In *Person Dimensions*: People are greedy*; people lust for power*; people are corruptible in the face of temptation*; people lack high moral standards.
In *Institution Dimensions*: Agencies do not control corruption sufficiently*; agencies recruit greedy people; agencies have generally poor management practices.
In *Cultural Dimensions*: Americans disregard own cultural values*; social pressures force people to seek instant success; the American spirit of competition breeds corruption.

Themes in Schools Schemas

In *Cause-and-Effect Dimensions*: Lack of money*; racial integration policies*; overcrowding; inadequate technological equipment; poor discipline; ban on physical punishment.
In *Person Dimensions*: Students are undisciplined*; teachers are incapable*; parents are uninterested*; students are unmotivated.
In *Institution Dimensions*: Schools offer poor quality programs*; Schools offer outdated curricula*; schools are poorly managed; school bureaucracies are

Fungible Narratives and the News

Mass media entertainment fare has far-reaching political implications. Most important is the extended social world that mass communication brings to us. If news tells us how real people like us cope with the drama of life, entertainment tells us how imaginary people cope with that drama. The distinction often blurs.

We infer many of our notions about human motives, problems, relationships, and their resolutions from entertainment; and those

Table 5-1—*Continued*

unresponsive to parents; school administrators lack an educational philosophy.

Themes in Pollution Schemas

In *Cause-and-Effect Dimensions*: Heavy road traffic*; heavy air traffic*; industrialization*; high cost of anti-pollution devices*; coal burning; pollution controls injurious to the economy; relaxation of controls due to bad economic conditions; nuclear testing; aerosol sprays.

In *Person Dimensions*: People drive cars needlessly*; people dump wastes carelessly*; people buy unduly large cars; environmentalists are overzealous; people smoke too much.

In *Institution Dimensions*: Heavy industry dumps industrial waste*; Big Business greed prevents adequate controls*; government does not enforce laws adequately*; enforcement agencies are inefficient.

In *Cultural Dimensions*: Americans are unconcerned about welfare of future generations.

Themes in Energy Policy Schemas

In *Cause-and-Effect Dimensions*: Exhaustible resources*; insufficient production*; excess population.

In *Person Dimensions*: People waste energy*; environmentalists prevent development of resources.

In *Institution Dimensions*: Government does not do enough research*; industry does not do enough research*; foreign governments manipulate supply*; government does not provide enough public transportation; Big Business greed prevents alternative fuels; greedy Arabs restrict supply.

In *Cultural Dimensions*: U.S. society is unduly oriented towards consumption; U.S. society is unduly wasteful.

*Themes used most frequently.
Source: Doris A. Graber, *Processing the News: How People Tame the Information Tide.* (New York: Longman, 1984), 188–89.

notions are fungible. We transfer them from the land of make-believe to our personal and political lives. Docudramas depicting persons and incidents often replace the original person and event. With the passage of time, we remember Watergate and the real Woodward and Bernstein less than we remember *All the President's Men* and the Robert Redford and Dustin Hoffman characterizations. If life for most black Americans in the 1950s was not as it was depicted in "Amos 'n' Andy," neither is it accurately depicted today in "The Cosby Show."

Our search for understanding leads us to relatedness searches of entertainment as well as news.

The morals and ethics of mass entertainment can become important elements of our political interpretations. If the political world is humanized and dramatized by the mass media, where better to learn the appropriate interpretive framework than through mediated human dramas? Unfortunately, the entertainment world's depiction of politics is almost totally amoral. When a program like "Dallas" affirms the suspicion that politicians can be bought by Texas oilmen, it complicates life for real people like John Tower and Jim Wright. When a miniseries like "Favorite Son" features sleazy, ambitious, libidinous, and murderous politicians, it undermines the legitimacy and perceived integrity of real people and institutions by affirming speculative narratives.

The role of fungible narratives is most evident in our conceptions of intelligence and national security. Few adults, no matter how politically disinterested, are without schemas for understanding espionage and international intrigue, largely because of the fact that real professional intelligence operations are the most secretive organizations on earth. Our interpretive framework for these matters is derived almost entirely from movies and novels.

James Bond novels and movies and the less romantic intrigues faced by Michael Caine's characters provide a framework through which periodic revelations and accusations of real espionage are interpreted. When the Soviets arrested *U.S. News and World Report* correspondent Nicholas Daniloff for espionage, was he a spy or an innocent victim? Our individual judgments largely reflected our taste in films. If your preferred narratives run toward "the totalitarian state rounding up innocent people, including a hero who single-handedly takes them on and escapes," then Daniloff was an innocent victim. But if your preferred narratives include "the shrewd spy masquerading as innocent professional who is apprehended and coolly traded for a shrewd enemy spy so that the chess game can continue," then Daniloff could well have been a spy. Either way, in this and other cases our notions of what is real and what is plausible are influenced by mass entertainment along with other sources of information.

Nimmo and Combs surveyed American films since 1930 and posited a relationship between the films and the politics of the decades (1983). Depression era films like *Mr. Smith Goes to Washington* embodied faith in ordinary people and America but distrust of institutions. By the 1940s, films like *Casablanca* were dealing with the issue of individual commitment to transcendent relations—people, institutions, causes, and allies. The 1950s brought a postwar world disturbingly unlike the one envisioned in the war-time fantasies, and Americans sought the culprits. Films like *Invasion of the Body Snatchers* dramatized the common fear of subversion by strange beings and the concern about paranoia. The upheaval and violence of the 1960s found its way into nation's theaters as characters like *Bonnie and Clyde* and Clint Eastwood's nameless westerner struggled to understand and apply the "American dream." Ultimately, the violence of the immediate world was transcended by peace and technology in films like *2001: A Space Odyssey.* Watergate and the fall of Saigon brought the disillusion-ment of the 1970s through films like *The Godfather* and *Taxi Driver*, which highlighted corruption, scandal, betrayal, and immorality. *Rocky* reversed the tide, reformed himself, and rose to the top to demonstrate the hopeful side of the America dream. But the strug-gling *Rocky* of 1976 became the victorious *Rocky II* and the com-placent *Rocky III.* In the 1980s, the Soviet evil was evident in *Rocky IV* and *Red Dawn.* A host of films sought to right the world either through direct action (like *Rambo*) or by correcting the past (like *Back to the Future*). There is discernible evidence of the correspondence between our films and our politics, but the relationship is probably less causal than it is reflective of our evolving interpretive systems.

Mass entertainment also transcends time and place to convey and embellish our heritage. Mass entertainment can recreate the life of prehistoric people (like *The Clan of the Cave Bear* and *Search for Fire*); it can create the lives of future peoples (like *Amerika* and *Star Trek*); and it can shuttle among time frames (like *Star Trek IV, Back in Time* and *Peggy Sue Got Married*). Mass entertainment can fantasize about reality (like *Franklin and Eleanor* and *Raid on Entebbe*); it can solidify the fantasy (like "Washington behind Closed Doors" and "Dallas"); and it can permit people to shuttle between fantasy and reality (like *The Purple Rose of Cairo* and *American Dreamer*).

The key is the audience's willingness to suspend disbelief. When disbelief is suspended we can literally believe anything and then later use it to interpret politics. Does President Reagan's penchant for nostalgia remind us of our real past or the past of our old movies? The sobering point is that we create our world from available information, and it matters too little where we get it.

The Nature of News

News may be one of those phenomena that are so pervasive and familiar that we do not understand them very well. What is news, and how do we know it when we see it? *News* is what we make of what we see and hear in those media that specialize in professional coverage of timely occurrences.

Consider the implications of this definition. First, it suggests the important role of availability. No event, no matter how important, is news if it goes unreported; and any reported event, no matter how trivial, is news.

Second, this definition of news reminds us that each of us relies on our personal interpretive systems to create our own news. We seek out some stories, passively follow others, and completely ignore others. Since each of us can sit through an hour of television news or wade through a whole Sunday newspaper and conclude that "there's nothing going on today," news must be more than what the producers and distributors provide. We process each news story through our interpretive systems to the extent that the headline "Reagan and Gorbachev Sign Arms Treaty" is historically good news to some and almost treasonous news, politics as usual, or interesting public drama to others.

The third aspect of the definition is that news is commonly defined by its source, whether newspaper or newscast. This in turn suggests the importance of form, since newscasts and newspapers are clearly recognizable apart from their content. Newspapers are oversized, have columns, headlines, and split-page stories and are divided into sections. Newscasts have well-groomed anchorpersons seated at a desk (usually in front of projected graphics), standing reporters out in the field, and short filmed stories. Both news sources rely on narrative discourse. Newspapers are parodied by copying their layout, and "Saturday Night Live" has long parodied television news. But while recognizing the form as newslike, we recognize the substance as parody when we realize that the quasi-reporters are specialists in entertainment, not news. We presume that those who specialize are best able to do it—an assumption that is often valid. The films *Broadcast News* and *Network* correctly suggested that the line between news and entertainment is a thin one and warned of the dangers of turning news reporting and production duties over to people trained in show business rather than journalism, political science, sociology, or economics.

Finally, news answers the question "What's new?" but it does not necessarily answer the question "What's important?" This is no small point. Remember that news production subsystems hire a staff of people to observe and report developments on a regular basis. Having paid them and having been paid by their advertisers and subscribers, the production subsystems must produce either a news program or a newspaper. Therefore, the reporters must find something new or risk being replaced. If nothing new and important occurs, they report the new and unimportant. But sometimes we misread "new" as "important," and problems arise.

Hundreds of reporters blanketing the Super Dome to cover the 1988 Republican Convention found the world's most carefully orchestrated presentation. The only loose thread to cover was the identity of the vice presidential nominee, and George Bush upstaged himself by announcing his choice mid-convention. As one of several hundred reporters interested in fulfilling your employer's confidence in you so that you might feed your family, where do you look for news? The only narrative possibility available to these reporters was "Who is Dan Quayle, and how do the delegates like him?" When some delegates failed to recognize or support him, the story mushroomed into a call for information about his National Guard and DePauw University experiences. The problem was not caused by Quayle, the Republican National Committee, or the reporters but by the social system that requires fragmented, dramatic, visual, personal stories, even when there is nothing important to report.

We have said that news is less concerned with "what's important" than "what's new," but of course its narrative must elevate some stories and subordinate others. In this sense "important" is implicitly equated with "interesting." When a 2-year-old Texas girl fell into a tiny, abandoned well in 1987, the nation watched her 48-hour entrapment, rescue, and recovery. The story was undeniably current, and it was undeniably interesting to caring human beings. But what was its importance? It was a single incident with no discernible historical, economic, technological, ideological, biological, spiritual, psychological, political, or educational significance. Nevertheless, the story dominated the nation's media for a week because it was a visual, personal drama requiring updates. About a year later, the world followed two whales trapped in arctic ice for many of the same reasons.

Indeed, even though editors must necessarily prioritize their stories, they are in a poor position to serve as ultimate arbiters of importance. Their focus is, and should be, on timeliness and interest. When they try to discern importance, they risk losing timeliness and interest. This is doubly unfortunate, because their profession does not permit journalists either the time perspective or the specialized knowledge available to scholars or authors. Even a network medical correspondent is less able to discern the importance of a prospective AIDS cure than can a professional medical researcher. Ultimate determinations of importance require time and specialized knowledge, which are very rarely within the job descriptions of reporters and editors. But then few historians, economists, or medical researchers could communicate regularly and effectively with a mass audience. Reporters and editors do their jobs, and it is unfair and unwise to hold them accountable for not doing a different job.

News, then, is the complex of our interpretations of what the people specializing in coverage of the new and interesting think their respective audiences will find new and interesting. It reflects who we are and what we have already found new and interesting, and it influences our interests and appetites for tomorrow's developments.

The Question of Bias

Bias has long been a topic of discussion and deserves our attention. A *bias* is a regular and predictable deviation. We can compensate for a bias by consistently adjusting our behavior. The charge that news is biased means that it has a predictable slant to it that could be compensated for by consistently adjusting our reading of it. This is different from inaccurate reporting, which involves random errors.

Now, the notion of biased news presumes the possibility of unbiased news. This sounds simple enough. But writers have been unable to decide whether "unbiased and objective" news refers to undistorted reality or to a balanced view of events. The problem is that journalists pursuing an accurate account of reality cannot balance, and those striving for balance cannot portray a single accurate reality. The case of Nazi Germany illustrates the point. If unbiased news is balanced news, then reporters should have fairly balanced stories charging the existence of extermination camps, Nazi denials, and extreme statements advocating the extermination of Jews. Could anything less be reasonably regarded as balanced? But if unbiased news is accurate news, then reporters should have scrupulously presented the "correct reality" and ignored the other two. But which was the "correct reality"? Hitler, Goebbels, and Streicher felt they were victims of bad press. In the final analysis, our appreciation of the press's ability to report the "correct reality" corresponds with our interpretive systems' ability to digest that reality.

Does this mean that American news is unbiased? Not exactly. It means that communication about life cannot be wholly divorced from the interpretive systems used by those who report and construe the news. Since reality can only be construed and shared with words, and since the choice and interpretation of words depends on people's interpretive systems, any verbally or visually conveyed depiction is necessarily interpretive. That does not mean that interpreted realities are evil, sneaky, partisan, intentional, destructive, or even consistent. They are, instead, unavoidably human.

Most studies have found no consistent pattern of partisan bias (Hackett 1984). Yes, individual investigations report particular biases, but the pattern is insufficiently consistent to indicate bias. The 1980 presidential campaign of Congressman John Anderson illustrates this point.

John Anderson was a liberal Republican who broke with the Reagan Republicans and ran as an Independent. Although he won about 9 percent of the popular vote, he won no electoral votes and never mounted a serious challenge to the front-runners in any state. Nevertheless, Anderson received widespread media coverage throughout his campaign. At one point President Carter skipped a planned Carter-Anderson-Reagan presidential debate because Anderson's candidacy trivialized it. Any partisan bias should have led the press to ignore, or at least to minimize, the Anderson candidacy. His candidacy divided Republicans, expanded the alternatives of undecided moderates, and presented yet another challenge to the Democratic incumbent. Yet the nation's press was the only real constituency John Anderson ever developed.

It is interesting that Americans see partisan biases of both kinds in their news, available research notwithstanding. Certainly much of it can be accounted for as a rationalization for developments otherwise at odds with our interpretive systems. When the press reports that "your candidate" did something you dislike, it is easier to lump the reporters with the opponent than to reevaluate your candidate.

But as this chapter has explained, American news is biased in favor of cultural norms, dramatic conflicts, interesting characters, ongoing melodrama, active visualizations, simplified confrontations, predictable events, and consistent newsmakers. Political news is shaped by the interaction of technological, cultural, organizational, and interpretive forces. The process has been summarized as

> (1) two sets of mutually dependent and mutually adaptive actors, pursuing divergent (though overlapping) purposes, whose relationships with each other are typically (2) role-regulated, giving rise to (3) an emergent shared culture, specifying how they should behave toward each other, the ground rules of which are (4) open to contention and conflicting interpretation, entailing a potential for disruption, which is often (5) controlled by informal and/or formal mechanisms of conflict management. (Blumler and Gurevitch 1981, 476–77).

The process and the system that we have developed to conduct it provide the bias.

A political community able to exploit these systemic biases appears to its adversaries to receive preferential treatment. Jamieson and Campbell pungently summarize the guidelines:

Likely to be covered or published [is] a single coherent statement clearly summarizing the issue in jargon-free English, written to be understood on first hearing or reading, which can be delivered clearly and dramatically in less than thirty-five seconds, requiring no additional information, available before deadline at a convenient place for newsgatherers, delivered in a symbolic setting or by a person who dramatizes the issue in a manner not subject to parody.

[Likely not to be covered is] a rambling statement skirting the issue in gobbledygook, written to be figured out by a cryptographer, which could not be delivered effectively by Laurence Olivier in less than four minutes, requiring at least a paragraph of clarification, available at midnight at the North Pole, delivered in a setting with no apparent relationship to the statement or by a nondescript person who mumbles in a manner that brings joy to the hearts of Art Buchwald and Garry Trudeau who hope the speaker will seek the presidency. (1983, 92)

Indeed, communities that exploit this formula do receive more news coverage to their liking than do others, but not because of the political preferences of the journalists.

The Political Effects of Mass Communication

Our frameworks for understanding effects have changed considerably over the years, as have the media themselves. Therefore, it is worth a moment to consider the theories of effects before we consider the effects.

Theories of Effects

The first conception of effects was a simplistic *stimulus-response model*. Writers presumed that mass media shot their messages at a target audience or injected their messages into the body politic. The target audiences fell over persuaded, and the society absorbed the substance and physically reacted to it. When directly tested during the 1940s, this model failed (Lazarsfeld, Berelson, and Gaudet 1948). The model was flawed because it overlooked the fact that senders do not "do" communication "to" a receiver, they "do" communication together. It failed to recognize that reading and listening are active processes in which thinking persons interpret the message for themselves.

The second view to emerge was the *social categories* model, which held that people with shared characteristics will similarly respond to mass communication. Indeed, researchers still point to the voting patterns, consumer behaviors, and media habits of various demographic groups. Unfortunately, this model was weak at explaining those tendencies. It is certainly stretching the point to say that chromosomes govern our television habits.

The *social relationships model* held that identifiable demographic groups exhibit patterned behavior, because all of us are most likely to interact with people who are like us in important respects. As we interact with similar people, we talk about styles, movies, politics, people, sports, or whatever; and we homogenize into interpretive communities. As noted in Chapter 2, we tend to seek out people like us and we try to move toward the people we like.

This model was built around the two-step flow principle of communication between the mass media and opinion leaders and between opinion leaders and everyone else (Katz and Lazarsfeld 1955; Katz 1957). *Opinion leaders* are not columnists but family, friends, neighbors, coworkers, and significant others, whose interpretations and evaluations matter to their associates. Subsequent research has suggested several modifications. We each have many opinion leaders—people with whom we discuss current movies, politics, fashion, or sports. But with increased access to mass media—more households reportedly own televisions than indoor plumbing—we now get the message firsthand and then check our interpretations with our opinion leaders. These opinion leaders provide a reality check and help us properly apply our chosen interpretive framework.

But even the social relationships model had its weaknesses. For one thing, it was difficult to predict or to explain the basis for interaction patterns, since many people clearly within one demographic group behaved more like the group to which they aspired. Moreover, the patterns of opinion leadership became so complex that the explanation became analytically inefficient.

Through the 1970s and 1980s, the *uses and gratifications approach* has received considerable attention. Because it holds that audience members use the form and content of mass communication to fullfill their personal needs, it explains effects more fully than could the earlier models. People experience some combination of cognitive needs, diversion needs, and identity needs, which motivate them to seek some kind of gratification through mass communication. *Cognitive needs* to reduce uncertainty can lead to news consumption or to the latest developments on a soap opera. *Diversion needs* can lead to escapist fare or to channel scanning and literally "watching TV" with secondary regard to program content. *Identity needs* can lead to ego-supportive programs like exercise and religious shows or to programs that help refine the sense of sociopolitical self. Televised political conventions, for example, can fulfill all three needs.

Researchers study the gratifications experienced by audience members and compare them to the gratifications sought. One relevant premise is the idea that audiences watch the *least objectionable program* rather than their most desired program. Fundamentally, this approach emphasizes what the audience needs from its media fare and what it does with what it gets (Blumler and Katz 1974).

The Political Functions of Mass Communication

Mass communication performs three political functions in America (Denton and Woodward 1985). First, we use it to *establish the political agenda*. It is primarily through mass communication that problems, solutions, and communities are discovered by society. In recent years we have seen mass communication alter the political agenda with discussions of deficit reduction, SDI, and child abuse, to name but a few issues. The important agenda-setting point was originally made by showman P. T. Barnum: "There is no such thing as bad publicity." Put differently, it is mostly the amount of coverage that an issue receives, not its balance, that influences its prominence in the public consciousness.

The second effect has already been discussed at some length—the role of mass communication to *define political realities*. Bitzer's conception of the rhetorical situation (1980) dealt with the ebb and flow of exigencies, resources, and constraints. It is primarily through mass communication that we learn about imperfections and their urgencies, about the ability of people to meet crises, and about the importance of acting within important constraints. This chapter has emphasized the fact that this information comes through both the news and entertainment arenas of mass communication.

The third effect of mass communication is its ability to *personalize the political world*. Through the human dramas of fiction, sitcoms, and movies, social and political problems and principles become personally meaningful to us. We develop an acquaintance with the people and issues of politics and can identify with them. As we identify, we subjectively understand them and the drama as a whole. This insight provides a particular kind of knowledge or information about the problem and gives us a sense of the critical dynamic of politics—human choice.

Conclusions

Mass communication is the process through which individuals create, sustain, and govern their society. Our mass media deliver a variety of narratives and symbolic forms, and they enable us to sense the political world. Indeed, several times daily, production systems set aside programming time to acquaint us with developments in the world around us.

But mass communication is also a community of interrelated interests. Without the day's news, Johnny Carson's jokes fall flat; and without Carson-like jokes, there is a diminished appetite for news. The system is highly transactional for producers, distributors, advertisers, regulators, audiences, and the general culture. As the process churns away, it is useful to remember that American mass communication balances on the fulcrum of interpretive communities.

This chapter discussed the relationship between politics and mass communication. It clarified the distinction between "media" as companies and as channels of communication. It explained the social system model of mass communication and explicated the technological, cultural, organizational, and interpretive influences on message production and dissemination. It explored the nature of news and charges of news bias, and it considered the political implications of mass entertainment. It summarized the theories of media effects and the major political functions of mass communication.

The bottom line is that the political implications of mass communication are not what many people expect. Many casual observers are still back at the "bullet model's" all-powerful transmitter, still presuming that messages mold people's minds. People choose their mass communication, and—especially with satellite dishes, remote controls, and push buttons—they change distributors when the message fails to fit their needs. We in the audience convey to the producers and distributors our preferences through our behavioral choices. They care more about our demonstrated preferences than about our professed preferences. We earlier said that mass communication is an imperfect mirror of our society—a point frequently made by others. It is too rarely said that mass communication is, on balance, a better mirror than we care to admit. After all, how many people really want to look into a perfect mirror?

References

Agnew, Spiro T. "Television News Coverage," November 3, 1969. *Vital Speeches of the Day* (December 1969): 98–101.

Bayley, Edwin R. *Joe McCarthy and the Press.* New York: Pantheon, 1981.

Bennett, W. Lance. *News: The Politics or Illusion,* 2d ed. New York: Longman, 1988.

Bitzer, Lloyd F. "The Rhetorical Situation." *Philosophy and Rhetoric* 1 (Winter 1968): 1–14.

———"Functional Communication: A Situational Perspective." In *Rhetoric in Transition: Studies in The Nature and Uses of Rhetoric,* edited by Eugene E. White, 21–38. University Park: Pennsylvania State University Press, 1980.

Blumler, Jay, and Michael Gurevitch. "Politicians and the Press: An Essay on Role Relationships." In *Handbook of Political Communication,* edited by Dan D. Nimmo and Keith R. Sanders, 467–93. Beverly Hills, CA: Sage, 1981.

Blumler, Jay, and Elihu Katz, eds. *The Uses of Mass Communication.* Beverly Hills: Sage, 1974.

DeFleur, Melvin. *Theories of Mass Communication.* New York: McKay, 1966.

DeFleur, Melvin, and Sandra Ball-Rokeach. *Theories of Mass Communication,* 4th ed. New York: Longman, 1982.

Denton, Robert E., Jr., and Gary C. Woodward. *Political Communication in America.* New York: Praeger, 1985.

Edelman, Murray. *Constructing the Political Spectacle.* Chicago: University of Chicago Press, 1988.

Epstein, Edward Jay. *News from Nowhere: Television and the News.* New York: Random House, Vintage Books, 1973.

Graber, Doris A. *Processing the News: How People Tame the Information Tide.* New York: Longman, 1984.

Hackett, Robert A. "Decline of a Paradigm? Bias and Objectivity in News Media Studies." *Critical Studies in Mass Communication* 1 (September 1984): 229–59.

Jamieson, Kathleen Hall, and Karlyn Kohrs Campbell. *The Interplay of Influence: Mass Media and Their Publics in News, Advertising, Politics.* Belmont, CA: Wadsworth, 1983.

Katz, Elihu. "The Two-Step Flow of Communication." *Public Opinion Quarterly* 21 (1957): 61–78.

Katz, Elihu, and Paul F. Lazarsfeld. *Personal Influence: The Part Played by People in the Flow of Mass Communication.* New York: Free Press, 1955.

Lazarsfeld, Paul F., Bernard Berelson, and Hazel Gaudet. *The People's Choice.* New York: Columbia University Press, 1948.

Matusow, Barbara. *The Evening Stars: The Making of the Network News Anchor.* Boston: Houghton-Mifflin, 1983.

McLuhan, Marshall. *Understanding Media.* New York: McGraw-Hill, 1964.

Nimmo, Dan, and James E. Combs. *Mediated Political Realities.* New York: Longman, 1983.

Siebert, Fred, Theodore Peterson, and Wilbur Schramm, eds. *Four Theories of the Press.* Urbana, IL: University of Illinois Press, 1956.

Chapter 6
ELECTION CAMPAIGNS

Election campaigns are the most blatant form of political communication. In no other profession do people speak, advertise, and travel to proclaim their superiority over others. In no other profession do people pursue and defend jobs by publicly boasting and attacking others. Campaign managers stay awake nights thinking of ways to reach the voters who avoid news of their candidates. It is little wonder that politicians have developed an unsavory professional image.

Perhaps because election campaigning is so blatant, strident, and intrusive, it is poorly understood by most voters. Americans averaging only five minutes of political thought or discussion per week are drenched with appeals and stories (McClister 1988). We therefore expend considerable effort lest politics intrude into the "more important" areas of our lives. The result? *Most of us accept the simplest available accounts of campaigns, candidates, and results.*

Our general disinterest rarely encourages us to develop specifically political interpretive systems. Instead, we borrow the interpretive systems developed for our other life pursuits—sports, warfare, drama, and crusades. We make sense of election campaigns as contests, battles, and moral quests rather than as processes for deciding which individuals can best transform our needs and preferences into social practice. Realizing that those schemas, rather than practical governance, keep us attuned to campaigns, the journalists and candidates frame campaigns in those terms.

Campaign communication is also misunderstood because the techniques and strategies change so quickly. It is a multimillion-dollar industry in which professionals try to stay one step ahead of each other. Each campaign brings new problems and new solutions that go undetected until the homestretch.

This chapter will present a useful framework for understanding campaigns by overviewing election campaigns from our interpretive perspectives, explaining the components of election campaigns, and discussing the media used by campaign managers.

Understanding Election Campaigns

Proper understanding of election campaign communication requires a grasp of its six rhetorical components: the rules, the candidates, the electorate, the issues, the resources, and the strategies used to adjust them to one another. Campaigners try to persuade voters to modify their interpretations of the components and of the relationships among the components.

Rules

Rules define an election, and they are determined before candidacies are announced. A candidate who misses the filing deadline or presents an invalid petition does not get on the ballot. A candidate who accepts illegal contributions or exceeds spending limitations risks prosecution and attack. A candidate who fails to understand what constitutes victory or how it is measured can win only by accident.

Candidates must first determine what constitutes victory. Presidential elections are won with electoral votes and require assemblage of a jigsaw puzzle of weighted state victories. Constitutional amendments are ratified by two thirds of the states, regardless of weighting. Presidential nominations are won with delegates and require a blend of informal party caucuses, winner-take-all primary votes, proportional primary votes, and the friendly support of party officials. Senate and gubernatorial contests hinge on a statewide plurality or majority, depending on the state. A local contest may require a majority of wards or precincts, regardless of the popular vote. Elections are won by accumulating a predetermined number or proportion of "victory units." Wise candidates, journalists, and citizens determine how results will be measured before assessing the campaign.

Winner-take-all primaries in California, Florida, Ohio, and Texas accounted for 40 percent of the delegates needed for the 1988 Republican nomination. George Bush apparently saw this more clearly than did his challengers Dole, Robertson, and Kemp, who concentrated on early contests in Michigan, Iowa, and New Hampshire, which provided few delegates.

Democrats in 1988 used proportional representation exclusively, usually with a 15 percent minimum vote needed to win delegates.

Finishing first in a Democratic primary was therefore less important than husbanding resources, beating the 15 percent minimum, and surviving to campaign in the next event. Paul Simon squandered his resources before the Super Tuesday of 20 contests and was a nonfactor when 34 percent of the delegates were determined. Al Gore geared his campaign toward Super Tuesday and quickly passed Babbitt, Hart, Simon, and Gephardt but was ill prepared to contest Dukakis and Jackson in northern industrial states.

Rules also govern fund-raising and expenditures. If the rules discourage a handful of financiers, wise campaigns solicit small contributions with a populist rhetoric. If the rules discourage small contributors, campaigns establish exclusive donors' clubs. The rules are the game, and the skillful player knows them better than the opposition.

Stories about the complicated Iowa caucuses, runoff primaries, the electoral college, voter registration reforms, and delegate selection reforms rarely stir the interests of the politically disinterested. CBS, for example, turned to Lesley Stahl for an afterthought report on the process following a 25 minute report on the Iowa caucus results. Why *then*? Precisely because the thrust of her story was that Iowa's rules were odd and confusing; it increased audience dependence on CBS analysts for the contests to come. Rules stories surface when a local rule provokes a personal confrontation that dramatizes a national theme, as in 1984, when Jesse Jackson attacked the delegate formulas in mid-campaign. Whether journalists spend too much or too little time explaining rules is a matter of interpretation. But experience suggests that relatively few voters learn enough to pass a pop quiz on election day.

Interesting or not, the rules define the race. Who may run, how they get on the ballot, who may vote, in what precinct their votes count, whether they cannot/may/must vote a straight party ticket, what resources may be spent on what kinds of activities, and how winners are determined constitute truly fundamental electoral decisions.

Candidates

News coverage centers on candidates, especially the front-runner. As in football and basketball, front-runners get the hot seat. Are they as good as they seem? Are they slipping? Are they repackaging themselves and their record? By how much do they need to win to retain front-runnership? By contrast, those toward the back of the pack can be boosted into contention with even modest success. There are two explanations for this phenomenon.

The organizational influences on news coverage require that reportorial resources be focused where they can do the most good—on the front-runner and on the dramatic surprise. The cultural and interpretive influences demand an interesting race, and third place draws little interest. In either case, candidates, especially front-runners and dark horses, are the centerpieces of election stories.

Almost anyone can run for office in America, but few can win elections. People considering candidacy should carefully and objectively examine their strengths and weaknesses. Why do they want the post? What have they done that suits them to the post? Which of their personal qualities do not suit them to the post? Are they well known to potential voters? Do they have a ready source of financial and volunteer support? What things in their (or their associates') past could be made to appear unseemly? Are they comfortable in an unending stream of handshakes and coffees? Again: Why do they want the office? Is that sufficient reason to risk indebtedness, public criticism, and possible humiliation? If they cannot enthusiastically answer these questions, they probably should avoid the race. *Good ideas alone do not make good candidates.* It may be wiser for them to support someone else's candidacy.

Once someone has decided to run, it is prudent to seek advice. Surgeons do not operate on themselves; barbers do not cut their own hair; and lawyers do not represent themselves. To paraphrase a saying, candidates who run their own campaigns have fools for campaign managers. Indeed, good campaign managers reject assignments that look too dismal, thereby saving the potential candidate time, money, and heartache.

The candidate should have a central *theme* that captures the essence of the campaign, like Reagan and Bush's "Together, a New Beginning." In 1988, Bush emphasized "experience," Dole stressed "leadership," and Gephardt proclaimed, "This is your fight, too!" If the Kemp, Haig, Babbitt, and Du Pont campaigns had central themes, they were not memorable.

The theme should be the candidate's single most important message. It should answer the voter's question "Why should I support you?" and it should differentiate the candidate from all of the others. Simple, dramatic persuasiveness is more desirable than complexity, because the theme must be memorable for all voters, regardless of their intellect or interest. The campaign theme should balance policy issues and personal qualities, and it should have potential for development during the campaign (Beaudry and Schaeffer 1986). Although a theme is important, campaigns can devote too much attention to their slogans and logos. The 1988 Dukakis campaign became consumed with the immigrant theme, playing Neil Diamond's song, "America," at every opportunity and leaving to the Bush campaign all sorts of Americana.

It is crucial that candidates understand that everyone cannot be satisfied. Candidates need to please their own electoral base and enough persuadable voters to outnumber the opponents' combination of base plus persuadables.

Values and policy issues are unquestionably important in elections, but likability is central. Elections pick people not policies. Most voters seem to prefer candidates with whom they can identify. Nasty, intense, unfriendly, secretive, or awkward candidates experience difficulty, even when their positions are compelling. Voters like confidence but not arrogance, with the result that it is often easier to be a confident challenger than a modest incumbent. Robert Dole won the 1988 Iowa caucus and headed for New Hampshire ready to knock George Bush out of the race. But the Bush campaign provoked Dole's anger, and, in defeat, Dole publicly accused Bush of lying about his record. Dole's edge evaporated, and Bush wrapped up the nomination on Super Tuesday. Nice beat nasty.

The Electorate

The *electorate* consists of those people who vote in an election, and it is better to be popular among those who vote than among those who stay home. An electorate comprises interpretive communities that need to be mobilized, transactionally or transformationally, into majority and minority constituencies. Each candidate can rely on an *electoral base* of bedrock supporters who need only be induced to vote. Important sources of base support frequently include party identification, ethnicity, and name recognition. Most contested campaigns are for *persuadable voters* (or *swing voters*).

The electorate's track record is an important starting point, because each campaign is conducted to win the adherence of particular audiences of voters who have demonstrated their preferencing patterns in past elections. But each electorate changes from year to year, and its needs and preferences change as well. Therefore, campaign managers search data bases to ascertain the distribution of votes in comparable elections. Early in the campaign they can project the county-by-county margins they will need to win. But even though electorates are stable, they do vary from election to election.

Campaigns rely on public opinion *polls* to estimate characteristics of the current electorate from the responses of a representative sample. Since every poll is an estimate, each includes a *margin for error* that varies with the sample size, usually plus or minus 4 percent. A poll of 48 percent with a 4 percent margin for error means that candidate A's support is in the range of 44–52 percent. A poll of 41 percent with a 4 percent margin of error means that candidate B's support is in the range of 37–45 percent.

The familiar horse race polls matter less to campaigners than do those reporting favorable and unfavorable reactions to the candidates and issues in particular communities of the electorate. The Times-Mirror corporation identified ten "tribes" of American politics, and some pollsters have as many as 300 demographic groups whose information and preferences they track with interest (Beiler 1988). Lee Atwater and his associates discovered in May of 1988 that swing voter support for Dukakis evaporated when those voters were told about Willie Horton's prison furlough and Dukakis's veto of the Pledge of Allegiance bill, leading Atwater reportedly to remark, "If we can make Willie Horton a household name, we win." Gerald Ford began his presidency with a firm commitment to reuniting America and an electorate 80 percent united around inflation as the country's primary exigence, suggesting a partial explanation for his loss in 1976. Voting histories, interpretive communities, and polls are critically important in campaigns. The microscopic tracking analyses, not the horse race overviews, reveal to campaigners which voters are responding to which issues.

Issues

Every campaign accuses its opponents of "ducking the real issues." Our journalistic watchdogs sniff around the campaigns and bark at the first sign of a "key issue." But what is an issue? An *issue* is a point of contention or source of disagreement, and points of contention in an election may be character or values or economic policy or social policy or foreign policy or—quite literally—anything else. Candidates, journalists, and voters form an interdependent system in which some symbols, narratives, preferences, and reasons fall flat and others chain out to unite an audience in a shared vision or preference. *Real issues* are those that ignite public interest and discussion and, most importantly, influence the voters' candidate preferences.

Electoral history is replete with examples of candidate positions that were simply out of step with their times. Candidates float potential issues, and journalists frame clashing issues for public discussion. But it is the public, through its social interpretive system, that ultimately defines the real issues and uses them to vote.

But precisely how do voters use issues? Consider the hypothesis that voters use issues to eliminate candidates rather than to support them. The *support model* presumes that voters search out and weigh candidate positions on the central issues, compare candidate records to their own preferences, and select the candidate closest to their ideal. It is an encouraging model of civic responsibility, but there is little evidence that voters actually do that. American voters spend little of their time on political thinking; few have expressly political interpretive systems; detailed policy information is hard to find; and polls usually show major, last-minute shifts.

Campaign behavior makes more sense when we view voters as eliminating or short-listing candidates. The one sure thing about any election is that someone will win office and that others will lose. It takes relatively little effort to scan news and interpersonal contacts for schemas that warrant eliminating a candidate from consideration. Questions about character, flip-flops even on unspecified policy questions, poor communication skills, and suspect electability can quickly lead to elimination. Emerging candidates with marginal credibility are particularly vulnerable to elimination, while incumbents and familiar candidates are more resistant. The *elimination model*, like the least objectionable program in broadcasting, fosters the emergence of a lowest common denominator candidate in the person of the least offensive candidate. In the 1988 Republican primaries, George Bush was less offensive to Republicans than were Dole, Robertson, Kemp, Haig, and Du Pont, and Michael Dukakis was less offensive to Democrats than were Jackson, Gore, Gephardt, Simon, Hart, Biden, and Babbitt. But Bush's depiction of the prison furlough and the Pledge of Allegiance issues made Dukakis the more offensive to the general electorate. Bush was ultimately preferred by an electorate that lamented the lack of "real issues."

Resources

The three resources of campaigns are *people*, *money*, and *time*. Candidates should estimate the people, money, and time available for the campaign, how much they want, how much they must have to campaign credibly, and how depleted resources can be replenished.

Today it is rarely too early to begin a campaign. An *election cycle* involves three phases. During the *surfacing phase*, potential candidates emerge, and their campaign organizations begin to amass resources (adapted from Trent and Friedenberg 1983). Some people are dubbed candidates by the press; others, by the political grapevine. This period can be used to associate the precandidate with issues and accomplishments and to enhance name recognition. Initial fund-raising activities and plans to get on the ballot with a petition, fees, or both often begin two years in advance. A candidate who announces early may dissuade potential rivals.

Candidates campaign initially in constituencies richer in volunteers and money than votes. A key to replenishing resources is "zip code targeting" through which computerized mailing lists are cross-referenced to identify zip codes that produce maximum contributions. The top contributing zip codes during the 1987 surfacing period included Manhattan's Upper East Side, the Cambridge and Brookline areas near Boston, and Greenwich, Connecticut.

The *nomination phase* relies on some combination of primary elections, runoffs, caucuses, and conventions to select a nominee. Obviously, this process is simplified when there is no opposition. This phase is ticklish since the nomination must be won to run in the general election, but party divisions handicap the general election effort and make conventions important reunification sessions.

The *general election phase* is a contest for the elective office itself. Other races may be decided on the same ballot, and the candidate's alignment with those candidacies and issues may be critical. Unless the candidate has alienated them along the way, most candidate partisans will join the campaign here because they view their party's candidate as preferable to the opposition party's candidate.

We have said that proper understanding of an election campaign requires a grasp of the rules, candidates, electorate, issues, and resources. These components comprise the exigences, audiences, and constraints of political campaigning. The task of the campaign is the formulation and implementation of strategies to win the appropriate victory units.

Campaign Strategies

Let us consider how political professionals devise and apply their strategies. As we do so, it is prudent to bear in mind that even the best-informed political managers armed with good candidates and ample resources lose campaigns.

Techniques are presented so that citizen readers can better understand the electoral process. Readers interested in campaign strategy in pursuit of political office should consult the political consultants' trade magazine *Campaigns & Elections* and books like Beaudry and Schaeffer's *Winning State and Local Elections* (1986) and S. J. Guzzetta's *The Campaign Manual* (1987), and they should volunteer to work in local campaigns. Sometimes a record of diligent volunteer work and known interest can get young workers an opportunity to work in higher-level positions.

Campaign strategies are the plans for adjusting the rules, candidates, electorate, issues, and resources to one another. Strategizing is a rhetorical process of thoughtfully adapting the components to maximize prospects for victory.

Strategy is based on the perceived strengths and weaknesses of particular candidates in the eyes of likely voters in the context of the applicable election rules. All of these elements are subject to modification through persuasion: candidates are repositioned; rules are reformed; issues are highlighted and marginalized; and voter registration and turnout are both encouraged and downplayed. A candidate who "plays well in Peoria" may be ill suited to election in Brooklyn or Malibu.

Every campaign should be approached as a unique system of components and relationships, but there are nevertheless some general guidelines. Let us briefly consider 14 basic strategic rules that govern most campaigns. As we discuss the following rules, bear in mind that as in football, basketball, and pinochle, all candidates are trying to win by using variations on the same strategic rules.

Fourteen Strategic Rules

1. *The winning candidate is the one preferred by the people who vote on election day.* It matters little to the outcome whether the winner is preferred because of her strengths or her opponents' perceived weaknesses; it matters simply that she is preferred. Negative commercials or "attack ads" focus voters' attention on their conceptions of reality and the preferable and reframe their alternatives by associating the target of the attack with undesirable sentiments that warrant elimination.

2. *It matters little who is preferred by nonvoters or who is preferred a month before the election.* Both factors are potentially useful, but potential needs to be realized. A candidate preferred among nonvoters should devote ample resources to *get-out-the-vote* efforts and to potentially influential exhibitions of support, like bumper stickers, lapel buttons, and yard signs. Candidates preferred weeks before the election might solicit resources for the stretch drive and publicize their lead to discourage opponents. Political consultant Joe Napolitan observed that, "An election is like a one-day sale" since votes only count on election night (1987).

3. *The key to being preferred is repetitive, persuasive communication with likely voters* (Beaudry and Schaeffer 1986). Obvious? It is astounding how many campaigns waste resources by dropping themes, boring voters, and addressing the wrong people. Wise campaigners study the electorate and target their issues to particular audiences before campaigning. Sometimes two or three

metropolitan counties are enough, while other contests require an unusual mixture.

4. *Campaign strategists target precincts and counties by emphasizing persuadable likely voters.* To find these persuadable voters, strategists rank the precincts or counties in question according to a calculation such as the following:

> number of registered voters X average voter turnout X (highest party vote percentage - lowest party vote percentage)

The formula prefers areas with many registered voters who vote (number X turnout). Attention goes to precincts that *often* vote for a particular party rather than to those that *always* vote for that party, since regulars need little persuading and are less susceptible to counterpersuasion. These same priorities are used in primaries, since the party can best find votes in its strongholds.

5. *Campaign strategists try to enhance registration and turnout in supportive precincts.* Can precincts be made more or less persuadable through the selection of issues and candidates? Registration and get-out-the-vote drives are rarely conducted with equal fervor in all precincts, and poll watchers may unintentionally initimidate opposition voters.

6. *Candidates should be depicted accurately, pleasantly, and in harmony with the interpretive systems of likely voters.* Distortions, exaggerations, and misrepresentations are both unethical and unwise. They will be noticed and reported, as Joe Biden can attest. Most voters prefer to vote for someone they can like and trust: they want an engrossing and believable storyteller. There may never be a better example than Ronald Reagan, whose popularity and approval remained impressive despite countless examples of misquotations and inaccurate information. Voters liked him.

7. *The campaign's message must be appropriate to the candidate, the rules, and the target voters.* The message must be accurate, clear, and understandable, without underestimating voters. This means simplifying difficult issues and not complicating familiar issues. Jack Kemp's discussion of "privatizing" Social Security and moving to the "gold standard" appealed to college audiences but confused most other audiences.

8. *A candidate needs to take on the role of either incumbent or challenger, using arguments appropriate to the role.* Candidates who stake out the role of incumbent can draw on the legitimacy, symbolism, and competence of their office; and they can run on their records. Candidates who run as challengers take the offensive by contrasting incumbent policies with traditional values and promising

a brighter future (Trent and Friedenberg 1983). Because these are rhetorical roles, we sometimes see incumbents running as challengers and challengers running as incumbents. For example, President Truman campaigned against the Republican "do-nothing" Congress in 1948 and won. In 1988, the leading Republican contenders all ran as incumbents: Pat Robertson was heir to the moral agenda; Alexander Haig was heir to the foreign policy of standing tall; Jack Kemp was heir to Reaganomics and SDI; Bob Dole was heir to the Reagan legislative successes; and George Bush was heir to the symbolism of the Reagan Presidency. The Dukakis campaign tied itself in knots by calling for change while putting his record in Massachusetts on the table for inspection.

9. *The campaign's message grows like an onion around the campaign theme.* The theme should memorably answer the central question "Why should I vote for this candidate instead of the opposition?" and it should be repeated throughout the dominant media so that all target voters learn it by election day.

10. *Campaigns emphasize visual and verbal symbols that reinforce the theme and avoid those that might contradict it.* Rufus Edmisten won North Carolina's 1984 gubernatorial primary with spots portraying his boyhood in the mountains. His switch to a suited attorney general posture for the general election was a harsh contradiction and contributed to his unexpected defeat. A message that works should be used until its returns diminish.

11. *Campaigns try to "dominate the dominant medium," whether that be television, handshakes, or yard signs* (Napolitan 1987). The dominant medium is where most voters get most of their information, and it pays to have the candidate's message in this traffic. But often, persuadable voters can best be reached through alternative media: Jimmy Carter advertised heavily on black radio stations in 1976 to reach potential supporters without reaching potential opponents.

12. *Campaigns are an inappropriate forum for deliberating complex, new issues, for teaching voters new priorities, or for telling them that their cherished beliefs and values are wrong.* When perception and reality conflict, reality must be explained. During the 1988 primaries, reporters and opponents repeatedly asked George Bush to explain his nonrole in the Iran-Contra affair and asked Richard Gephardt to explain his "flip-flops." Both had reasonable explanations, but both lost time, money, and votes because they had to influence perceptions. Remember that voters interpret new information through their interpretive processes as far as they can, and they are likely to resolve unpleasant interpretive dilemmas by eliminating the candidate who caused them. Citizens and journalists need cam-

paign messages that fit their available schemas and narratives if they are to be understood.

13. *Message delivery should coincide with the targeted audiences' decision making.* In most races this rule translates into "Save resources for a big finish." Consultants advised candidates 20 years ago to make their major arguments early and often to establish support (Bailey 1988). Now they advise candidates to concentrate their spots at the end for greatest impact. If they have nothing new for the end, they repackage old material (Bailey 1988). Most voters in most elections now decide at the last minute.

But recent presidential races are evidencing a different trend: our preferences crystallize much earlier. The huge number of undecided voters in 1988 was a popular theme among journalists that did not withstand close scrutiny, since undecided voters split into votes for candidate A, votes for candidate B, and nonvotes. Dukakis, Mondale, and Carter resources saved for a stretch run were wasted. That is why this strategic rule recommends that candidates provide messages appropriate to persuadable voters' preferencing at the time when those voters are scanning the news to reduce their uncertainty.

14. *Double-check everything.* The little things can matter greatly, and the big things always merit care. Does the theme really appeal to potential supporters? In what counties does the candidate have unusual, nontraditional appeal or vulnerability? In what areas does the candidate run better or worse than expected? Which messages and characteristics are mentioned by voters, and how do they feel about the candidate? The campaign should have a first-rate communication system among its key people, and they should have a designated top-level "reaction unit" to respond to unexpected developments.

Political Consultants

Campaign strategizing is a serious, complex, and significant task. These strategic choices influence voters' judgments since they position the candidates with respect to our interpretive systems. But individual voters make individual choices based on their personal preferencing processes. Campaign strategists cannot control or determine our votes. They present candidates in ways that fit our preferencing processes so that on election day a majority of us will prefer, and vote for, their candidates rather than their opponents.

The field of political consulting has grown into a multimillion-dollar profession during the last quarter century, and it is rightfully subject to careful scrutiny. But its depiction in movies like *Power* is misleading. Advertising agencies dominated during the 1950s and

1960s and plied their wares for both parties. But the field became so specialized that today's political consultants specialize in politics, and most work exclusively for candidates of a particular party. Philosophy and principle are important to most consultants.

The legitimate concern that consultants pay too much attention to "what works" and insufficient attention to the "quality" of the person and issues running for office is exaggerated. Lawyers are obliged to provide the best possible defense for their clients, even those known to be guilty. Physicians are obliged to save patients, even those known to be criminals. Teachers are obliged to teach all students as best they can, even when they suspect possible misuse of that knowledge. Political consultants are retained to help serious candidates for public office to communicate with the citizenry. As a professional community, they are no more or less ethical than lawyers, physicians, or teachers. Strategy is important, and the alternative to skilled consultants is to entrust strategizing to amateurs. The stakes are extremely high to be left to public relations experts, but they are too high to be left to novices.

Media for Campaign Persuasion

The campaign strategy is implemented through the media of mingling, printed matter, rallies, speeches, radio and television spots, and joint forums or debates. Each medium offers novel opportunities and dangers and should be used wisely by the campaign.

Mingling

We will coin the term *mingling* to encompass all campaigning that initiates or consolidates personal contact between a candidate and citizens. This includes door-to-door canvases, walking across the district, handshaking at factory gates, telephone calls to spelling-bee champions, and throwing the ceremonial first pitch of the World Series. Mingling is most important during the surfacing stage, when potential candidates need recognition, contributors, volunteers, and narrative anecdotes that dramatize the issues ("While walking across the state I met . . . "). Mingling is easiest for incumbents, who need it least, but such are the advantages of incumbency. Anyone can invite the senator, congressman, or mayor to their pancake breakfast, but mingling with challengers smacks of political activism.

The keys to effective political mingling are advance work and follow-up. *Advance work* scouts the situation and spreads word of the candidate's visit. Before shaking hands at a shopping mall, advance people verify that the opponent will be elsewhere, that all permits are in order, that signs and handbills announce the visit, that volunteer and contribution cards are available, and that brochures and bumper stickers are available. *Follow-up work* contacts everyone who filled out a card or expressed interest. When candidates ring doorbells on a street, their advance people provide the names of contributors or influentials, and the follow-up people invite the newfound supporters and undecideds to the next campaign event.

Mingling is simple, but effective mingling is not. The campaign carefully selects promising haunts for potential voters. This frequently means visits outside the target precincts to reach target voters in factories, shopping malls, stadiums, or fairs. The candidate smiles at each passerby, offers a firm handshake and says something inspirational like, "Hi! My name is Jane Johnson, and I'm running for city council. . . . I'd appreciate your support" and lets the voter go on with his or her life. If voters want to chat, the candidate listens and sees that they all take brochures and volunteer or contributor cards. Genuinely interested voters deserve more attention than a handshake, and the candidate needs to make contact with as many different people as possible.

Mingling is the best opportunity for identifying with real people, and it recruits volunteers. It can be especially helpful for disarming voters who envision the candidate with horns and a pitchfork.

But mingling is badly suited to the discussion of issues, especially complex ones. A candidate who gets drawn into detailed conversations about issues or gets easily angered cannot afford to mingle very much. One who can smile and avoid depth is a natural mingler, which may go a long way toward explaining the nature of our electoral politics, since only skilled minglers accumulate sufficient resources to advance to the other media.

Printed Matter

Printed matter includes newsletters, brochures, mailings, and display items like bumper stickers, yard signs, and campaign buttons. Former journalist Paul Simon relied heavily on the distribution of multipage typed and stapled single-issue position papers in his 1988 campaign to spell out his positions; Richard Gephardt relied on a glossy, folded full-color brochure of smiling American workers and impressive testimonials; and Michael Dukakis husbanded his resources.

In most cases, it seems that the tangible souvenir quality of the printed matter is its most important quality for the voter. Without these souvenirs the voter may not remember the candidate's name or contest on election day. Printed matter is customarily distributed at every opportunity.

Printed matter can have a symbolic dimension beyond its substance. Simon's position papers prevented his quick elimination by those voters scanning the field for candidates stressing policy questions. The simple availability of the position papers achieved this effect, whether or not the papers were actually read. In fact, lengthy, typed position papers actually discourage careful reading as compared to graphically interesting and succinct brochures. Perhaps this is because voters can easily eliminate candidates with no discernible issue positions and those with clearly incompatible issue positions, leaving in the running those candidates with poorly understood issue positions.

Display items are useful indicators of acceptance. Voters who display Bush-Quayle yard signs, bumber stickers, and lapel buttons are unlikely to risk embarrassment by changing their preference on election day. Moreover, the balance of display items in a precinct suggests community preferences. Candidates who are miserly in their distribution of display items enable their adversaries to nurture the appearance of widespread support.

Rallies

A *rally* is a campaign gathering that brings together supporters and activists. Whereas mingling takes the candidate to citizens, rallies bring potential supporters to the candidate. Such events serve important rhetorical functions that cannot be performed well through other vehicles. Rallies are capable of generating more excitement and enthusiasm than mingling, debates, or television spots because the favored candidate is interacting with enthusiastic supporters who are further excited by the shared enthusiasm.

The rally is a pure example of fantasy chaining as the candidate's vision is shared with supporters. The collective identity comes from both the shared vision and the act of sharing it. Rallies can be a critical means for rebuilding morale among supporters late in a campaign.

Because a rally's most important potential is excitement, a boring rally is disastrous. At good political rallies, bands and cheerleaders abound, celebrities appear, favored politicians endorse, precinct leaders introduce, followers wave signs, and speakers call for audience answers. Well-heeled campaigns offer free food. Moreover, they do all of this at a snappy pace. When it mattered most in late October of 1988, there were snappy, energetic Bush rallies and lengthy, droning, repetitive Dukakis rallies.

A candidate's rally speech hammers at the central theme and the issues appropriate to the audience. Extended, single-issue addresses are rally killers. The rally audience comes not for a detailed analysis but for fun, excitement, and camaraderie. They are already on the bandwagon and need further ego-involvement in the campaign to prevent counterpersuasion and to induce contributions of time and money. The advance and follow-up people distribute position papers, pledge cards, buttons, and bumper stickers at the rally so that souvenirs will fuel the excitement of being there and subsequent reflection will recall the candidate, theme, and excitement.

Speeches

Campaign speeches are unique because political campaigning is a unique exigence. Each candidate is expected to visit a variety of audiences comprising potentially conflicting constituencies, to address the issues that each audience defines as central, to spell out detailed, practical positions on each, to avoid conflicting positions, to say the same thing everywhere without getting repetitious, to undermine opponents without seeming unfair, to defend against attack without seeming defensive, and to demonstrate leadership without seeming power hungry.

The best available approach to these complex tasks is the use of *modular speeches*. A candidate prepares modules, or minispeeches, on each important issue or theme. Each of these modules is used so often that the candidate can remember it and convincingly deliver it. George Bush spoke of his desire to become the "education president." Richard Gephardt launched into his $48,000 Hyundai module. Jesse Jackson asked audience members who knew drug users to stand. Jack Kemp spoke of the gold standard.

Modules offer several advantages beyond memorability and consistency. Clarifications and new material can be worked into the repertoire without unnecessarily disturbing the other modules. Advance people scouting an audience can advise the candidate of the need to use certain modules rather than others.

But modular structures are not magic. Bruce Babbitt traversed Iowa and New Hampshire in 1988 with his "courage to raise the difficult issues" module and quickly staked out the Democratic cellar. Sadly, even those American voters who worry about difficult issues rarely support candidates who say that the choices are difficult, especially during an election. Unpopular arguments cannot be saved by modular structures.

The use of modular speeches dovetails with the polls that tap subtle changes in the approval and disapproval of candidates and issues. These are the polls that enable a campaign to tell whether it is gaining ground among voters who have heard its candidate, gaining ground among voters who have not heard its candidate, or losing ground among voters who have heard its candidate. These polls, not the horse race polls, tell the campaign which modules are working and which are not working so that the candidate's message can be revised.

Campaign speeches use *creative ambiguity* extensively so that conflicting interpretive communities can all interpret the message positively. In Richard Nixon's 1968 pledge to quickly end the Vietnam War, hawks heard military escalation and doves heard negotiation and withdrawal. Votes from both quarters were vital to his narrow victory over Hubert Humphrey and George Wallace, but Nixon's eventual policy pleased neither community. His campaign fed an ambiguous pledge to varied interpretive systems.

Since elections are matters of preference, campaigns are replete with attacks and defenses, and the balance between attack and defense speeches can be treacherous. Attacks put one's likability at risk and highlight the opponent, but elections are comparative. Responding to charges escalates the controversy, but silence allows them to build momentum. Candidates need to remember that "target voter concern" about the issue should guide their strategy. George Bush's supporters were unconcerned about his alleged involvement in the Iran-Contra scandal and rallied to his defense whenever he was asked about it. Pat Robertson's supporters dismissed Paul McCloskey's allegation that favorable treatment had saved him from combat duty. But Joe Biden's supporters, who admired his eloquence and idealism, were deeply distributed by his unattributed use of another's speech and his embellished academic record. And people who supported Michael Dukakis because of the "Massachusetts miracle" were vulnerable to accusations about his handling of taxation and the pollution of Boston Harbor. The key to handling accusation and defense is for the campaign to address the interests and concerns of its targeted voters.

Radio and Television Spots

Political advertising has been around since the 1840s; and since 1952, television spots have evolved into a million-dollar enterprise that can make or break many campaigns.

Each spot costs anywhere from $10,000 to $50,000 to produce, and each campaign needs several of them. *ID spots* introduce the candidate and theme, usually stressing biographical materials and pictures. *Argument spots* establish constructive points and associate the candidate with one or more issues, events, and people. *Attack spots* direct voter attention to flaws or contradictions in the opponent's record (Diamond and Bates 1984). Each type of message performs an essential function for the campaign.

But spots must be aired, and air time is scarce. Stations must agree to sell equal amounts of time at an equal price to all candidates in a race, but that price is usually top dollar. Moreover, everyone wants his or her time just before the election, and there are limited minutes available.

The prevalence of campaign spots and public aversion to them have fostered the notion that spots are improper, misleading, corrupting, and manipulative. It may be comforting to blame election outcomes on campaign techniques, but it is unfair to do so. Television is the dominant medium of our age, with radio right behind. Spots are the only means by which candidates can get their preferred messages to a large audience of target voters. Fundamentally, spots are properly adapted to the concerns of an electorate that is both politically disinterested and inclined to interpret civic responsibilities in melodramatic terms. The people who create political spots understand clearly how their targeted voters decide to vote, and they speak precisely to those concerns because that is their role. It bears repeating that our mass communication is a better mirror of our society than we care to admit.

Joint Forums or Debates

Many thoughtful observers during the 1964–76 period felt that the superficiality of campaign spots, rallies, modular speeches, and mingling undermined the selection of effective leaders. The ideal solution, they thought, would be debates like those in 1960 between Nixon and Kennedy. These efforts produced an explosion of "debates," which proved that such forums can achieve significant popularity when they, too, become superficial.

A true *debate* is a "confrontation in equal and adequate time of matched contestants on a stated proposition to gain an audience decision" (Auer 1962). The familiar candidate forums entail neither a stated proposition nor an audience decision. Worse, they typically deny candidates either the right to define the issues or the right to directly question opponents. Instead, allegedly expert panelists define the issues and pose the questions. Any candidate who fails to answer a panelist's question directly, however weak it might be, is considered evasive.

The panel format presumes that candidates for government service must be forced by representatives of a nongovernment elite to commit themselves on matters of policy with spontaneous responses to planned questions. We are told by our journalists to look for quick, concise, and rhetorically memorable, substantive answers that respond directly to the question. Why? Don't questions about weapons systems and homelessness, and taxation and treaty commitments merit a moment of reflection? Might not a future president grasp the civic issues more clearly than a future anchorperson?

Consider the different kinds of information we would gather if we adopted a different approach to candidate forums: (1) each campaign would give a set of questions to the other; (2) after a week, each would provide its answers to the wire services for distribution; and (3) after another week, there would be a live forum in which the candidates could evaluate the answers and a panel of topically relevant congressional leaders, professors, journalists, and community representatives could press for elaboration. The point is not that such forums would provide better candidates but that they would provide fundamentally different bases for choosing among candidates.

But candidates tend to like the familiar approach, despite its problems, because it safeguards their images on two fronts. No candidate can be directly humiliated by an opponent, and no candidate need risk likability by asking harsh questions (Martel 1983).

Candidate forums are carefully staged, and the wise candidate realizes the nature of the performance. Asked after his first debate if he had been nervous on stage with President Carter, Ronald Reagan quipped, "No, I've been on the same stage with John Wayne." Myles Martel's *Political Campaign Debates* (1983) is a treasure chest of advice for candidates by one of the foremost campaign forum consultants. These tactics are the fundamental behaviors of political "debates," and we should understand the techniques if we are to use political forums to select leaders. Table 6-1 summarizes ways of responding to various types of questions, a typology that can be useful when analyzing a debate.

Considerable research suggests that candidate forums help voters develop political interests and learn political information. These effects seem particularly pronounced among nonpartisan voters, although it is unclear whether they are independent thinkers or simply apolitical (Kraus and Davis 1981). It should also be noted that the information voters learn from forums does not necessarily differ from the information they learn from other vehicles, since the same citizens use the same interpretive schemas to scan the tide of campaign information.

My 1984 political communication class—a group of solid students— prepared for the first Reagan-Mondale "debate," watched it, and discussed it in class. After 30 minutes of discussing Reagan's age and

Table 6-1
Ways of Responding to Difficult Questions

Type	Example	Major Options
1. Hostile	"How do you expect more liberal groups to support you with your rotten record on the environment?"	1. Point out hostility. 2. Show cool, non-defensive disagreement, taking exception to terms chosen. 3. Project righteous indignation, short of losing composure.
2. Speculative	"What do you expect union membership to be in this state in four years?"	1. Label question as speculative. 2. Generally, don't predict with any attempt to be precise; stick with optimistic generalities (if, of course, they apply).
3. Hypothetical	"If interest rates drop to 12 or 13 percent within the next year, would you still propose raising the state sales tax?"	1. Point out hypothetical nature of question. 2. Refuse to answer because of phrasing. 3. Answer directly.
4. Picayune/ Overspecific	"What has been the percentage of growth of the Department of Transportation budget since 1978?"	1. Label question as overspecific. 2. If you don't know, say so. (Sometimes you may need to explain in a nondefensive manner why you don't know.)
5. Leading	"Why can't this state attract more industry with one of the best labor forces in the nation?" This question carries three assumptions? 1. The state is not attracting new industry as it should. 2. The state has one of the best labor forces in the nation. 3. The labor force should attract more industry.	1. If you agree or disagree with any of these assumptions, let it be known.

Continued on next page

Table 6-1—*Continued*

Type	Example	Major Options
6. Value	"Which is a better choice for energy conservation, carpools or public transportation?"	1. Apply your definition of "better" without drawing attention to this term. 2. Point out the value term, define it and then answer the question. 3. Ask questioner to define it and then respond.
7. Question Begging	"Isn't the main reason why we have so little available energy because there are significant shortages of the types of energy we normally rely on?"	1. Point out politely that the question in essence argues in a circle—it answers itself without probing further.
8. Multifaceted	"How many workers are unemployed in this state? How has this level changed over the past four years? How does this state's unemployment compare with that of neighboring states? What do you plan to do about the unemployment problem?"	1. If each facet can be remembered and answering all won't cause harm (assuming there is ample time), then answer fully. 2. If harm can be caused by answering a remembered facet, it is probably best to "forget" it. 3. Don't hesitate to ask for a facet to be repeated if you are reasonably certain you forgot a "safe" one. 4. You may want to refer humorously to the number of questions asked. 5. If the questions cannot be realistically answered within the time allotted, say so, e.g., "Perhaps it takes only a minute to ask all those questions, but it will take a lot more than that to answer them."

Continued on next page

Table 6-1—Continued

Type	Example	Major Option
9. Vague, Unfocused	"What do you plan to do, if elected, to make this a better state in which to live?"	1. Define the question the way you wish— consistent with your persuasive goals. 2. Ask the questioner to clarify his focus.
10. "Yes-No"	"Your campaign has been funded mainly by PAC contributions, yes or no?"	1. If "yes" or "no" is safe by itself, answer accordingly. 2. If risky, point out how the forced alternatives can interfere with a presentation of "the full truth." Then answer the question.
11. Nonquestion	"Unemployment is climbing; inflation is still spiraling; we are in a depression and ought to admit it."	1. Ask for a question, noting the nonquestion. 2. Respond to the nonquestion in whole or in part.

SOURCE: Myles Martel, *Political Campaign Debates: Images, Strategies, and Tactics.* (New York: Longman, 1983), 109–12.

Mondale's humor, a comment about substantive policy arose. Embarrassed by their inattention to policy, the class tried again on the second "debate," and it worked; it only took 25 minutes to draw a substantive observation! The point is that viewer interpretive systems govern the selection and interpretation of information regardless of the persuasive medium. We can convince ourselves that our interpretations of forums are inherently more rational, substantive, reliable, and respectable than interpretations of mingling, printed matter, rallies, speeches, or spots. But that is a potentially dangerous assumption.

Conclusions

Any election campaign consists of rules, candidates, issues, resources, an electorate, and strategies for adapting them to one another. At the center of the process are voters, who scan their environment for information that enables them to eliminate candidates who disturb their interpretive systems.

Candidates need repetitive persuasion with their likely voters, especially those who swing from party to party. But it is difficult and expensive for them to reach us, since most of us duck their messages. They rely on mingling, rallies, printed matter, speeches, spots, and candidate forums to articulate their themes and positions. The objective is to be preferred on election day by a plurality specified in the rules.

In *The Candidate*, Robert Redford plays a liberal, social activist son of a former governor who is enticed by a political consultant to run for the Senate. The consultant assures the candidate that he will not be packaged and that he can use the unwinnable campaign against a popular incumbent to draw attention to his favorite issues. In many ways, the movie reflects the average campaign more closely than does any single real campaign. But in the end, Redford's candidate pulls the Hollywood upset. In the bedlam of the victory celebration, the new senator pulls the consultant into an empty hotel room and asks, "What do we do now?"

References

Auer, J. Jeffrey. "The Counterfeit Debates." In *The Great Debates: Kennedy versus Nixon, 1960*, edited by Sidney Kraus. Bloomington: Indiana University Press, 1962.

Bailey, Douglas. "Famous for 15 Minutes." *Campaigns and Elections* 8 (January 1988): 47–52.

Beaudry, Ann, and Bob Schaeffer. *Winning State and Local Elections: The Guide to Organizing Your Campaign.* New York: Free Press, 1986.

Beiler, David. "Times Mirror's Ten Tribes of Politics." *Campaigns and Elections* 8 (January 1988): 10.

Diamond, Edwin, and Stephen Bates. *The Spot: The Rise of Political Advertsiing on Television.* Cambridge, MA: MIT Press, 1984.

Guzzetta, S. J. *The Campaign Manual: A Definitive Study of the Modern Campaign Process*, 2d ed., rev. Alexandria, VA: Political Publishing, 1987.

Kraus, Sidney, and Dennis K. Davis. "Political Debates." In *Handbook of Political Communication*, edited by Dan Nimmo and Keith Sanders, 273–96. Beverly Hills, CA: Sage, 1981.

Martel, Myles. *Political Campaign Debates: Images, Strategies, and Tactics.* New York: Longman, 1983.

McClister, Michael. "American University Campaign Management Institute." Washington, D.C.: C-SPAN, 1988.

Napolitan, Joseph. "Joseph Napolitan's Greatest Hints." *Campaigns and Elections* 8 (May/June 1987) 48–53 and (July/August 1987): 40–47.

Trent, Judith S., and Robert V. Friedenberg. *Political Campaign Communication: Principles and Practices.* New York: Praeger, 1983.

Chapter 7
CONGRESSIONAL DELIBERATION

Legislatures are generally misunderstood. Comedians, commentators, and the rest of us often deride legislatures for their slow pace, their quibbling, their inefficiency, and their apparent inability to deliver the executive's request. This chapter will suggest that these apparent shortcomings perform several positive functions intended by the Framers of our Constitution. We shall also see that legislative communication differs functionally in several fundamental respects from executive and judicial communication.

Most of the legislative deliberation principles discussed in this chapter apply to state and local legislatures as well. But because of this book's nationally dispersed audience, our concern will be with the United States Congress, which provides abundant examples, embodies diverse interests, and prepares us to consider the presidency in Chapter Eight. These general principles will affect particular legislatures in unique ways, and you may want to study the ways in which they influence a specific state legislature or city council.

The Founders and Planned Inefficiency

Unpleasant experiences with King George III left the Framers wary of executive power. Their British history taught them that problems arise when unwise or repressive monarchs rule unchecked and that the best corrective is to create checks and balances by distributing legitimate power between a monarch and Parliament. Because their interpretive systems emphasized the single leader's tendency to impose unwanted demands and restrictions on the colonial citizenry, they concluded that America should be governed by a kind of parliament unencumbered by any single executive. By making it extremely difficult for government to do anything, government could only do those things on which there was broad consensus.

The Framers intended the legislature to make only those laws necessary to the nation's survival. We could almost say that they designed the legislature to *obstruct* laws. This requires us to reverse our assumptions about congressional lawmaking. Legislative government minimizes the possibility that a law offensive to a majority of those represented will be enacted by minimizing the possibility that any law will be enacted. Legislatures are not designed to function as quick, efficient, productive institutions; for that one wants a more autocratic leader, like Mussolini, who made the Italian trains run on schedule. In short, a legislature is an assembly of representatives who *deliberate* about policy questions and pass only that legislation on which there is a consensus.

The Framers chose to further complicate the process by dividing their legislature into two chambers, each reflecting different constituencies: a Senate based on states and a House based on population. Moreover, no bill could be enacted into law without a majority vote from both chambers. If we are to assume that the Framers created this bicameral legislature to efficiently enact all possible laws, we must judge their Constitution a gross miscalculation. We can see the genius of their construction only if we recognize their fear of unwanted repressive government. The Senate and House each hold veto power over every proposed bill. If a bill is opposed by a majority of the population-based representatives, it dies. If it is opposed by a majority of the state-based senators, it dies. If the two chambers cannot agree on a compromise version, it dies. Only after a bill has survived all three tests can it advance to the president. Legislatures are indeed slow and unproductive, and they were made so by design.

Of course, the failure of the Articles of Confederation had taught the supporters of legislative government that the nation would need some sort of single executive. They therefore created an amazingly restricted presidency: one that would be selected by an electoral college that mirrored the legislature. The state representatives (Senate) would ratify presidential appointments and treaties and would declare war. The people's representatives (House) would initiate all taxing and spending measures. Bills already accepted by the House and Senate would become law, whether the president signed or ignored them; his veto could be overridden by a two-thirds vote of both chambers, and the legislature could impeach a president it suspected of high crimes and misdemeanors. This was not a system designed for efficient and decisive action!

The legislative, executive, and judicial branches can each be viewed as systems within the federal or state government suprasystem, each constructed to represent different subsystems. Today's Senate represents the nation by allocating two at-large seats to the majority of voters in each state. Imagine how different the Senate would be if we seated a Democrat and a Republican from each state, if we created two Senate districts in each state, if we elected regional or national senators, or if we returned to the old style of state-appointed senators. The House essentially ignores states and today divides the nation's population into 435 districts, making it at once the most representative and least manageable subsystem.

The president is the only authority-wielding official elected at large and is, therefore, the most efficient but least representative official. The judiciary represents those who study, practice, and use the law. Government in America is based on an initiative's acceptability in all quarters. Our governmental system is based on the tension between the doctrines of separated powers and checks and balances. As Louis Fisher succinctly wrote, "An institution cannot check unless it has some measure of independence; it cannot retain that independence without the power to check" (Fisher 1981, 4).

The Framers envisioned the protections of planned inefficiency as House and Senate weeded out unwanted bills and sent the acceptable few on for presidential approval and judicial application. Judicial review and the growth of executive power have complicated the governmental process beyond their dreams but perhaps to their satisfaction. Indeed, a young political scientist named Woodrow Wilson wrote in 1885 that congressional government had become stalemated and required major changes (Wilson 1960).

Our contemporary view of government is based on the now dominant doctrine of executive supremacy that began to emerge under Presidents Theodore Roosevelt and Woodrow Wilson (Tulis 1987). Wilson's personal involvement in the League of Nations and his inability or unwillingness to negotiate with Congress advanced the notion that Congress should deliver the president's agenda. This argument was advanced by Franklin D. Roosevelt to respond to the Great Depression and World War II and was embraced by his successors to achieve their own goals. By the 1950s presidents were initiating the budget; and by the 1960s, presidents were routinely committing American soldiers without seeking declarations of war. In the 1980s, members of the National Security Council not only failed to inform Congress of their covert activities, they intentionally deceived Congress and disdained its effort to serve as "535 secretaries of state." Their urgency to get things done was much the sort of executive juggernaut feared by the Framers, who would have wanted only those foreign entanglements acceptable to most of the states. Yet the arguments and institutional trends are powerful and likely to continue during the Bush years. The doctrine of executive supremacy and the notion of a "rhetorical presidency" will be further developed in Chapter Eight.

The Framers imagined a government in which the House, Senate, president, and judiciary must be satisfied of a policy's wisdom and legality in order for it to achieve full legal force. But each branch is capable of espousing a doctrine of government that subordinates one or more of its counterparts: Congress investigates alleged overextensions of executive power, even as the executive branch decries legislative inefficiency and acts alone. The Framers sought a protective tension among their government's subsystems, but the complex demands of the twentieth century and the modern doctrine of executive supremacy too often resolve that tension by obscuring its purpose and undermining the legitimacy of the system itself.

Representative Roles and Relationships

Legislatures are based on *representation*. Voters in each legislative district create a representational relationship by electing someone to perform the role of legitimate surrogate. But since the reelection rate among U.S. representatives exceeds 80 percent, it seems unlikely that these electoral choices are made with surgical care.

Representation is a relational role, and we cast it much as we cast people in our interpersonal relationships. We scan the available people and rely on our interpretive schema to prefer one of the alternatives: Do we have reason to feel that the challenger will be any better than the incumbent? Unless the incumbent has died, resigned, or been disgraced we usually are satisfied. Most Americans mistrust Congress but support their own representatives.

The impressive level of support for one's own representative is attributable largely to the ease of rhetorical adaptation within each congressional district. Presidents adapt to the whole nation, but representatives need to adapt to only 1/435 of the nation, and even Senators need to adapt to only 1/50 of the country. Each legislative district is a relatively homogeneous audience.

Hannah Pitkin defined representation as "acting in the interests of the represented, in a manner responsive to them" (Pitkin 1967, 429). Aspiring representatives try to articulate the essential needs, symbols, preferences, and arguments that unite a majority of their constituents. But Pitkin's definition raises three questions: How are the *interests* determined? What is meant by *acting?* and What constitutes *responsiveness?*

Representives interpret interests, actions, and responsiveness in personal ways, influenced by their conception of proper representation. At one extreme is the *delegate* model in which representatives ascertain their constituents' desires, translate these desires into action, and report their performance back to the constituents. At the other extreme is the *trustee* model in which representatives exercise personal judgment and seek a vote of confidence on election day (Pitkin 1967). The representatives' role interpretation directly influences relations with constituents, because it defines the proper role of constituents as well as representatives. The delegate is subordinate to constituents; the trustee, superior. The delegate asks, the trustee tells.

We may elect representatives on the basis of policy issues but find them either too dependent on us for guidance or too distant and unresponsive. The district's culture often seems to influence representative selection more than does ideology. For example, North Carolina sent conservative trustee Jesse Helms and liberal trustee Terry Sanford to the Senate two years apart, both times defeating well-known and more moderate candidates who were perceived by voters as too "wishy-washy".

Few representatives are either pure delegate or pure trustee. Most strike a balance that leans toward trustee. Individual representatives' votes are influenced by the convergence of six factors: (1) the intensity with which local interests are felt, (2) the vulnerability of a vote to exploitation by challengers, (3) what a challenger might do once in office, (4) perceived obligations toward various organized and unorganized interests, (5) the influence of trusted colleagues, and (6) public and private appeals by the president or party leaders (Fisher 1981, 182). In short, congressional voting is more trustee than delegate, but individual representatives' preferences are influenced by the demands of multiple constituencies.

Representatives try to fulfill their conception of their role in one or more of the following ways. First, they *act* on the district's essential interest by using it as a litmus test for legislative votes. For example, a representative of an agricultural district might vote for every bill that seemed to help agriculture, regardless of its weaknesses; or a representative of a depressed urban area might vote for all city-related measures and against rural measures. Voting behavior is rarely so clearcut; representatives act in their constituency's interest as it interacts with a variety of other considerations. Notice also that representatives vote not to affirm or deny broad principles but to accept or reject very specific measures. Representatives often vote against a mild bill in the hope of getting a stronger one passed, even though this gives rivals an opportunity to charge betrayal of the constituents.

Second, representatives *articulate* the essence of their constituency's interest by talking about it at every opportunity. John F. Kennedy, Gary Hart, and Jesse Helms are less notable for their legislative impact as senators than for their advocacy of principles and issues (Reedy 1986). The representative raises public consciousness of an issue, perhaps attracting media attention, and thereby representing the interests of the district. This is functionally important because few issues strike the nation all at once, and districts afflicted with a problem first serve as an early warning line of defense. Since 1974, Congress has welcomed more and more new members who are attuned to television and who articulate interests for the public while their staffs polish legislation and build alliances (Smith 1988).

Third, representatives *perform*, or enact, their constituency's interest by living it. Ralph Perk, former Mayor of Cleveland, remained an avid bowler while in office, and Senator Sam Ervin played the simple country lawyer despite his Harvard Law background. Representatives have been known to perform their constituents' interests by teaching Sunday school, by working a different job one day each month, by attending meetings of veterans or other community organizations, and by living frugally and using an old snowblower. Representatives' performance may obscure their voting record and/or their ability to argue for their constituents' interests. It is this dimension of representation that is undermined by accusations of personal misconduct, although it should be remembered that some representatives who take "the pursuit of happiness" to excess may be enacting quite accurately the norms and interests of a Heffnerian constituency.

Notice that action, articulation, and performance are three distinct ways to represent a district's interests. A good representative is able to balance action, articulation, and performance; while lesser representatives settle for less.

However representatives choose to perform their role, the delegate and trustee models provide them with rhetorical resources. When voting with their constituents, representatives can expound on the will of the people and their responsiveness to it. And when compelled to disagree with constituents, they can claim the moral responsibility and courage of trusteeship. Floor debate, as we shall see, provides representatives with an opportunity to frame their votes in a manner acceptable to their constituents.

The Framers devised a bicameral legislature to maximize neither efficiency nor expertise but representation. Many of us find our interests represented by individuals elected elsewhere, like the late representative Claude Pepper of Florida who represented the interests of aging Americans wherever they live. This serves as a reminder that representatives articulate, vote for, and embody the interests of an interpretive community that—in an era of mass communication— may be less concentrated geographically than their individual constituencies. Their national community can help support reelection efforts, but representatives must, nevertheless, be preferred by a majority of the voters in their respective districts. Notable legislators like Senators J. William Fulbright of Arkansas and Lowell Weicker of Connecticut eventually found themselves more popular nationally than among their own voters, ending their legislative careers.

The Framers' goal was to create a government that would continue to represent the hopes, fears, and aspirations of the nation over time. Their multitiered selection process ensures varied representation, which promotes the consideration of proposed legislation through a variety of interpretive frameworks.

The House and Senate Compared

A bicameral legislature would be pointless if the two chambers were absolutely identical. The Framers created two parallel, but distinct, deliberative bodies by distributing Senate seats on the basis of statehood and House seats on the basis of population. This initial decision established different organizations that spawned other differentiating characteristics. Although an evolutionary history of the House and Senate is beyond the scope of this book, we can profitably examine evolutionary differences in the House and Senate over the last quarter century.

Students of Congress in the 1960s saw eleven differences between the chambers (Froman 1967). The House was larger, more formal, more hierarchically organized, faster acting, more rigidly rule based, more impersonal, and more conservative. Its power was less evenly distributed, it entailed a longer apprenticeship for new members, it reflected fewer important constituencies, and it conveyed less prestige to its members.

The House had evolved an organizational structure that enabled competing local representatives to work out their differences in tightly run committees chaired by veteran members of the House, cooperation with whom could lead to similar seniority and power. It was a legislative machine geared to the examination of detailed information, reflected in the practice of limiting floor debate to the committee members who had worked on the bill (Polsby 1979).

The watershed year of 1974 brought about many changes in Congress and its operations. A decade of untrustworthy behavior by Presidents Johnson and Nixon significantly undermined congressional trust in its institutional relationships; and when trust is undermined, people take formal precautions. Congress asserted its power relative to the presidency in a variety of areas: by enacting legislation requiring consultation by the CIA regarding the commitment of American troops and covert operations, by banning presidential impoundment of funds authorized by Congress, and by establishing the Congressional Budget Office to provide a non-presidential data base on economic questions. The House then dismantled the seniority system that had concentrated power in the hands of committee chairs and created a host of subcommittees that would be chaired by newer, usually younger, members. In the wake of President Nixon's resignation, America elected 75 new Democrats who altered the power balance in the House. Increasingly, nonpartisan, ticket-splitting voting patterns rendered voters more reliant on personal judgment, which in turn enhanced the importance of television and those representatives able to use it to their advantage. All of these changes altered institutional relationships and rules, and in the proliferation of power centers that followed, special interest groups and their political action committees took on increased importance (Smith 1988).

By 1988 the House had become more like the Senate. As Hedrick Smith writes, within the constitutional system,

> the rules of the power game had been rewritten, and the old power relationships had been dramatically shaken up. What emerged was a more fluid system of power, one which made the American political system harder to lead than just a couple of decades ago. (Smith 1988, 21)

Issue leadership may come from anyone since so many members are now financially supported on the basis of their sympathy toward particular causes. Advocacy of so many proposals has fueled the proliferation of subcommittees, with the result that leadership positions now come more quickly. Television coverage on C-SPAN, PAC interests, and the fast life cycle of congressional careers all mean that member aspirations are more likely to run toward the Senate and presidency than toward a career in the House (Ornstein 1981). For these reasons, as well as the fact that the House was the last bastion of Democratic influence during the Reagan years, the House has become the more liberal legislative body.

By virtue of its smaller size, the Senate of the 1960s had evolved as less formal, less hierarchically organized, slower, more flexible, more personal, more liberal, and more prestigious, with a shorter apprenticeship, a more even power distribution, and more important constituencies (Froman 1967). Largely because the Senate originally consisted of a handful of representatives chosen for six-year terms by their state legislatures, it developed neither the House's short-term electoral pressures nor its chaos. The Senate became the arena for forging a national consensus on broad policy questions, the details of which were developed in the House (Reedy 1986).

But the Senate, too, has evolved since the 1960s. Perhaps forgetting its fundamental role, the Senate reformed its rules to increase its efficiency. The dramatic increase in bills and votes has resulted in less careful deliberation and less time for the development of interpersonal relations. The heavier workload demanded new rules that have depersonalized and formalized Senate life and have increasingly involved senators in legislative detail (Ornstein 1981).

In short, the Senate has become more House-like, while the House has become more Senate-like. Both chambers have decentralized their responsibilities to the point where they can best be described as "subcommittee government." The basic obstructionist function recently performed by entrenched and powerful committee chairs is now performed by the more chaotic tendencies of decentralized subcommittees and by maverick representatives like Jesse Helms (Smith 1988).

Nevertheless, the House remains the chamber most likely and best suited to the refinement of legislative detail because of the larger and more diverse pool from which committee members can be drawn. Action is still relatively fast paced because so many members with so little time are interested in so many issues. Similarly, the Senate remains the forum best suited and most able to develop a national consensus because of its smaller size and long-term view.

The problem is that each branch is moving in a direction that makes the performance of its fundamental role more difficult. Why is this happening? The doctrine of executive supremacy, which glorifies decisive action, has nurtured the impression that the legislative function is to quickly enact the executive's agenda rather than carefully develop and screen proposals around which there is a consensus. This is all the more difficult when congressional organization is becoming decentralized around a proliferation of subcommittees and political celebrities. Executive-legislative relations have, therefore, increasingly become a struggle for policy leadership, and Congress has adapted itself to that struggle.

The election of a delegating president might have significantly redressed the executive-legislative imbalance had President Reagan used the managerial style with Congress that he applied to the executive branch: Delegate authority and don't interfere. But the president pushed for very specific policy positions: a 30 percent tax cut, deep cuts in federal spending, aid to El Salvador and—later—aid to the Nicaraguan Contras, and the "Star Wars" defense system. His strong policy preferences and his insistence on action further undermined public understanding of the legislative function.

Now that the House, Senate, press, and public seem to have internalized the doctrine of executive supremacy, it will be interesting to see how President Bush approaches Congress. His early calls for negotiation and cooperation were contradicted by his steadfast support of the steadfastly opposed nomination of John Tower for secretary of defense.

Deliberation

To *deliberate* is to carefully weigh the arguments for and against a proposal. Deliberation is purposeful and cautious. It benefits from a full airing of questions and reservations and, therefore, from broad participation. The more representative a body is, the more likely it is to uncover troublesome reservations.

Deliberation also benefits from multiple reconsiderations. Some legislatures cannot pass a bill until its third reading, and the bicameral structure requires every bill to be passed by two separate bodies. But most important to the deliberative legislative process is the committee system, which subjects each bill to intense scrutiny before it reaches the full chamber. Congressional committees get most of their public attention when they block a controversial bill or when they investigate a public scandal.

Legislative deliberation, therefore, occurs in three distinct arenas: interpersonal conversations, committee sessions, and floor debates. It is the mix of the three that differentiates legislative deliberation from executive deliberation. Let us discuss each in turn.

Interpersonal Conversation

Political parties and their factions provide important interpersonal networks in Congress. Conservative Republican senators have the Steering Committee, moderate Republicans have the Wednesday

Club, and some House Republicans belong to the Chowder and Marching Society; while Democrats have the Conservative Democratic Forum, the Arms Control Caucus, and the House Democratic Caucus. Another important network is the freshman class of representatives seated in the same year. State and regional concerns nurture sectional networks, and congressional committees constitute important communities. But one of the earliest findings in organizational communication was that informal networks carry information faster and more accurately than formal networks.

Whatever the question on the floor or in committee, representatives and their staffers walk down hallways and ride the shuttle together; they jog, golf, or play raquetball together; they meet at the coffeepot and watercooler; and they attend the same parties and speak at the same forums. They converse. "Bill didn't help his cause much with that tirade today, did he?" "You know I support what you're trying to do with that bill, but I just don't see how it can work." "I was back home for a commencement address, and nobody seemed to know or care much about that bill." Ideas and reservations are floated informally, and waters can be tested before plunging in. These informal relationships frequently transcend ideological and partisan differences. The Congressional gym nurtures such cameraderie:

> [Massachusetts Democrat Barney] Frank, a Jewish bachelor in his late forties whose pudgy cheeks once bulged around horn-rimmed glasses, lost seventy pounds through strict dieting and weight lifting. Now, at two hundred pounds, he has shoulders like a New England Patriots tackle. He mixes with the other side: One of his weight lifting partners is Vin Weber, a staunch Republican right-winger from Minnesota and from the far end of the ideological spectrum. That is typical of the gym. The regular pickup basketball games are bipartisan: plenty of hard-court razzing goes on, but serious partisanship is left off the court. (Smith 1988, 101–2).

Ideological opponents who value each other as persons are better able to understand the opposing viewpoints than are those who simply dismiss their adversaries.

These personal relations are particularly important in the Senate because of the six-year terms, the cozier organization, and the more flexible committee structure. Each Senate colleague constitutes 1/51 of a majority for six years whereas each congressional colleague is but 1/218 of a majority for a scant two years. Senators have fewer like-minded colleagues and must work with their adversaries for several years. In this environment, relational flexibility is a useful asset. Indeed, The Senate is often viewed as a club in which sensitivity to other senators, as well as to the body's formal and informal rules, is the key to membership and success.

Conversely, all members of the House have about thirteen months to satisfy their constituents before the primary campaign. This pressure toward chaos is countered by a strict committee structure, a frustrated and heated rhetoric, and less time to informally develop collegial relations. The two-year congressional term puts a premium on the very sort of quick action that is made unlikely by assorted constituent pressures. In this climate, every colleague becomes a source of potentially dangerous delay. The rigid committee system has become the only way to combine action and deliberation.

Committees

Committees and subcommittees do most of the congressional work by hammering out bills on which there is a consensus and losing those on which there is none, and they function somewhat differently in the House and Senate. It may be helpful to relate congressional committee work to two topics discussed in most introductions to group decison making: group roles and the standard agenda.

The *task roles* of legislative committees pertain to the production of sound legislation. They include the initiation of communication about issues, the exchange of information through personal knowledge, staff research, and committee hearings. Legislative task roles also include the elaboration, evaluation, and coordination of information and issues and the monitoring of the committee's progress and procedures over time. Task role specialization is more likely in the House, where local interests, a diverse talent pool, a specialized committee structure, and PAC support all facilitate individuality.

Socioemotional roles create and sustain working relationships. In the legislative setting these roles include encouraging others and expressing support for members embroiled in difficult debates, as well as relieving tensions and negotiating compromises. They also include coordinating the flow of quality information into, through, and out of the committee's decision-making process so that all members feel needed and influential. These socioemotional roles are especially apparent in the Senate, where senators who delay adjournment by railing against a consensus bill or who adopt a short-term, high-pressure, winner-take-all path are held at arm's length from "the club."

But every group has *both* task and socioemotional needs to fulfill if it is to both remain a group and be productive. The point here is that legislative committees need all of these group roles performed, but

House committees emphasize task roles and Senate committees emphasize socioemotional roles. Effective legislative service requires effective performance of one's committee responsibilities; however, representatives who only act on, articulate, and perform their constituents' interest may not be well suited to the committee work that is so central. One could reasonably argue that congressional candidates should be judged on their technical expertise in relevant policy areas and their ability to assimilate and evaluate great quantities of conflicting information, while prospective senators should be judged on their ability to maintain working relationships and to negotiate compromises with their adversaries.

Each committee brings together a small group of representatives who bring interpretive frameworks, constituent demands, and staffs. The fundamental task facing any committee chair is the blending of these divergent forces for the creation of a sound group decision. It is rare for all committee members to enthusiastically support the same policy position, and when they do they often lose on the floor. Although we like to think of ourselves as highly rational, we are more likely to rationalize our preferences. Legislative committees are one of the arenas in which people try their best to make rational decisions about some very emotionally charged issues. Who could make a "cold rational policy judgment" about a woman's right to an abortion, the future of the family farm, American support of Israel, or the proper level of taxation and social services? For that matter, would "coldly rational decisions" on these issues be desirable? Indeed, is there such a thing as a "coldly rational decision"?

Legislative committees, like most other serious decision-making bodies, rely ideally on some form of standard agenda to keep themselves as rational as possible. There are many versions of the *standard agenda*, all of which advise a committee to (1) define its task, (2) find facts, (3) analyze the problem, (4) establish criteria and limitations affecting solutions, (5) generate possible solutions, (6) evaluate possible solutions according to the criteria and limitations, (7) review the preferred solution(s), and (8) develop plans for implementing the solution and monitoring its effects. It is important for the group to move deliberately through the steps of the standard agenda in sequence. This ideal is sometimes realized in congressional practice.

It matters whether a committee is expected to analyze the causes of a problem, to solve the problem, or to review the effects of a previous solution. Ideally, committee members agree on the nature of their task. More commonly, individual members interpret the problem from their constituencies' perspectives and undertake parallel tasks.

Committee staff members compile legislative histories, examine court rulings, research opposing arguments, analyze pertinent statistics, identify authoritative experts, and take testimony. Their divergent interpretive systems often cause committee members to disagree over the facts: If my statistics clash with your beliefs we will both be slow to change. Committees, therefore, develop their own central files, which serve as a library for discussion of the policy proposal. Journalists and others scoff at the thousands of pages of evidence generated by committees like the Inouye-Hamilton Iran-Contra committee, but the accumulation of evidence is a monumental task that provides a common foundation from which the committee members can work. The fact-finding process itself can involve adversarial members in a shared effort that enhances their incentive to work together. The committee ends this portion of its deliberations by reaching an agreement on the facts, which is to say that they legitimize some claims as factual and leave others subject to challenge.

Ideally, analysis of the problem traces the past, describes the present, and projects the future. Notice that even committees in agreement about their facts can differ over the values to be preferred in the narrative that explains past, present, and future directions. Consensus on the nature of the problem is difficult to attain, and most committees ultimately produce majority and minority views that tend to resemble, but not quite mirror, party affiliation.

Most texts tell us that only groups willing to court disaster knowingly move directly from analyzing a problem to solving it. A group should establish the criteria and limitations by which it will solve the problem. But a committee of members and staffers with divergent interpretive frameworks and divergent interpretations of the problem may be able to agree only on broad working guidelines. The committee should formulate criteria to focus its deliberations so that it frames the reasons before tackling solutions; in practice, however, a roomful of delegates often rationalize their constituents' interests in accordance with the committee's broad guidelines and definitions.

Texts tell us that the best solutions emerge when participants dispassionately generate a list of possible solutions. But committee members elected by voters during heated campaigns, lobbied constantly by interest groups, and interviewed frequently by reporters have ideas about potential solutions before reaching this point. In practice, it is a legislator's and a committee's staff members who prepare lists of ideas to be circulated, discussed, and embellished.

Textbook decision making calls for a dispassionate comparison of the potential solutions to the committee's shared definition of its task and its shared preferences. But since legislative committees are unlikely to have shared definitions of either task or objectives, this step is problematic. In practice, members pursuing their particular definitions of task and objectives oppose solutions that endanger their interests. Much like television's least objectionable program approach and voters' short-listing of prospective candidates, this adversarial system produces least objectionable bills. Members who want the task accomplished are held at the mercy of difficult committee members. The proliferation of subcommittees has increased the number of points at which a bill can be held hostage by opponents, thereby increasing the tendency to expedite passage by avoiding clauses objectionable to committee members (Smith 1988). This obstructionist tendency is consistent with the Framers' system of checks and balances.

Congressional committees typically deal with matters of implementation by granting broad powers to executive agencies and by involving themselves in the oversight of particular programs. Congress exercises several administrative controls: personnel policies, appropriations, resolutions directing the appropriate agency's actions, advice, investigations, and private bills to correct administrative mistakes (Fisher 1981). It is not unusual for Congress to pass a bill in one session that is later implemented in a manner representative of different preferences.

The standard agenda is designed to guide decision making from the problem to its objectives and solutions so that a group can reach a rational consensus before tackling solutions. Its purpose is to make the deliberative process as rational as possible, despite the tendency of humans to react emotionally when their interests are threatened. In legislative practice, of course, few groups achieve that ideal. Legislative committees are the primary guarantors of deliberation. Prevalent images like the windbag senator in the comic strip "Shoe" miss the mark. We scoff at representatives who say that "We must always support our friends and allies in their struggles, while recognizing that our resources are not unlimited and that our first responsibility is to those Americans who know hope only as a stranger." But representatives are responsible for reconciling conflicting values, goals, and images and for honing acceptable laws that embody those beliefs.

An executive speaks like the captain of a ship—decisive, commanding, and with an eye on the horizon. But a representative stands on a floating log—constantly running for election on a slippery base and vulnerable to any wave that may come along but better suited to the shallow waters of small inlets and in danger only of getting wet, not sinking the ship of state. Yes, representatives want to have their cake and eat it too. Yes, they spend much time reconciling apparently small points. No, they cannot agree very often. Wouldn't the Framers be pleased?

Floor Debate

Visitors to the Capitol have long been surprised by the nature of congressional floor debates, and when C-SPAN began televising House proceedings, that surprise reached many living rooms as well. "Why is this guy talking?" we asked "There's nobody there! No wonder the country is such a mess."

Having learned that Congress debates proposed bills, many of us surmised that all 435 members sat around en masse all the time. Were they to do so, they could not study the bills, develop policy expertise, meet with constituents, shape bills in committee, gather expert testimony, or interpersonally fine-tune their working arrangements. In short, if we had a system that relied exclusively, or even primarily, on floor debate, representative government would crush itself to death like a beached whale.

Nevertheless, floor debate serves several important functions, not the least of which is to *refine legislation.* Members other than those on a bill's committee now speak regularly, and floor debate is more wide ranging than it used to be. Sometimes this is good, especially when a committee has been careless about gathering information or representing diverse interests. Members of a committee's minority use floor debate to advocate their positions before a larger audience in the hope that non-committee members will amend, fine-tune, sharpen, or soften the bill's objectionable features.

Second, floor debate serves to *obstruct legislation.* Senate rules permitting the filibuster allow any senator to obstruct a bill by speaking unless three fifths of the Senate votes for *cloture*—to close debate. The filibuster is a reminder that the Framers worried more about a national government trampling state governments than an inability to pass laws. Annoying as they are, filibusters protect minority interests against the onslaught of majority whims.

Although the filibuster is the major instrument of obstruction in floor debate, it is especially valuable as a bargaining chip. A committee aware that its preferred solution will draw a filibuster or presidential veto sands its bill to smooth the rough edges, both to avoid the filibuster and veto and to mobilize the votes needed for cloture and override. Obstruction through floor debate is less important in the House, where that function is served by size, diversity, and competing pressures. The House has developed rules that determine in advance the total time allowed for debating each bill, and obstruction occurs as bills await their respective turns on stage.

Floor debate is also used to *position the representatives' personal interpretive stance* in the wide range of political communities. Members use these debates to frame their votes and to enact conviction. Assume, for example, that you must vote for a small tax increase as an unwanted and unpleasant, but nevertheless necessary, response to even more unwanted and unpleasant alternatives. You need to explain your vote to your constituents because your opponents will characterize you as a deceitful, unresponsive spendthrift. Your statements during floor debate can explain and clarify how the reasons for your vote represent your constituents' interests. When 435 interpreting members must vote for or against a motion, there will be roughly 400 different interpretive reasons for those votes.

It is worth noting that some members exploit floor debate now that it is televised by speaking on almost every issue, while others avoid the limelight. An effective committee representative may go completely unnoticed by the public, while less able representatives address the House and ignore their other responsibilities.

Neither the House nor Senate is likely to begin floor debate until the votes are assured, and those votes are won at the interpersonal and committee level. This arrangement is only paradoxical if we view legislative deliberation as the work of congress en masse rather than as the activity of a complex and highly differentiated institutional system.

The fourth function of floor debate is to *direct subsequent legislation and debate*. Legislative deliberations sift down to the following positions: (1) there is no problem to solve, (2) there is a problem but this bill makes it worse, (3) there is a problem but it is unsolved by this bill, (4) this bill solves this problem but creates even more serious new problems, or (5) this bill seems to solve this problem for now. These positions provide members with *topoi*, or argumentative topics, that are articulated by different members on different bills. Through floor debate, one or more of these topoi become publicly understood as the important reason to favor and to oppose the bill. This is the beginning of the next phase of legislative deliberation, as members prepare to pursue the rest of their program. Often, this means carrying the fight to the Appropriations Committee, where the money to implement, enforce, and continue programs is considered separately from the legislation. Floor debate helps to direct these discussions by foregrounding some considerations and by marginalizing others.

Finally, floor debate is used to *influence votes* on the bill. But since the specialists have a grasp of the issue before they propose the bill and since most other knowledgeable and interested representatives form their views during the committee period—whether through the committee process or interpersonal conversations—few votes are susceptible to conversion. Floor debate can reinforce, undermine, or activate a representative's stance on the bill. Someone desiring legislation on the topic but uncertain of the particular bill may decide to vote for it until something better comes along. Floor debate can indicate the grounds on which a representative's subsequent vote can be won. One side's handling of the floor debate may so antagonize representatives that they refuse to join that coalition. But overall, influencing votes is probably the least important function of floor debate.

In short, floor debate helps representatives to refine legislation, to obstruct unwanted legislation, to clarify their positions and intensity, to direct the course of subsequent deliberations, and to influence a few votes. But floor debate occurs after the issues have been framed, after the facts have been gathered, after goals and criteria have been developed, after potential solutions have been compiled and evaluated, after technicalities have been considered, and after votes have been corralled. Floor debate is important, but it is not the essence of legislative deliberation.

Legislative-Executive Relations

Because the Framers created three institutions to share power, it is important to examine legislative-executive relations. The president and Congress need one another. Congress needs the president's signature if they want to avoid mustering two thirds of each chamber for every bill, and the president needs the help of Congress to fulfill his agenda (Fisher 1981). Some people wish for a more productive and efficient legislative apparatus and believe they could get it if the president and a majority of both chambers belonged to the same political party. But forgetting the dangers of legislative efficiency for the moment, what is the nature of presidential influence in Congress?

The Framers did their best to ensure legislative-executive tensions by giving the president, Senate, and House different constituencies (national, state, and local) and time perspectives (four-, six-, and two-year terms). From these beginnings, each institution developed a unique internal structure, as well as differing areas of expertise and information access. For example, President Washington denied a

House demand for papers related to the negotiation of the Jay Treaty with Great Britain on the grounds that the Constitution required Senate, not House, ratification of treaties and that his administration had fully complied with the pertinent constitutional provisions. The Supreme Court held that President Nixon misapplied this doctrine of executive privilege during Watergate by denying assorted executive papers to investigators pursuing their constitutional and statutory responsibilities.

In his careful empirical study of *Presidential Influence in Congress*, political scientist George C. Edwards III (1980) clarified several myths about congressional behavior. First, he found that from 1953–1978 congress sided with the president on 72.9 percent of the clear presidential stands that came to a vote. But presidents are most likely to take clear stands on bills that are likely to pass—to claim credit for passage and to avoid looking like a loser. Most, but not all, clear presidential stands came long after Congress had framed the issues and developed the specifics. In other words, we could say that these presidents bet on the winning horse in 72.9 percent of the races. The sobering point is that under these success-inflating circumstances, presidents *lost* an average of 27.1 percent of the policy votes on which they took clear stands. The presidential batting average of .729 is less impressive than it looks.

The presidential batting average during the 1953–1978 period was highest on questions of national defense, better than 50-50 on other foreign policy matters, and less than .500 on domestic questions where every representative and senator had affected constituencies. Vetoes were rarely overridden, and 97 percent of the nominations were approved largely because these presidents strategically anticipated opposition and adapted to it. The nominations to the Supreme Court of Judges Haynesworth and Carswell by Nixon and Judges Bork and Ginsburg by Reagan and the nomination of Senator Tower to secretary of defense by Bush were monumental failures because the presidents did not present the best possible, *confirmable* nominees. They apparently forgot that politics is the art of the possible.

Presidents get higher support levels from members of their own party (65 percent on the average) than from the other party's representatives (44 percent). An obvious finding? Notice that presidents from 1953–1978 won 44 percent of the other party's votes and lost 35 percent of their own partisans! Party alignment is important in Congress, but it is much less deterministic than most citizens probably believe it to be. This partisan disorder stems from the fact that partisanship provides an opportunity for shared interpretations of the political world, but votes are cast by individuals who have other competing community frameworks. Edwards also demonstrated that presidential coattails are less important to legislative reelection than is often believed and that it is difficult for presidents to use partisanship to win congressional support.

According to Edwards, the two most important, manageable sources of presidential influence in Congress are the president's popularity among each legislator's constituents and the president's ability to maintain a healthy and productive working relationship with the Congress. Ironically, recent presidents have put these two resources in conflict. Rather than carefully nurturing their relationships with representatives, with the leadership in both chambers, and with the citizenry, our presidents have become greedy. They have bypassed elected representatives and have used television to urge voters to pressure their representatives into supporting the presidency. As we shall see, Presidents Wilson and Roosevelt first used this strategy, and it was used almost exclusively by President Reagan, who seemed to perfect it.

But even Reagan, the arguably "Great Communicator," incurred two forms of backlash. His partisan pressuring left him with a Democratic House more hostile than necessary and made the Senate's return to Democratic control unnecessarily problematic. Even worse for President Reagan, the audience for his televised addresses declined markedly (Foote 1988). A House and Senate miffed by presidential pressure was unfavorably disposed toward the Reagan administration's record of ignoring and deceiving them about the Iran-Contra dealings, its efforts to seat controversial judges Bork and Ginsburg on the Supreme Court, and its strident appeals for aid to the Nicaraguan contras. Moreover, most Americans opposed the president on these issues even as they stopped watching his speeches and became decreasingly susceptible to his personable appeals.

The history of presidential-congressional relations is replete with dramatic conflicts: the impeachment proceedings against President Andrew Johnson, Woodrow Wilson's advocacy of the League of Nations, and Senator Joseph McCarthy's pursuit of suspected communists in the executive branch all preceded the Vietnam War, Watergate, and the Iran-Contra hearings. In each case, the interinstitutional tensions built into the system by the Framers reached pathological proportions, and both institutions became determined to reassert themselves. In such times, all of us—especially the active participants—forget that the Framers gave us a system that values disagreement, tension, and compromise rather than compliance, like-mindedness, and power. Proper legislative-executive relations prevent traumatic upheavals by building a consensus for policies rather than force feeding them to the public. When these cataclysmic struggles occur, they are relational struggles in which all parties bear some responsibility.

President Bush began his administration with calls for negotiation and compromise but aroused considerable suspicion and antagonism with his hardline stance on the Tower nomination. The Tower episode divided Congress; and in its aftermath, Newt Gingrich of Georgia, a conservative well known to the cameras, became the Republican whip in the House. The whip's function is to round up a voting majority for its party, which means that Gingrich will need to corral Democrats as well as Republicans until Republicans gain a majority of seats. Whether Gingrich whips moderates away from his coalition or, through his public visibility, generates public pressure on moderates to move toward the right, he will go a long way toward shaping the politics of the 1990s.

Conclusions

The Framers created a governmental system of checks and balances by devising functionally overlapping institutions. The bicameral legislature was devised as the arena for careful representative deliberation. Bills offensive to a majority of state governments would be weeded out in the Senate, bills offensive to populous areas would be weeded out in the House, and only those bills acceptable to both chambers would reach the president.

The intended differences between House and Senate caused them to evolve additional differences. But their recently acquired role as the presidential delivery system has encouraged Congress to gird itself for battle with the White House, suggesting the degree to which the doctrine of executive supremacy has taken root.

Legislative deliberation occurs through interpersonal relationships and committees as well as floor debates. When the process works, our representatives are able to reconcile conflicting constituent needs and visions, to fine-tune substantive policy details, and to frame necessary policy adjustments through appropriate interpretive systems. When the process runs aground, the relationship between citizens and their government can become strained, as their representative liaisons lose their ability to translate interests into policy or to relate policy to interests.

References

Edwards, George C., III. *Presidential Influence in Congress*. San Francisco: W.H. Freeman, 1980.

Fisher, Louis. *The Politics of Shared Power*. Washington, D.C.: Congressional Quarterly Press, 1981.

Foote, Joe S. "Ratings Decline of Presidential Television." *Journal of Broadcasting and Electronic Media* 32 (Spring 1988): 225–30.

Froman, Lewis A. *The Congressional Process: Strategies, Rules, and Procedures*. Boston: Little, Brown, 1967.

Ornstein, Norman J. "The House and the Senate in a New Congress." In *The New Congress*, edited by Thomas E. Mann and Norman J. Ornstein. Washington, D.C.: American Enterprise Institute for Public Policy Research, 1981.

Pitkin, Hannah Fenichel. *The Concept of Representation*. Los Angeles: University of California Press, 1967.

Polsby, Nelson. Strengthening Congress in National Policymaking. *Yale Review*, 59 (Summer 1970): 481–97

Reedy, George E. *The U. S. Senate: Paralysis or a Search for Consensus?* New York: Mentor Books, 1986.

Smith, Hedrick. *The Power Game*. New York: Random House, 1988.

Tulis, Jeffrey K. *The Rhetorical Presidency*. Princeton, NJ: Princeton University Press, 1987.

Wilson, Woodrow. *Congressional Government*. New York: Meridian Books, 1960.

Chapter 8
PRESIDENTIAL LEADERSHIP

The single most important political communicator in contemporary America is the president. He speaks and writes several times daily, his words are harvested for publication in *The Weekly Compilation of Presidential Documents* and the annual *Public Papers of the President*, and the files and background briefings of every president since Hoover are housed in a series of presidential libraries.

Presidential talk today pervades our news-based political consciousness. Usually, presidents speak on television to get the public's attention, but such addresses had become so overused by 1979 that President Carter had to cancel a television address to get the public's attention. Presumably, reporters and film crews follow presidents to convey their insights to the public, but for the better part of eight years they conveyed mostly footage of President Reagan smiling, waving, and cupping his hand to his ear as helicopter motors drowned out the reporters' questions. These examples reveal our national expectation that presidents talk. It was not always so, and this chapter will explain the evolution of the contemporary rhetorical presidency and the nature of presidential discourse.

Presidential Character versus Presidential Role

Because the American presidency combines a person and a role, presidential leadership is influenced by both role and personality variables. But in what ways do individual personality and character dominate or conform to the role? And in what ways does the role empower or imprison its caretaker? Let us consider the competing perspectives of James David Barber and Bruce Buchanan to understand how motivated, symbolizing, preferring, reasoning persons interpret and enact the presidential role.

Presidential Character

Barber's thesis is that the *power situation* and *climate of expectations* define presidential options, but what a president does depends upon his character, his worldview, and his style. *Character* is one's enduring stance toward life, which develops in early childhood. During adolescence, character shapes one's *worldview* of beliefs about human nature, social causality, and moral conflicts. As young adults begin to engage in public affairs, they develop a habitual *style* for handling their three political tasks: rhetoric, interpersonal relations, and homework. A president's early childhood influences his understanding of the world and his means for coping with it, all of which combine to influence his response to the power situation and climate of expectations.

Barber presents four presidential character types that approach the presidency in particular ways and with predictable results. *Active-positives* enjoy life and invest energy in it, and achievement is an important source of motivation. People like Franklin Roosevelt, Truman, Kennedy, Ford, and Carter were well suited to the role, says Barber, because of their enjoyment of the unavoidable demands, their flexibility, and their positive desire to succeed. *Passive-positives* are other-directed and response oriented. Because they need affection, passive-positive presidents like Taft, Harding, and Reagan were ill-suited to leadership on unpopular topics but well suited to unify the nation. *Passive-negatives* do not enjoy what they do, so they do as little of it as possible from a sense of duty. They avoid confrontations and emerging issues by withdrawing into established procedures, thereby making life difficult for the presidents who follow them: Coolidge left a depression-prone economy to Harding; Eisenhower left racial conlicts to Kennedy. *Active-negatives* expend great energy on tasks they dislike. Irrational? That is precisely Barber's point. Active-negatives are obsessed with the need to prove themselves to themselves and others, so they act compulsively. Active-negatives are driven by a fear that the world they dislike will get even worse unless they push themselves. Where active-positives see opportunities, active-negatives see crises. Active-negatives rigidify and have avoidable confrontations that cost them important decisions that could have been won with flexibility.

The active-negative record is sobering. Wilson's refusal to compromise with moderate senators killed his League of Nations Treaty. Hoover's refusal of a government safety net during the Great Depression led to the sweeping New Deal. Johnson's refusal to compromise his Vietnam policy endangered his domestic policies, cost him a second term, and resulted ultimately in the fall of Saigon. Nixon's need for appoval, his unwillingness to admit mistakes, and his inability to compromise with investigators appointed by him led to his resignation in disgrace. Barber concludes that the active-negative is the personality most likely to seek political power and the worst suited to its exercise. Active-negatives, he says, damage themselves and the country (Barber 1985).

Barber's perspective suggests that the prospects for presidential leadership are shaped by the early childhood, adolescence, and first adult success of the persons we elect. We have not a presidency, he says, but one president after another; each leading the country with an interpretive worldview and characteristic style of rhetoric and management that fulfills personal needs.

The Presidential Experience

Bruce Buchanan argues that even active-positives are capable of self-destructive and rigidifying behavior, and, therefore, Barber's emphasis on character is misplaced. Buchanan reminds us that Franklin Roosevelt behaved like an active-negative when he tried to reform the Supreme Court because it held parts of his New Deal unconstitutional. Buchanan argues that Roosevelt's behavior was indistinguishable from the Wilson, Hoover, Johnson, and Nixon cases (Buchanan 1978). That being the case, why prefer active-positives over any other character type?

Buchanan attributes Roosevelt's behavior to the psychological experience of the presidential role. The role is defined by its accumulated legal-constitutional responsibilities and its normative expectations (Corwin 1957; Rossiter 1956). These responsibilities and expectations often conflict, exposing presidents to *stress, dissonance, frustration,* and the expected *deference* of others (Buchanan 1978). The cumulative psychological pressures are modified by the president's self-concept or character, so that some people are better equipped to cope with the office than others. But from Buchanan's perspective, character is only a modifier of the presidential role experience.

The character-versus-role controversy stems from the fact that every president is a person interpreting and enacting a role. The oath of office changes the president into a former president and the president-elect into a president. Ronald Reagan lost very little of his personal charm and style on January 21, 1989, but his speeches are less valued and his words are quickly forgotten. Now America listens for the words of President Bush. In short, we listen for the president regardless of his style, but an effective rhetorical style can enhance the prospects for success.

The enactment of the presidential role depends heavily on the character, worldview, and style of the individual president. The actors' interpretations of the role contribute to different interpretations of the unique opportunities and constraints facing them.

Because contemporary presidents cannot enact the role without mass communication, the presidency is wedded to the cultural biases of American news—fragmented, personalized drama reinforcing cultural norms. The Carter administration tried to depersonalize, undramatize, and synthesize politics for the press and public with disastrous results; whereas the Reagan administration played to the camera, dramatized the mundane, simplified and personalized complex phenomena, and fed information to the press and public in usable form.

Finally, the personal enactment of the presidential role by each president leaves a legacy for the next. Theodore Lowi summarized "three general laws of politico-dynamics" since 1961:

1. The Law of Effort:
   A. Presidents spend the first half of their terms trying sincerely to succeed according to their oath and promises.
   B. They devote the second half of their terms trying to create the appearance of success.
   Refinement 1: The second half is starting earlier and earlier.
   Refinement 2: The onset of the second half is indicated by White House complaints about bad press and White House efforts to plug leaks and otherwise manage the news.
2. The Law of Outcomes: The probability of failure is always tending toward 100 percent.
   Refinement: Given the exalted rhetoric and high expectations surrounding the presidency, a partial success is defined by the mass public as a failure.
3. The Law of Succession: Each president contributes to the upgrading of his predecessors.
   Corollary: This is the only certain contribution each president will make. (Lowi 1985, 11):

Lowi's laws are closer to the mark than many of us might care to admit. His Law of Effort matches the record since 1961, and the Law of Outcomes prevails only because the Framers made it so. But the Law of Succession is less sound, since it is difficult to see how Ford upgraded Nixon, how Carter upgraded Ford, how Reagan upgraded Carter, or how Bush upgraded Reagan. With deference to Lowi, the sure thing is that presidential performance reshapes the role for the successor, who will either upgrade or blame the predecessor in accordance with the variables of character, worldview, and style. Let us see how the office has evolved into its present rhetorical role.

The Evolution of the Rhetorical Presidency

The Framers of the Constitution worried that rule by a single executive could turn out as badly as British rule, but their experience under the Articles of Confederation had convinced them of the need for a single executive. Their solution was an office with few powers. *The Framers defined the functions of an office rather than designating George Washington as executive.* Imagine the power struggles, corruption, disbanded legislatures, and rewritten constitutions that could have occurred as aspirants jockeyed to become Washington's successor. Lest the person serving temporarily as president try to exercise too much influence, the Framers supplied checks and balances: three branches of government.

The Constitutional Presidency

The presidency was a low-profile office for its first century. The Framers had feared demagogues who would whip crowds into hysteria with emotional appeals to prejudice, and early presidents rarely addressed the public. Even their required messages to Congress were written and read aloud by aides. When those presidents did attempt to exert influence they explicitly invoked their constitutional powers (Tulis 1987), enabling us to refer to the nineteenth century as the *constitutional presidency.* John Quincy Adams published his lectures on rhetoric but gave only one speech per year; populist Andrew Jackson confined his presidential appeals to written messages to Congress; Abraham Lincoln refused to talk publicly about the Civil War; and Andrew Johnson's "intemperate, inflammatory, and scandalous harangues" were the tenth article of impeachment brought against him (Tulis 1987).

Government during our first century was primarily congressional, with presidents fulfilling mostly ceremonial tasks. By the 1880s Congress had checked and balanced itself into a gridlock. When the Hepburn Act to regulate the nation's railroads generated demagogic arguments about sinister conspiracies, President Theodore Roosevelt began redefining the proper role of presidential rhetoric.

The Rhetorical Presidency: Initial Phase

In Theodore Roosevelt's revised view, the constitutional order needed periodic refounding to square actual practice with the Framers' intent. By speaking responsibly on political principles and issues of the day, Roosevelt argued, presidents could inform the public and counteract community demagogues (Tulis 1987). Presidential addresses began to become acceptable as something other than ceremony.

Woodrow Wilson took Theodore Roosevelt's view of presidential rhetoric considerably further. Wilson began the *rhetorical presidency* in which presidential influence derived not from constitutional powers but from the president's ability to articulate persuasively the interests of The People. Beginning with Wilson, (1) speeches replaced written messages, and (2) speeches to the public replaced messages to Congress (Tulis 1987).

Advances in transportation and mass communication after 1920 made it increasingly convenient for presidents to "go public." But it was Theodore Roosevelt and Woodrow Wilson who redefined the role of presidential rhetoric and legitimized presidential policy addresses to the public (Tulis 1987). These two presidents so changed the presidency that 1900 has become a watershed, with the presidency being largely a twentieth-century concern. But even the twentieth-century rhetorical presidency has evolved from this *initial phase* into modern and contemporary phases.

The Rhetorical Presidency: Modern Phase

The *modern phase* of the rhetorical presidency began with Franklin Roosevelt's inauguration on March 4, 1933. Federal regulation of radio broadcasting in 1928 had cleared the way for the growth of networks, and by 1933 radio had become a viable medium for presidential speech. Only Presidents Harding, Coolidge, and Hoover had even been able to use loudspeakers, and only Hoover had any sort of meaningful radio network available to him. Roosevelt took advantage of radio's potential. His inaugural address and his first "fireside chat" about the economy oriented, directed, and reassured a distraught American public. America began to cope with difficulty by listening to the president.

Additionally, political scientists and historians regard Franklin Roosevelt's administration as the beginning of the "modern presidency" because of three interconnected changes: (1) the Great Depression created a more complex economy under the mildly watchful eye of government, (2) World War II involved America in international affairs, and (3) efforts to deal with both emergencies led to the centralization of presidential authority over people and issues traditionally regarded as nonexecutive matters. Especially on matters relating to the depression and war, the American public came to rely heavily on direct addresses by their president. The result was that post-Roosevelt presidents like Truman and Eisenhower were expected to communicate with the American people about matters of policy. Public opinion began to matter nearly as much as congressional opinion.

The Rhetorical Presidency: Contemporary Phase

Richard Neustadt's analysis of this new presidency, *Presidential Power* ([1960] 1980), provided the springboard into the *contemporary phase* of the rhetorical presidency. It provided presidents with a user's guide to the office. Presidential power was defined as the power to persuade, which was in turn defined as the power to bargain. Presidents were advised to build and to protect their personal power in three ways: (1) by enhancing their professional reputation among "Washingtonians," (2) by enhancing their public prestige, and (3) by making choices carefully to build and to conserve their prospective influence. Neustadt's landmark book turned attention from constitutional powers to personal influence, from presidential command to presidential persuasion, from the lobbying of legislators to the rallying of the people; and it led to a perception of presidents under siege by those who would steal their influence.

The transition to the contemporary phase in 1960 required more than a book, however. Live, coast-to-coast television began in 1959, and a popular, grandfatherly president would be replaced in the 1960 election—a new president, a new approach, and a newly developed technology. President Kennedy's youthful vigor is given much of the credit for the move toward presidential television, but it is important to remember that Richard Nixon was enamored of television and would himself have used Neustadt's book and television. Television provided the medium, Neustadt wrote the manual, and the election of 1960 provided the opportunity.

The contemporary rhetorical presidency differs markedly from the rhetorical presidencies of the two Roosevelts. Transportation developments make it possible to jet around the world to affirm, directly and personally, relations with constituents. Communication satellites make it possible to address directly either the entire nation or selected gatherings. The declining influence of political parties and the growth of PACs encourage temporary, single-issue coalitions rather than broad and enduring coalitions, making personable presidents more the rallying point of the governing coalition than its delegate (Kernell 1986; Lowi 1985).

Where modern presidents bargained with congressmen and political insiders, contemporary presidents mobilize public opinion to pressure their adversaries into supporting them (Hart 1987; Kernell

1986). Where modern presidents spoke informally with reporters in the Oval Office, contemporary presidents stage televised news conferences as necessary. Where modern presidents relied on the advice of professional politicians, contemporary presidents rely on pollsters, image specialists, and speech-writing teams. All of these changes have evolved from sociopolitical and technological changes—there is no return. The game and the rules of presidential leadership have changed: modern presidents tried interpersonally to persuade influentials; contemporary presidents try telegenically to persuade the American public. President Bush tried to change the process by meeting informally with senators and representatives in the White House living quarters and by waiting eight months to deliver a televised address. It will be interesting to see whether he can change the office before the office changes him.

The contemporary rhetorical presidency poses at least five potential problems for the political system. First, presidents who pressure their adversaries silence even valid policy reservations and stifle deliberation. Second, pressuring is more likely to antagonize than to calm presidential adversaries, provoking avoidable confrontations. Third, "going public" requires the emphasis of familiar, ambiguous themes and values like "doing the right thing because it's the American Way" so that diverse, modestly informed persons can interpret the president's position as consonant with their own. Fourth, pressuring undercuts constitutional checks and balances by treating the legislative branch as a simple nuisance while simultaneously undercutting any attempt to stimulate thoughtful public deliberation. Fifth, the dramatic increase in presidential speechmaking has been accompanied by a declining public awareness of policy alternatives and by a declining sense of dialogue between citizens and their president (Hart 1987). Nevertheless, that is the presidency that has evolved and the one to which we as a nation respond.

Characteristics of Presidential Rhetoric

The presidential role contributes to characteristically presidential rhetorical behavior. Several dimensions of that behavior were revealed in a series of studies that examined systematically presidential speech acts, audiences, values, language, calls for action, and rationales for those requests from the administrations of Presidents Truman, Eisenhower, Kennedy, Johnson, Nixon, Ford, Carter and Reagan. Let us consider the regularities of presidential rhetoric before discussing distinctive presidential styles.

Presidential addresses reveal a variety of regularities that cut across considerations of party, personality, and exigence. These characteristics are summarized from systematic content analyses of presidential speaking from 1945 to 1985, with particular emphasis on 1964 to 1985. (Hart 1984, 1987; Smith 1983, Smith and Smith 1985). The normative data suggest that anyone who becomes president in contemporary America will

1. Speak frequently, averaging one speech per work day with a clear trend toward multispeech days;
2. Speak at ceremonies about once in every three speeches;
3. Speak more when his programs are in trouble than when they are meeting with success;
4. Speak in Washington to special interest groups, the press, and invited guests when his party controls Congress;
5. Speak relatively more often to citizen audiences in domestic cities located in densely populated states when the other party controls Congress;
6. Speak more often in neutral or contested states than in states loyal to the president's party;
7. Speak about diffuse, multiple topics rather than focus on single issues;
8. Refer to himself more frequently than do other speakers (specifically corporate executives, social activists, religious leaders, or political campaigners);
9. Express greater optimism than do other speakers;
10. Express himself in concrete, practical—rather than abstract, idealistic—language;
11. Express himself in direct, simple language even if he previously used more complex language;
12. Express himself more cautiously than do other speakers;
13. Explain policy neither as clever nor prudent but as morally proper;
14. Frame his message with consistent, core values (such as morality, peace, patriotism, effort/optimism, and progress/change);
15. Exhort us to work hard and optimistically without promising material comfort, financial success, or equality of opportunity.

Within these institutional regularities these studies identified the following evolutionary changes in presidential rhetoric:

1. A steady increase in the number of presidential speeches per year.
2. A steady increase in the number of self-references per speech.
3. A steady increase in presidential caution, as their language became less certain.
4. Ceremonies were essentially discovered by Kennedy, relied on by Johnson, and institutionalized by his successors.
5. Presidents since Ford are more likely than their predecessors to directly address their critics, their party, racial and ethnic groups, intellectuals, religious groups, and farmers.
6. Presidents since Ford are less likely than their predecessors to address Congress.

In short, the results summarized here demonstrate that presidential rhetoric entails something more than a political figure speaking his mind. To speak *as president* is to speak often and in ways constrained by the public expectations nurtured by one's predecessors. These expectations of the presidential role homogenize personal rhetorical style in many ways.

Anyone who has heard more than one president speak can testify to the importance of personal style. The eclectic nature of this book precludes thumbnail analyses of individual rhetorical presidents. Readers interested in such critiques should begin with the entries in *American Orators of the Twentieth Century* (Duffy and Ryan 1987), and progress to *Essays in Presidential Rhetoric* (Windt and Ingold 1987). The larger point is that individual stylistic differences occur within the institutional pattern of presidential speech.

The American presidency, then, is a unique rhetorical role that homogenizes presidential utterances on several levels: the type and frequency of speech acts, the audiences, values, language, and the requests and rationales. Once a president has conformed to the role demands, there is some room left to adapt to partisan, generic, and evolutionary norms.

Genres of Presidential Rhetoric

The responsibilities of the presidential role in the general policy areas of national security, economics, and domestic programs include seven fundamental tasks or responsibilities. The president is responsible for (1) crisis management, (2) symbolic and morale-building leadership, (3) priority setting and program design, (4) leadership recruitment, (5) coalition building, (6) program implementation and evaluation, and (7) general oversight (Cronin 1980). The tasks overlap, and the splash from one presidential action ripples through the others.

The outstanding performance of one presidential responsibility can help the president to perform some of the others. Presidents Reagan and Kennedy used their symbolic and morale-building leadership to set priorities and design programs. Presidents who appear to respond well to crises—even if they themselves contributed to the crisis—galvanize support for their priorities and programs. Presidents often fulfill their responsibilities in different arenas: Reagan's international crisis management and economic morale building gave him greater freedom to create domestic policy coalitions and priorities.

Most presidential responsibilities are often routinely performed. But some of these twenty-one responsibilities—seven tasks in three policy areas—will periodically conflict. That conflict may derive from the needs of conflicting communities or from the scarcity of resources. That conflict creates a rhetorical exigence that invites presidential persuasion.

Bitzer's notion of the rhetorical situation holds that diverse speakers responding to similar exigencies and constraints produce *genres* of speeches. Presidents, like the rest of us, look to generic patterns for guidance. But it is worth remembering that presidents have a considerable advantage over others; often, they define the exigence. By defining the exigence, a president indirectly defines the applicable constraints and, therefore, its potentialities and pitfalls. Richard Nixon, for instance, introduced the 1974 energy crisis as a bridge from his precarious Watergate defense to the sort of international crisis that enhances our reliance on presidential leadership. Let us consider briefly three genres of presidential rhetoric.

Inaugural Addresses

The Constitution requires only that the president report annually on the state of the union, but presidents feel the need to speak after taking the oath of office. The primary exigence underlying inaugurals is the tension between the president's roles as the combative partisan and the unifying leader who is "above politics." We need help with this symbolic transformation, and the inaugural provides it.

Karlyn Kohrs Campbell and Kathleen Hall Jamieson explain that inaugurals are *epideictic* addresses because they are

> delivered on ceremonial occasions, fuse past and future in present contemplation, affirm or praise the shared principles that will guide the upcoming administration, ask the audience to "gaze upon" traditional

values, employ an elegant, literary language, and rely on . . .
amplification and reaffirmation of what is already known. (1985, 24)

But the inaugural brand of epideictic addresses is an *investiture* of
legitimate quadrennial authority in the president that requires the
president to establish his suitability for the role.

Campbell and Jamieson identify five characteristics of inaugural
addresses. First, inaugurals unify the country by reconstituting
supporters, opponents, and undecideds into "the people," who invest their power in their president. Second, inaugurals discuss
shared values and standards rather than divisive issues. Third,
inaugurals interpret and announce the new administration's
general principles and themes, grounding them in the shared values
while avoiding particular policy statements. Fourth, inaugurals establish presidents' suitability for their role by noting the awe in
which they hold the office, the potential for power excesses, and
their personal humility. Finally, inaugurals accomplish these four
objectives with epideictic rhetoric: praise for the office, nation,
people, and values and a fusion of past and future in the ceremonial
and contemplative present.

Inaugural addresses facilitate both president-president and can-
didate-president transitions. They provide the president with a highly
symbolic moment in which to address history, as well as his constituents. For this reason, a great or empty inaugural can affect
perceptions of the whole administration. The inaugural addresses of
Presidents Lincoln, Franklin Roosevelt, Kennedy, and Reagan are
quoted frequently; whereas the addresses of Presidents Eisenhower,
Carter, Bush, and most others have been forgotten.

Crisis Addresses

Much as we rely on a doctor when we are ill, we rely on the
president during a crisis. But much as a physician needs sick
patients to pay for her or his house, car, and a vacation, a crisis
orientation enhances a president's power. The pattern is a decline in
presidential performance ratings, broken only when an international
event associated with the president briefly rallies the public (Lowi
1985). The political implications are unmistakable: "Don't just stand
there: do something," advises Thomas Cronin, "Appear resolute and
dominant and accentuate the sense of crisis" (1980, 105-10).

Theodore O. Windt describes four generic characteristics of
presidential crisis addresses (1973). First, the president explains how
international events constitute a crisis for America. Through his
narration, the president takes command of the crisis, because the
new facts are known only to the president and his close advisors. The

president has considerable latitude to depict the facts and to frame America's options.

Second, the presidential narration contrasts American innocence and propriety with the deceit, secrecy, and devilishness of our adversary. The net result is a depiction of a particular incident as the straw that broke the patient president's proverbial back. A military or political episode becomes part of the good versus evil melodrama, thereby protecting the president from charges that he himself precipitated the crisis.

Third, the president frames America's response to the crisis as even more than a matter of policy, of military preparedness, or of good versus evil; the crisis is a test of our national character and will. To fail in the crisis is to fail as Americans. Thus, people who question the facts, interests, or responses are challenged on the basis of their character and patriotism.

It is important to note, as does Windt, that crisis addresses announce rather than propose action. They are designed to mobilize support for the president's action, not to initiate public dialogue. Responsible discussion of policy must somehow slice through the suspicions that the critic failed the character test, sympathizes with the evil forces, or both. That is a heavy burden for anyone who wants only to fine-tune understanding of the facts or interests.

The pattern identified by Windt is apparent in President Roosevelt's 1941 declaration of war, President Truman's 1947 "Truman Doctrine" address, President Kennedy's 1962 Cuban Missile Crisis speech, President Johnson's 1964 Gulf of Tonkin address, President Nixon's 1970 Cambodia address, the Ford administration's 1975 Mayaguez statements, President Carter's 1980 statement on the hostage rescue mission, and President Reagan's addresses on KAL 007 and Grenada, to name only a few.

Crisis addresses bolster a president's popularity, and his decisive action can improve or worsen the situation; and it is the president himself who identifies crises for us. The crisis mentality gives the president a power edge that is essential during real crises and hurtful during fabrications.

Presidential Defenses

Buchanan's notion of a presidential experience marked by stress, frustration, deference and dissonance describes a climate that tempts most presidents to tug at the constitutional leash. Extremely popular presidents acting questionably in extenuating circumstances—like Abraham Lincoln and Franklin Roosevelt—are usually praised for their leadership.

But opposition to policies evolves periodically into criticism of the president himself, which can lead to a legitimacy crisis. American news thrives on dramatic, personal, and fragmented stories like charges of misconduct by prominent officials. Significant or not, the appeal of such charges to readers makes the investment of reportorial resources worthwhile, and reporters confirm charges often enough to justify the chase.

A president charged with misconduct often can ignore the charge. This *avoidance* strategy works when the credibility of the office and of the occupant combine with the sheer quantity of other news to outlast the accusations. Accusations that fail the tests of narrative rationality—coherence and fidelity to the audience's experience—rarely demand presidential responses. But well-organized and rhetorically sophisticated critics with compelling evidence of a serious transgression benefit from presidential avoidance. By the time the president decides to respond, his critics have gained the momentum.

When addressing charges against themselves presidents have several options (Ware and Linkugel 1973). First, a president may admit the act, deny it, or sidestep it. Second, the president can frame the act for his audience by arguing (1) that the act was actually proper, (2) that it seemed proper at the time, (3) that it was preferable to the available alternatives, or (4) that it was inexcusable. Third, the president can justify his conduct in terms of transcending concerns like national security.

Finally, whatever else he has said, the president can express pride, satisfaction, ambivalence, or remorse for the act. If he has admitted and defended the act, then he probably should be either proud or satisfied with the outcome. Sometimes he will be ambivalent, as when the plan works imperfectly or at great cost. And in some cases the president will express remorse: "Whether I realized that I was doing it, whether I meant to do it or not, whatever my reasons, I truly regret that it turned out as it did." It is remarkable how rarely politicians apologize for obvious transgressions, considering our religious tradition of sin and atonement.

Kenneth Burke has described the dramatistic ritual through which disagreement leads to guilt and redemption through the destruction of some guilt-laden vessel (1966). Our president and press regularly enact this Burkean drama. Reporters, special prosecutors, and congressional investigators try to find the person, agency, or statute responsible for an improper act. That vessel is heaped with public scorn and driven out to purify America. The symbolic drama is as old as the Crucifixion and as unlikely to be forgotten.

The Rhetorical Legacy of the Reagan Presidency

Ronald Reagan's rhetoric quickly earned him the moniker "the great communicator," and he provides a useful case study through which to summarize this chapter on presidential leadership.

Ronald Reagan's character, worldview, and style prepared him almost eerily to play the role of president in the 1980s. His childhood nurtured the passive-positive appetite for affection that produces popular presidents. His experience recreating entire baseball games from ticker-tape summaries for radio audiences prepared him to help the public envision his goals. His acting experience prepared him to use the ever-present cameras, lights, microphones, and teleprompters to full advantage. His days as General Electric's spokesman for free enterprise prepared him to make simple ideological statements and to answer questions with disarming wit and charm. And his experience as governor of California provided him with significant experience as a political executive. Preparation does not always translate smoothly into performance, but in Reagan's case it did. He was consistently more popular than his policies and he maintained solid approval ratings even through the lengthy Iran-Contra scandal.

Ronald Reagan narrated life for America as he had narrated "Death Valley Days" on television for 20 Mule Team Borax. He was a good narrator who could simplify events for the television public and, thereby, incur their favor and establish a seemingly personal relationship. President Reagan's first-term rhetoric conveyed a sense of place, tradition, and momentum (Hart 1984). It was built on the bedrock of a community we might call "MisteReagan's Neighborhood," a land populated with ordinary people identified by their economic roles who bore the brunt of taxation, high prices, unemployment, and government regulation. They made things happen by speaking out and by acting heroically. Heroes abounded in the neighborhood, and nobody who lived there caused its problems. When neighbors made poor decisions, their intentions were always above reproach. The neighborhood faced two adversaries: an "evil empire" that caused all wrongs and the neighborhood's own government (Smith 1987). "MisteReagan's Neighborhood" boasted a proud heritage based on its freedom. He emphasized that Americans could do anything through faith in that heritage and that failure occurs only when Americans have insufficient faith in their heritage to act boldly, because America's actions are self-evidently moral and necessary for the betterment both of America and of the world.

Essentially, President Reagan gave epideictic addresses in almost every kind of situation. If presidents could unify the nation with ceremonies that stress past glories and rehearse traditional values, why save such rhetoric for the commemoration of D-day and Super Bowl triumphs? The president and his advisors sensed that epideictic addresses foreground the unifying symbolic side of the presidential role, whereas other kinds of rhetoric foreground the divisive political side of the role. The rhetoric of "MisteReagan's Neighborhood" interwove Reagan's themes into a seamless tapestry: We have a proud heritage because of our moral purpose and heroic ordinary people; we can accomplish anything because of our heritage and moral purpose; our moral purpose is evident in our proud heritage and the otherwise inexplicable accomplishments of humble people; our people are great and heroic because they are heirs to a great moral and heroic tradition; and so on. Each of Reagan's themes justified the others and left responsible critics without a foothold.

President Reagan even used epideictic rhetoric to defend White House policies. Rather than respond to specific challenges, he would muse about the essential meaning of the neighborhood, so that criticism of his policy seemed an attack on our people, heritage, morality, and commitment. When a suicidal terrorist killed hundreds of marines in Beirut, President Reagan deflected policy questions as (1) attacks on heroic young marines, (2) attacks on our heritage of selfless heroism, and (3) signs of timidity that threaten to betray our bold heritage before (4) calling for us to live up to our heritage by standing tall in Lebanon:

> I think that young marine and all his comrades have given every one of us something to live up to. They were not afraid to stand up for their country or, no matter how difficult and slow the journey might be, to give to others that last, best hope of a better future. We cannot and will not dishonor them now and the sacrifices they've made by failing to remain as faithful to the cause of freedom and the pursuit of peace as they have been (Reagan 1983, 1502).

The wisdom, feasibility, and propriety of the decision to send American marines into Beirut, as well as the wisdom and competence of the administration, were insulated from scrutiny by the honor of the young marines and by the implicit equation of caution with cowardice.

It was against this rhetoric that the Iran-Contra revelations burst in 1986. The president addressed his public and even held a press conference, but nothing seemed to work. He appointed the Tower Commission, but their report failed to stifle criticism. A joint House and Senate committee held televised hearings through the summer of 1987, and the public began to doubt their president's competence and trustworthiness.

The Iran-Contra scandal grew directly from assumptions nurtured by the president's first-term rhetoric: Act boldly in a good cause that you believe in, and you will be a seen as heroic. The scandal revealed flaws in the presidential management style and forced him to choose between images of competence and trust. The complicated dealings defied the Reagan staples of simplification and vivid language, since he could not describe simply and vividly decisions he could not recall. Finally, although President Reagan could have partially rehabilitated Iran for the public, his only public reference to Iran in the six years prior to the disclosures was in a strident antiterrorist address to the American Bar Association.

Ronald Reagan took office at a time when presidents had made the American presidency a speaking office (Hart 1987; Tulis 1987). Public speaking had become so central to the role that a president able to deliver moving speeches seemed the perfect choice to many. The fact that this particular speaker was familiar, likable, folksy, and fashionably conservative made him all the more desirable. Elected largely on a wave of anti-Carter frustration, Reagan quickly transformed his landslide into a *personal* mandate by articulating America's hopes and dreams as he had done for Chicago Cubs fans and by building the credibility needed to sell policies as he had done for General Electric.

The Iran-Contra scandal undermined public confidence in President Reagan's abilities but not in Ronald Reagan himself. Nevertheless, our diminished confidence in his ability greased the skids for his subsequent failures in the Bork and Ginsburg nominations to the Supreme Court and the late 1988 budget reconciliation bills. Had the Reagan term ended just before the 1986 mid-term elections, he might have been regarded as a rhetorical giant. But his high-energy, low-yield campaigning in 1986, his Iran-Contra defense, his Bork debacle, and his inability to control the deficit demonstrated the limits of even Ronald Reagan's rhetoric. His staunch supporters generally blame those failures on Congress, which raises an interesting question: Is a president who cannot persuade congress a truly "great communicator"?

Conclusions

This chapter examined presidential leadership as a communicative phenomenon. We saw that constitutionally separated institutions sharing power put a premium on cooperation and, therefore, persuasion. We learned that constitutional responsibilities and public expectations create an office and psychological experience that homogenize the conduct of presidents, whatever their character, worldview, or style. We concluded that the presidency is a rhetorical role and examined the recurrent patterns of presidential rhetoric. We then considered the generic features of inaugural addresses, crisis addresses, and presidential defenses. Finally we attempted to explain the sources of President Reagan's rhetorical success and his problems during the Iran-Contra investigations.

References

Barber, James David. *Presidential Character: Predicting Performance in the White House* 3d ed. Englewood Cliffs, NJ: Prentice-Hall, 1985.

Buchanan, Bruce. *The Presidential Experience: What the Office Does to the Man.* Englewood Cliffs, NJ: Prentice-Hall, 1978.

Burke, Kenneth. *Language as Symbolic Action.* Berkeley: University of California Press, 1966.

Campbell, Karlyn Kohrs, and Kathleen Hall Jamieson. "Inaugurating the Presidency." *Presidential Studies Quarterly,* 15 (Spring 1985): 394–411.

Corwin, Edward S. *The President: Office and Powers, 1787–1957.* New York: New York University Press, 1957.

Cronin, Thomas E. *The State of the Presidency,* 2d ed. Boston: Little, Brown and Company, 1980.

Duffy, Bernard K., and Halford Ross Ryan, eds. *American Orators of the Twentieth Century: Critical Studies and Sources.* Westport, CT: Greenwood Press, 1987.

Hart, Roderick P. *Verbal Style and the Presidency: A Computer-Based Analysis.* New York: Harcourt Brace Jovanovich, Academic Press, 1984.

———*The Sound of Leadership: Presidential Communication in the Modern Age.* Chicago: University of Chicago Press, 1987.

Kernell, Samuel. *Going Public: New Strategies of Presidential Leadership.* Washington, D.C.: Congressional Quarterly Press, 1986.

Lowi, Theodore J. *The Personal President: Power Invested, Promise Unfilled.* Ithaca, NY: Cornell University Press, 1985.

Neustadt, Richard E. *Presidential Power: The Politics of Leadership from FDR to Carter.* New York: John Wiley and Sons, 1960, 1980.

Reagan, Ronald. Address to the nation on events in Lebanon and Grenada, October 27, 1983. *Public Papers of the Presidents: Ronald Reagan,* 1517–22. Washington, D.C.: Government Printing Office, 1983.

Rossiter, Clinton. *The American Presidency*, revised edition. New York: Harcourt Brace Jovanovich, 1956.

Smith, Craig Allen. "The Audiences of the 'Rhetorical Presidency': An analysis of Presidential-Constituent Interactions, 1963–1981." *Presidential Studies Quarterly* 13 (Fall 1983): 613–22.

———. "'MisteReagan's Neighborhood': Rhetoric and National Unity." *Southern Speech Communication Journal* 52 (Spring 1987): 219–39.

Smith, Craig Allen, and Kathy B. Smith. "Presidential Values and Public Priorities: Recurrent Patterns in Addresses to the Nation, 1963–1984." *Presidential Studies Quarterly* 15 (Fall 1985): 743–53.

Tulis, Jeffrey K. *The Rhetorical Presidency*. Princeton, NJ: Princeton University Press, 1987.

Ware, B.L., and Wil A. Linkugel. "They Spoke in Defense of Themselves: On the Generic Criticism of Apologia." *Quarterly Journal of Speech* 59 (October 1973): 273–83.

Windt, Theodore O. "The Presidency and Speeches on International Crises: Repeating the Rhetorical Past." *Speaker and Gavel* 2, no. 1 (1973): 6–14.

Windt, Theodore Otto, and Beth Ingold. *Essays in Presidential Rhetoric*, 2d ed. Dubuque, IA: Kendall-Hunt, 1987.

Chapter 9
COMMUNICATION AND
THE COURTS

In this chapter we will see how courts serve unique governmental and political functions. The legal community is a social group with shared goals, a common language, an ideology that values precedent and procedure, and a logic that emphasizes evidence and narrative form. Courts *adjudicate* conflicts by interpreting (1) laws and previous rulings and (2) specific cases as depicted by the concerned parties and (3) by matching a specific case to the pertinent aspects of established law to resolve the dispute. These tasks necessitate arguments and decisions that differ in many respects from those found in the legislative, electoral, and journalistic arenas.

This chapter will consider courts as arenas of political communication before discussing the rhetorical features of courtroom argument and the inescapably political role of an institution that strives to be "above politics."

Political Communication and the Courts

We have defined political communication as the process of negotiating a community orientation through the interpretation and characterization of interests, of power relationships, and of the community's role in the world. It is in our courtrooms—or at least in the corridors leading to them—that this negotiation reaches its pinnacle. The courtrooms of the land are reached only by irreconcilable positions that cannot be amicably resolved short of a legal hearing.

Communicative Functions of the Courts

Judge and jury refine for a community the nature and reach of its laws. They do this by interpreting the law and an act in relation to one another. For example, a court will decide (1) whether "malice" should be construed in a manner that encompasses the defendant's actions and (2) whether the defendant's actions were malicious. Judge and jury hear competing depictions of the conflict framed with the applicable points of law; they negotiate a judgment that refines the law for the community and clarifies its power relationships.

Courts serve three fundamental political functions in America (Meadow 1980). First, courtrooms *embody legitimate political authority.* A court's legitimacy is enhanced by its symbolic trappings, as Robert Meadow explains:

> Overall, the architecture of the courtroom is a symbolic political message [with its] majestic settings, flags, robes, gavel, bailiffs, and so on. The strength and authority of the government is on the line in the courtroom; proceedings are open to the public, so every effort is made to underscore the fairness and impartiality of the event. The . . . message is clear: the government is fair but strong. All efforts are made to seek out the truth. Social order is extremely important. And, of course, deviance is punished. (1980, 140)

These symbolic dimensions are especially apparent in the U.S. Supreme Court. Marble halls, a high bench, black robes, a locked box for recording votes, the ritual process, closed deliberations that remain confidential in a tradition of secrecy among justices and their aides—all of these factors enhance the Court's legitimacy by elevating the justices, obscuring their disagreements, and dramatizing the traditions and continuity of the government.

Second, courts *legitimize narratives* as accurate and truthful and deny legitimacy to alternative narratives. Judge and jury listen to competing depictions of a dispute, and they either embrace one narrative and reject the other or construct a composite narrative from pieces of the competing arguments. Either way, the court sanctions one version of truth and accuracy. We will return to this topic later in the chapter.

Third, courts *provide an avenue for political participation* to people with grievances. Black Americans, women, and others have used the courts to argue that society's laws have been improperly interpreted and unfairly applied. When the courts rule in favor of such challenges, they legitimize the plaintiffs' narrative and orient subsequent courts toward the new interpretation. When a court upholds the prevailing legal interpretation and application, it often crystallizes public sentiment for new legislation. For example, the Court's decision, in *Roe v. Wade* that some abortions were permissible under existing law spurred the antiabortion community to reverse its tactics by lobbying for a constitutional amendment to outlaw abortion. People unable to lobby effectively for legislation may be able to challenge effectively the legitimate interpretation and application of existing law.

It is also important to note that the symbolic presence of the judicial process has contributed to the resolution of many disputes. The risk that one could "wind up in court" has encouraged many a grudging compromise. Those risks are dramatized for us in countless courtroom dramas where the only question is, "Will the court get it right?" It is largely because the guilty sometimes go free and the innocent sometimes lose all that we settle so many of our disputes without legal hearings. If we all believed the judgment of the courts to be inerrant, we would probably rush into court with every grievance, since most people construe their own actions as justified.

In short, the court system embodies the constitutional system, legitimizes one narrative and rejects alternatives, provides a means of political participation, and indirectly encourages people to resolve their differences.

Written Opinions and Legal Language

Courts issue written opinions intended for an audience in the legal community. Both the restricted nature of the legal community and the technical points decided serve to encourage a highly jargonized, verbose, and heavily footnoted writing style (Berkson 1978). That rhetorical style, in turn, keeps the legal community restricted (Edelman 1964).

The ambiguity of legal language is significant. Lack of clarity can lead to additional legal actions, erroneous interpretations, or simple noncompliance. Moreover, the public's understanding of a decision—influenced by the press—can differ markedly from the legal community's technical understanding of the same decision (Grey 1968).

But judges, like legislators, frequently use ambiguous language to resolve political conflicts (Edelman 1964). Ambiguity enables judges (1) to protect the sense of legal precedent and continuity, (2) to resolve the dispute before them, (3) to influence, but not determine, the resolution of similar disputes yet to come before them, (4) to insulate the legal community from broad public interference, (5) to preserve the symbolic mystique of the courts, and (6) to allow interpretive latitude to future generations of judges.

Court decisions have been criticized for their specialized language, length, and lack of clarity; and these are distinct risks. But to specially trained elite readers like law professors and judges who constitute the court's primary audience, that style is rated positively.

Moreover, this rhetorical style performs many political functions for the legal community.

Adjudicative Judgments

When an unresolved difference finds its way into court, the interested parties seek adjudication. *Factual judgments* grant the accuracy of a depicted reality; *value judgments* affirm a preference; and *adjudicative judgments* affirm the conformity of a depicted reality to an explicitly agreed upon code of behavior (adapted from Arnold 1974). Courts specialize in factual and adjudicative judgments, leaving value judgments to presidents, legislators, journalists, movements, and candidates.

Judges rule on the admissibility of evidence and decide whether the facts are open to discussion. Recall that Chaim Perelman's theory of argument defines a "fact" on the basis of its universal acceptance. In the familiar Christmas film *Miracle on 34th Street*, for example, the judge must decide on the existence of Santa Claus on behalf of the state. He invites arguments on both sides, and when the post office delivers all of its mail addressed to Santa to the defendant, the judge affirms the federal government's decision and finds in favor of the defendant.

Real judges determine whether confessions have been coerced, whether evidence has been obtained illegally, and whether a plaintiff has established a sufficient case. Judgments can be appealed and convictions overturned on the grounds that the judge ruled improperly on these factual and procedural questions.

Ultimately, a judge and/or jury adjudicate a dispute by comparing the facts of the case to the explicitly stated and agreed upon formal code of conduct—the law. The law consists of the Constitution, subsequent statutes, and the body of legal opinions explaining court decisions in similar cases. Each of us has had occasion to squirm when a verdict fails to square with the expectations we had formed through newspaper accounts. This usually occurs because we are generally unaware of the relevant points of law. Let us consider two recent examples.

William Hinckley shot President Reagan on March 31, 1981. Most Americans saw a film of the incident, and the public outcry was deafening when the court found Hinckley not guilty by reason of insanity. But the point of law holds that people cannot be found guilty if they are incapable of discerning right from wrong. It is interesting to speculate about a society wherein a person can be judged guilty by reason of insanity, but that is not the legal code by which American courts can adjudicate cases. The public used press accounts to conclude that Hinckley committed a despicable act, but that was not the adjudicative question.

In 1988, two activists occupied a newspaper office in North Carolina and held several employees hostage to dramatize charges of racism and corruption in the area. After a lengthy standoff with police, they escaped, were captured, tried, and acquitted. They claimed that the acquittal vindicated them and legitimized their claims of political corruption. Observers were stunned, because it was well known that the defendants had occupied the newspaper office. But they had been accused of violating a federal hostage law that outlawed demands on the U.S. Government. Because the defendants had made no such demand, they had not violated that particular law. Much of the public was predictably outraged by what they perceived to be the permissiveness of the courts, and questions about the prosecution's strategy were largely ignored. The defendants can be tried on other charges, like kidnapping, but conviction could again be complicated because they did not try to abduct the hostages.

In each case, guilt and conviction seemed clear enough, because the general public understood the narrative and judged it according to general value preferences of right and wrong. The public was unprepared to adjudicate largely because the press found little reason to interrupt such powerful melodrama with little details such as pertinent laws.

Fortunately, the legal system has developed several mechanisms to facilitate sound adjudication. Jurors are instructed and advised by the judge, for example, and the trial attorneys frame the charges so as to address crucial legal points. Law schools and bar examinations ensure that lawyers surpass a minimum level of technical competence, and judges are carefully screened.

But technical specialization in the adjudicative process restricts its usefulness in two indirect ways. The first restriction is costliness. Legal education requires considerable time, effort, and money; and it is not surprising that most lawyers capitalize on their investments. Moreover, the adversarial nature of legal battles puts a premium on those lawyers and law firms who win their cases, and the market reflects this demand for winners. But one byproduct of this competitiveness is that some people cannot afford to go to court. It also means that wealthy defendants can drag out the adjudicative process until a less prosperous plaintiff drops a case or settles out of court. Courts can be an avenue of political participation for the politically disadvantaged but only if they can afford it.

The usefulness of the legal system is also restricted by its technicalities. Simply, the laws in your neighborhood may not relate to the wrongs inflicted on you. This clearly returns us to the deliberative function of government and the legislature's need to anticipate as many scenarios as possible. In the meantime, while legislatures correct present problems and plan for the future, courts draw on the past to decide the present.

Trials and Narratives

The interested parties in a legal dispute seek a favorable adjudicative judgment from the court by advancing a narrative. Each side attempts to win the judge and/or jury's adherence to its claims by telling a convincing story. It is this reliance on storytelling as the primary means of argument that enables ordinary citizens to reach legal decisions, since they have been interpreting narratives every day of their lives. Narrative form is the means through which jurors organize and test the competing arguments (Bennett 1978).

Lance Bennett suggests that stories help jurors perform three interpretive operations (Bennett 1978). First, the story helps each juror to identify the *central action*, or "key behavior around which the point of the story will be drawn" (Bennett 1978, 5). What kind of story is it? Robbery, murder, rape, embezzlement, plagiarism, or espionage? The identification of a central action is facilitated by the narrative "bookkeeping devices"—verb tense, pronoun usage, flashbacks and flashforwards—that enable listeners to understand "what happened, to whom, and when." The story highlights a particular kind of action and marginalizes other actions. The identification of the central action evokes in the juror a relevant interpretive framework constructed during a lifetime of experiences.

Armed with a relevant personal framework, each juror uses the story to *infer relationships* among the elements that affect the central action. These inferences are of five types (Bennett 1978, 11–18). *Empirical connections* are the juror's interpretation of observable events, like "the bartender saw the defendant leave at midnight" or "that is her car." "Descriptions are taken literally," warns Bennett. "Terms that would have to be changed to produce a sensible version of an incident . . . become possible indicators of 'made-up' versions of reality" (1978, 12–13).

Categorical connections, or "language categorization" connections, tie the story into the juror's personal construct system, relating words to one another to create clusters of coherence. If the categorization permits a clear and sensible inference about the connection among symbols, says Bennett, listeners will accept the categorization that connects most obviously to the central action. For example, an attorney might undermine the credibility of a witness by asking about the interested party as "your *friend*" or "your *employer*" so that the label suggests a possible bias in the testimony.

The empirical and categorical connections permit still other narrative connections. Each verbal categorization permits *logical connections* derived from the nature of the category. If you accept the prosecutor's categorization of the defendant as the witness's employer, then you infer that the witness's testimony might be influenced by her uncertain job security or her stormy working relationship with her employer. *Normative connections* in the story pose for the juror questions of right and wrong, fair and unfair, excusable and inexcusable acts to be answered within the juror's social interpretive processes. Finally, *personal and aesthetic connections* are facilitated by stories that use presentational techniques or cultural stereotypes so that the relationships among story elements become "targets for emotional release or personal identification" (Bennett 1978, 17–18).

Each story establishes a web of empirical, categorical, logical, normative, and aesthetic connections that explain and justify its account of the central action. Was the loss of life attributable to an accident, self-defense, justifiable retaliation, or premeditated murder? Did the police harass protestors who were merely exercising their constitutional freedoms of assembly and speech, or did they restore order in the midst of an unlawful public disturbance? The interested parties frame their positions in narratives that connect the elements of the case in ways that encourage juror identification with their actions.

Finally, each juror *tests the competing narratives* as narratives, judging their coherence and fidelity. We expect stories to be internally consistent, adequately descriptive, and complete (Bennett 1978, 5), and most jurors reject arguments that fail to satisfy these tests. Much as Doris Graber's television viewers scanned newscasts for bits and pieces of stories that fit their interpretive schema, jurors scan arguments and testimony for narrative coherence and fidelity. The scanning process enables each juror personally to test the arguments and testimony, presumably within the legal guidelines set forth by the judge.

If courtroom success requires the presentation of sound narratives, it is small wonder that courtroom drama has become popular as entertainment. Novels, movies, and television series such as "Perry Mason" and "LA Law" offer viewers a drama stemming from the tension between conflicting narratives, each of which can be constructed to maximize the requirements of good narrative form. Responsible journalists are increasingly following the lead of the tabloids in chronicling all manner of divorces, palimony suits, and other trials that provide ongoing personal dramas in narrative form. And afternoon television graces viewers with "real-life" small claims court cases. The adjudicative aspect of the legal process is marginalized, and the melodramatic aspect is emphasized by concealing pertinent legal considerations until the judgment is announced. The process comes full circle when the "Peoples' Court" viewer and tabloid reader are selected for jury duty.

The U.S. Supreme Court's Communication Process

The Articles of Confederation included no national court, and there were no Supreme Court cases for the first three years of the constitutional system until Chief Justice John Marshall energized the Court and established the doctrine of judicial review in the *Marbury v. Madison* decision of 1803. Marshall recognized that the Constitution was the supreme law in America, that new laws could conflict with the Constitution, and that these challenges to the supreme law would need to be adjudicated by the Supreme Court.

The Court is both insulated from and dependent on public support. It is insulated from the public by the selection process and its elite rhetorical style. The Constitution provides for justices to be appointed by the president with the approval of the Senate. Individual justices, therefore, derive their legitimacy and credibility from the other federal institutions, not from the public at large. This process involves elected representatives in the selection process but conveys only indirect legitimacy. Moreover, life tenure affords justices an insulation from public accountability that is unique in our system, although the permanence of the appointment makes it susceptible to political dispute. We will explore the legislative-executive tussles over Supreme Court nominations later in this chapter.

Despite its insulation from the public, the Court is highly dependent on public support. The Supreme Court has no police force to enforce its rulings, and it relies instead on voluntary compliance. Without public support, this compliance is unlikely, and offenders must be found and arrested by local authorities and then charged and tried in lower courts. There is more than a little margin for error in this process as a variety of individual and social interpretive systems come into play.

Given its need for voluntary compliance, the Supreme Court needs a clear grant of legitimacy from society. Fortunately, the abstract notion of "The Supreme Court" symbolizes the ideal of justice for most Americans. Popular support for the abstract institution runs higher than support for any current court, for individual justices, or for specific decisions (Mason 1980). But why?

It seems reasonable to suggest that the Court maintains respect by not soliciting public opinion. The Supreme Court's public information office engages in little image building (Berkson 1978). Justices neither throw out ceremonial baseballs nor call the Super Bowl champions' locker-room celebration. Justices welcome neither returning astronauts nor prisoners of war. Justices neither address the nation on television nor campaign for public support. By not engaging in ceremonies designed to entice the public, the justices remain cool, detached, and dignified. The Court participates only in its own ritual dramas.

A second reason for the credibility of the abstract Court is its apparent decisiveness. Congress wrestles with the budget night after night on television only to miss its deadline. But the Supreme Court deliberates in private, thereby avoiding the melodramatic coverage that dogs Congress and the president. We never see the Court in disarray, and the justices always appear to reach decisions, even if those decisions are narrow and technical.

Stages of the Court's Communication Process

Presidents and elected representatives can initiate rhetorical efforts on behalf of issues that concern them. But justices can only review the cases brought to them by others, almost always on appeal. The practical effect is that presidents can discuss their priority issues on prime-time television and elected representatives can introduce and advocate legislation, but justices must await cases that warrant appeal. Such cases are rare. During the 1984–85 term, for example, the Supreme Court handed down full written opinions in only 4 percent of the 4,269 cases it considered (Abraham 1987).

The Oral Argument Stage

Attorneys file 40 copies of their briefs with the court clerk. Oral arguments are presented by specially certified lawyers, usually in half-hour presentations. Arguments are presented in the 300-seat chamber, with some seats available to the general public. Justices may interrupt counsel with questions, and there is no formal sequence as in legislative hearings.

Oral argument performs an obvious function of helping all parties in the dispute to *obtain and clarify information* (Wasby, D'Amato, and Metrailer 1976). Oral argument also helps attorneys to *focus attention on their chosen legal points*. Every dispute potentially involves many elements, and it is the job of an attorney to interpret a client's story through the interpretive system of the law. The written brief provides each counsel an opportunity to highlight a client's important points and to marginalize those useful to the opponent. A brief is organized so as to present the facts of the case and the pertinent legal points; indeed, briefs often advance every conceivable legal possibility. Oral argument allows counsel and justices to assess the most important elements of the brief by responding to the opposition's narrative.

Third, oral argument can help justices to *focus on the pivotal elements* of the case. Justices frequently put counsel on the spot during this phase with questions such as, "That is the sole basis of your case, is it not?" This is an important function, because nine judges can conceivably interpret the case before them as tests of nine different points of law. This focusing is important, because the justices' decision will turn on the pivotal point of law.

Fourth, oral argument *assures lawyers that their case has been heard*, a function less cynical than it may seem. The Court has evolved from strictly oral arguments through optional written briefs to mandatory written briefs and, in recent years, optional oral arguments. It has even been suggested that oral arguments be dropped altogether. Like the student who wonders how carefully the C+ paper was read, lawyers and clients have no way to ensure a careful reading of their briefs. This can be especially worrisome when briefs are filed late or when the Court faces an unusually busy session. Oral argument assures the lawyers that their arguments have been heard by all the justices prior to the moment of decision.

Similarly, *legitimation of the judge* is a fifth function of oral argument. Oral argument personally introduces the justices into the dispute and enacts the full ceremonial ritual of the Court. If we were ever to reduce Supreme Court rulings to a process of submitting written briefs and reading written opinions, we would come close to transforming Supreme Court justices into government bureaucrats on the order of IRS auditors.

A sixth function of oral argument is to provide for *communication among the justices*. Sometimes one justice will tell the others that a pivotal legal point cannot be seriously considered until a more basic point, such as jurisdiction, has been fully settled. At other times, a justice might draw attention to an overlooked aspect of a case. Clearly, it can be helpful to raise these questions when counsel has an opportunity to answer.

Oral argument also enables the justices to *select a strategic approach* to the case. By "strategy," we expressly do not mean to say that justices decide what they wish to rule and then justify it. Instead, strategy refers to the Court's plan for fulfilling its task without creating a needlessly disruptive, or needlessly restrictive, precedent for future courts (Hahn 1973).

The Court's strategic options are varied. It can uphold lower- court rulings either by refusing to review a case or by reviewing the case and issuing an opinion. A second strategic choice concerns the number of cases to be reviewed and their grouping by legal point (like right of privacy) or by topic (like segregated facilities). Third, the Court must decide how to deal with lower-court rulings, since it will bear responsibility for implementing the ruling. Finally, the Court will choose to present either a summary ruling or a longer opinion that clarifies the Court's thinking and provides the bases for future disputes. Additionally, detailed opinions are likely to invite concurring opinions and dissenting opinions from other justices. The development of oral arguments enable the justices to determine the wisest strategic approach to the cases before adjudicating them.

The Deliberation Stage

After the oral argument phase, the justices enter a locked room for the deliberation stage. A number of procedural regularities constrain this process. There are no pages present, and no record of the conference is kept. Indeed, justices rarely speak publicly about the Court's activities. Each justice presents his or her view of the case, beginning with the chief justice and continuing in order of descending seniority; then the order is reversed to cast the first tentative vote. The dynamics of this process maximize the influence of the senior justices by isolating the least senior justices: the least experienced justices speak and vote only after the Court's general direction has been revealed.

The Court considers four guidelines when deliberating a case (Abraham 1987). Foremost is the legal doctrine of *stare decisis*, which commits the Court to presume the legal validity of precedents established in earlier decisions. This standard differs markedly from that used by elected representatives.

The Court also insists on several procedural matters: (1) the case must involve a definite case of controversy, (2) the Court must have jurisdiction, (3) the parties must have legal standing, (4) there can be no advisory opinions, and (5) all remedies below the Supreme Court must have been exhausted.

The Court's third guideline is the presumed constitutionality of all legislation. Finally, the Court—as a matter of policy—acts on the basis of what is legally correct rather than what it might deem to be fair, wise, or democratic. Justices exercise their sense of fairness after the appropriate legal points have been resolved. But these standards are usually merged to depict the decision as correct, fair, wise, and democratic.

Opinion Stage

When issuing a full written opinion, the Supreme Court must do more than simply decide a case; it must carefully present the rationale for its decision. The Court wants an opinion that is "right" in the sense that it accurately conveys the facts, laws, and reasons expressed by the justices. The Court wants an opinion that can be understood so that it can guide subsequent public conduct and trials. The opinion must be persuasive, and perhaps even eloquent, if it is to convince all parties and induce voluntary compliance. Finally, the opinion should foster unity rather than conflict among the justices and other legal practitioners (Abraham 1987).

The chief justice decides which justice will write the opinion. Communication between justices and their staff has received little scholarly attention because of the tradition of privacy that extends over the entire deliberative process. The precise balance of justice and staff input is unknown, but it is safe to say that the justices write more of their own material than do presidents or representatives. The draft opinion is printed on the Court's private printing press and circulated to the justices.

After reading the drafted opinions, the justices bargain and compromise to work out a majority opinion. The Court is unanimous only in about 30 percent of its decisions. Therefore, justices need to persuade their fellow justices to muster the majority vote. Coalitions form around similar judicial and ideological conceptions. These ongoing coalitions have occurred throughout the Court's history. It is aided by the life tenure of the justices, which makes continuing working relationships both desirable and likely. As with Congress and the president, single actors need support from their institutional colleagues. This process of building support requires persuasion among the justices, but the specifics of their discussions remain private.

Finally, the Court publicly presents its decision. The author speaks from the bench and may paraphrase the opinion, lecture about it, read it, or simply note it. The opinions are recorded in *U.S. Reports.* The Court's final decision is distributed to the press without elaboration or background briefing. The procedure states implicitly (1) that the Court speaks to the legal profession, not to the journalists, (2) that the Court is always on its own turf, and (3) that the Court itself, not the press, offers the definitive narrative.

In summary, the rhetoric of the Supreme Court is strongly influenced by the undemocratic elements of appointment and life tenure. Legitimacy and credibility are crucial for an institution dependent on others for the enforcement of its decisions. The public's highly symbolic attachment to the Court is maintained by a rhetoric—unfathomable to most citizens—that mystifies the judicial process (Edelman 1964). Written briefs and opinions influence which cases are heard and how the lower courts will implement the decisions. Oral argument and interpersonal deliberations influence the opinion; and written communication influences the impact of the opinion on society.

Politics and the Courts

The U.S. Supreme Court is one of the three separate institutions sharing power, and it has periodically come between Congress and presidents. Let us consider briefly the political battles over the efforts of Presidents Roosevelt, Nixon, and Reagan to shape the direction of the Court.

Roosevelt's Court-Packing Scheme

The New Deal used extraordinary measures predicated on a depiction of the Great Depression as an emergency comparable to war, and Franklin D. Roosevelt's administration worried about the Supreme Court (Leuchtenberg 1963). Roosevelt's supporters said that the Court was comprised of "nine old men" appointed by the Republican presidents whose economic and political philosophies were challenged by the New Deal.

The vigorous executive anxious to tackle the nation's problems and the legislature willing to write the appropriate legislation were blocked by a Supreme Court whose long view and commitment to precedent unanimously ruled the National Industrial Recovery Act unconstitutional on May 27, 1935. Even the liberal justices agreed that the case involved both a reckless delegation of legislative power to regulatory agencies and a federal intrusion into intrastate commerce. A 5–4 loss was one thing, but a 9–0 decision against a major program devastated Roosevelt; and with his 1936 landslide as a mandate, he moved to reform the Supreme Court. The problem, according to Roosevelt, was that the justices had become too old to function properly. He proposed legislation that would enable a president to appoint an additional justice for every justice who failed to announce his retirement within six months of his seventieth birthday. It was not coincidental that all four conservative justices, and one of the swing justices, were over seventy. Under the plan, Roosevelt would have been able to appoint five sympathetic justices to the Court, thereby creating a 9–5 New Deal majority.

Roosevelt's court-packing scheme was an unqualified disaster. Intoxicated with his public support and frustrated by the Court, he failed to heed his advisors' warning against the plan, failed to prepare Congress for his radical proposal, but pushed the Court plan relentlessly for the first six months of 1937. A president at the peak of his popularity had run full speed into the marble ethos of the Supreme Court and created more problems than he had dared to imagine. Public reverence for a Supreme Court believed to be "above politics" withstood the attacks of an extraordinary politician. Roosevelt's actions disillusioned some of his supporters and demonstrated his unanticipated ability to lose a battle (Ryan 1987).

The court-packing scheme transformed public perceptions of the Supreme Court in a way that endures today. Whether one blames the holdover conservative justices or the activist president, America now worries about a "political" Supreme Court. Presidents Eisenhower, Nixon, and Reagan fretted about Democratic holdovers who were, in Roosevelt's phrase, "out of step with the times," just as today's Democrats worry about the efforts of Presidents Reagan and Bush to "pack the Court" to overcome what they perceived as the "wisdom and stability" of aging liberal justices. The Roosevelt case focused greater attention on the process of selecting Supreme Court justices.

Nominees and Presidential Prerogative

The Constitution provides for the president to appoint Supreme Court justices with the advice and consent of the Senate. The Framers could have let the president appoint justices without anyone's advice or consent if they had wished to do so, or they could have let the legislature staff the Court without disturbing the president. But they did neither of these things.

The Framers protected the citizenry against unwanted laws by complicating the system to create a Supreme Court independent of any other single institution. Basically, people who are to interpret the law are chosen by the chief enforcer of laws and approved by those who write the laws; a reasonable way to ensure that the legislative, executive, and judicial functions are performed by people with roughly harmonious interpretive systems.

Vacancies on the Supreme Court occur rarely, and the president's nominees are usually confirmed. From 1900 to 1969, for example, the Senate rejected only one nominee for the Supreme Court. This has led some observers to argue the existence of a *presidential prerogative* argument that all presidents should have the right to pick their own Supreme Court justices. Predictably, this position is heard most frequently from presidents and their partisans.

But the presidential prerogative argument is flawed. It underestimates the Framers' decision to require the advice and consent of the Senate. Alexander Hamilton warned in *The Federalist* that presidents might use their appointive powers for personal rather than societal advantage unless checked by the Senate, and Yale Law Professor Charles Black wrote that judges should be as independent of the president as they are of the Senate, "neither more nor less" (Simon 1973).

A second problem with the presidential prerogative argument is that many presidential appointees have been rejected by the Senate—roughly one in five by one count (Simon 1973). Simply, presidents have no prerogative to staff the Supreme Court, although they like to argue that they do. Their argument did seem convincing during the middle part of this century, when presidential nominees were accepted.

But the period of presidential success came during the period when presidents were increasingly active and credible with the Senate and when presidents personally consulted—and compromised—with congressional leaders. Simply, prudent presidents listen to the advice of the Senate before asking their consent to a nomination. Presidents win when they assess the Senate, compile a list of confirmable justices, and then select the one they prefer.

Earlier, we saw how presidents, especially since 1961, have moved from consultation and compromise with congressional leaders toward indirect public pressure. The process appears to have similarly influenced Supreme Court nominations as recent presidents claimed their presidential prerogative and pressed for confirmation, only to have their nominees rejected. Presidents Nixon and Reagan picked their nominees, claimed presidential prerogative, and spurned the advice of the Senate.

Richard Nixon's 1968 campaign used public concern that the Supreme Court had become dangerously permissive, especially with regard to crime. Nixon defeated Hubert Humphrey by half a million votes largely because George Wallace polled ten million popular and forty-six electoral votes. To win reelection, Nixon would need to attract Wallace supporters, and one way to do so would be to appoint conservative southern justices to the Supreme Court.

But his nomination of Judge Clement F. Haynesworth to the Court in 1969 encountered immediate controversy. Although Wallace had won ten million votes and carried the South just nine months earlier, it had been only sixteen months since the death of Martin Luther King, Jr., and many other Americans worried that the major advances of the 1960s could be lost through a conservative Court and a muted civil rights movement.

The debate over the Haynesworth nomination came to center around a series of questionably ethical decisions and his apparent "insensitivity" to racial discrimination (Vatz and Windt 1974). The Nixon administration sidestepped the charges and asserted the mythical presidential prerogative, and the nomination was defeated.

Nixon then nominated G. Harrold Carswell to the Court. After originally questioning Carswell's ability to deal with racial discrimination cases, the confirmation hearings broadened into a test of his judicial competence; Carswell was inclined to disregard precedent and suffered an unusual number of reversals. Oddly, Carswell's supporters admitted that he was a mediocre judge and tried once again to win on the grounds of presidential prerogative (Vatz and Windt 1974). Again, the argument seemed to dissuade key senators, some of them Republicans, and the Carswell nomination was also defeated.

It had seemed impossible for a president to lose two successive nominations to the Supreme Court. Southerners, conservatives, and Republicans charged that Haynesworth and Carswell had been defeated simply because they were southern conservatives. But President Nixon knew, or should have known, that the appointment of any southern conservative to the Supreme Court in 1969 would be terribly controversial. He could have heeded the advice of the Senate and chosen a confirmable justice like Harry Blackmun, whom he eventually nominated; or he could have nominated southern conservative judges less tainted and more distinguished than Haynesworth and Carswell. Certainly, Nixon could have been less imperial by answering the charges against the nominees more directly and by qualifying the presidential prerogative. But he did none of those things, and he was publicly embarrassed.

Perhaps the most surprising thing about the Haynesworth and Carswell rejections was their reenactment by President Reagan. Eager to leave America in conservative hands and flushed with the glow of his 1984 landslide, President Reagan nominated Judge Robert Bork to the Court. Judge Bork was a brilliant law professor and judge, popular among conservative intellectuals. Judge Bork had previously espoused a variety of controversial positions—from socialism to libertarianism—and, like many scholars, he enjoyed mental gymnastics and argument for argument's sake.

But the mind that made Robert Bork a provocative professor made him a discomfiting nominee for the Court. His writings and testimony questioned the legal points on which many civil rights decisions had been based. Bork believed that the same rulings could be more properly based on different legal points, and many Americans feared, worried, or hoped that he might overturn important precedents. Reagan asserted the prerogative argument, and the nomination was defeated.

President Reagan then nominated Judge Douglas Ginsburg to the Court. Like Carswell an apparently certain nominee, Ginsburg withdrew his nomination in the face of revelations that he had smoked marijuana during his younger days. On the third try, President Reagan nominated Judge Anthony Kennedy, who was confirmed.

There are several similarities among the Nixon and Reagan failures. Both relied heavily on the fallacious argument of presidential prerogative. Both presidents, like Roosevelt before them, tried to use political strength to mold the Supreme Court to their agenda, and both failed because they would not hear the advice of the Senate. Both failed to realize that the presidential prerogative argument invites Senate opposition, if only to preserve its constitutional role.

Three popular presidents—Roosevelt, Nixon, and Reagan—all had serious confrontations involving the Supreme Court, and all three lost. Public respect and the complicated constitutional process for staffing it protected the Supreme Court from Roosevelt's, Nixon's, and Reagan's efforts to shape the Supreme Court in their own image. The court-packing scheme heightened concern that the Court would be politicized, and the Nixon and Reagan appointments were debated and decided in that context. The result has been that the Supreme Court continues to function as a stabilizer, the keel on the ship of state, resolving disputes through interpretation whenever possible.

Conclusions

This chapter discussed the judiciary, particularly the Supreme Court, as an arena of political communication. We saw that our courts adjudicate conflicts by considering narratives that frame the facts and legal points in dispute. We discussed the communicative implications of the process by which the Supreme Court operates and examined the political nature of the Court's role in the larger federal system.

The model of political communication elaborated earlier in this book emphasized that individuals form communities of shared motives, values, language, and narratives and that they struggle for the right to define reality for everyone else. In this process, we have given our courts the ultimate political power. The law is quiet, dignified, technical, expensive, and inaccessible to many citizens. Oral arguments are less melodramatic than presidential press conferences or investigative hearings, and judicial opinions are far more difficult to follow than are presidential addresses or campaign commercials. But it was the U.S. Supreme Court that restrained the procedural excesses of the New Deal and ended legal segregation of the races.

References

Abraham, Henry Julian. *The Judiciary: The Supreme Court in the Governmental Process.* 7th Ed. Boston: Allyn and Bacon, 1987.

Arnold, Carroll C. *Criticism of Oral Rhetoric.* Columbus, OH: Bell and Howell, charles E. Merrill Publishing, 1974.

Bennett, W. Lance. "Storytelling in Criminal Trials: A Model of Social Judgment." *Quarterly Journal of Speech* 64 (February 1978): 1–22.

Berkson, Larry Charles. *The Supreme Court And its Publics: The Communication of Policy Decisions.* Lexington, MA: Lexington Books, 1978.

Edelman, Murray. *The Symbolic Uses of Politics.* Urbana: University of Illinois Press, 1964.

Grey, David L. *The Supreme Court and the News Media.* Evanston, IL: Northwestern University Press, 1968.

Hahn, J. "The NAACP Legal Defense and Educational Fund: Its Judicial Strategy and Tactics." In *American Government and Politics,* edited by Stephen L. Wasby. New York: Scribner's, 1973.

Leuchtenberg, William E. *Franklin D. Roosevelt and the New Deal.* New York: Harper and Row, 1963.

Mason, Alpheus Thomas. "Eavesdropping on Justice: A Review Essay." *Political Science Quarterly* 95, (Summer 1980): 295–304.

Meadow, Robert G. *Politics as Communication.* Norwood, NJ: ABLEX, 1980.

Ryan, Halford Ross. "Franklin Delano Roosevelt." In *American Orators of the Twentieth Century,* edited by Bernard K. Duffy and Halford Ross Ryan. Westport, CT: Greenwood Press, 1987.

Simon, James F. *In His Own Image: The Supreme Court in Richard Nixon's America.* New York: David McKay, 1973.

Vatz, Richard E. and Theodore Otto Windt, Jr. "The Defeats of Judges Haynesworth and Carswell: Rejection of Supreme Court Nominees." *Quarterly Journal of Speech* 60 (December 1974): 477–88.

Wasby, Stephen L., Anthony A. Amato, and Rosemary Metrailer. "The Functions of Oral Argument in the U.S. Supreme Court." *Quarterly Journal of Speech* 62 (December 1976): 410–22.

Chapter 10
FOREIGN POLICY RHETORIC AND NATIONAL ORIENTATION

This chapter will examine foreign policy rhetoric as a vehicle for orienting America to the world by linking together the rhetorics of disparate domestic communities. It is impossible to cover adequately 200 years of foreign policy in one chapter, even a long one. Choices must be made. This chapter will follow major arguments, doctrines, and symbols as they have evolved through major state documents like presidential addresses. Historical causes and trends, policy analyses, and matters of international law will be treated superficially. This chapter is not about American foreign policy; it is about the political functions performed by foreign policy rhetoric.

Major Themes

Two themes undergird this chapter. One is the relationship between a policy and the rhetoric with which it is framed. Why did President Johnson send troops to Vietnam? Was it (1) to retaliate against attacks on American ships and marine barracks, (2) to contain the spread of communism, (3) to pave the way for free elections, (4) to symbolize American power, (5) to demonstrate psychologically his own strength of character, or (6) to protect American economic interests? The policy might have used any of these frameworks, since the framework defines the nature of success and failure.

This chapter will examine several cases in which long-standing frameworks were reinterpreted to frame policies on which an informed public consensus had yet to emerge, and it will examine cases in which presidents enunciated clearly and forthrightly new justifications for ongoing policies. Remember the distinction between the policy and the rhetoric through which it is argued, but also remember that policies are only understood by people through their symbolic interpretive systems.

The second theme underlying this chapter is that foreign policy addresses mold symbols, arguments, and needs into narratives to merge disparate communities into a nation united behind a policy. Nations expect coherent, reasonably consistent foreign policies from one another—elusive qualities in a system of separated institutions of diverse elected representatives sharing their legitimate powers. Every two years the American ship of state is rocked by a wave of electoral changes.

Coherence and consistency are achieved—when they are achieved at all—by presidents who depict their policies in rhetorical frameworks that are (1) familiar to the public and (2) articulated by the opposition. It has been said of President Carter that he thanked the wrong people because "he thanked the people whose advice he took." Rhetorically sensitive presidents bestow their symbolic rewards on their spurned advisors to soothe their needs for inclusion, affection, and control.

In the same sense, presidential speech writers often use the arguments and symbols of a spurned policy to justify a new policy—a new substance in a familiar package. Opponents cannot immediately argue against the policy without contradicting their own rhetoric, and supporters of the new policy swallow the rhetoric to achieve the policy. Problems arise when speech writers are excluded from the policy discussions and when they write ideas into the speech that failed in those discussions. These processes contribute to the increasingly frequent disjunctions between foreign policy rhetoric and actions, as when several recent presidents vowed never to deal for hostages while doing just that.

Let us consider the ways that presidents, in particular, have depicted American foreign policy for domestic and international audiences. American foreign policy rhetoric has moved through three evolutionary phases. From the framing of the Constitution through World War I our rhetoric stressed isolation and moralism; from World War I until 1947 we stressed the need to make the world safe for isolation; and from 1947 until at least 1988 we have engaged in a rhetorical cold war. Much as you remember only major incidents from your childhood and adolescence and nearly everything that happened to you during the last two days, our national interpretive system for foreign policy is built on old landmarks and a flood of recent events. This chapter will treat the three phases accordingly.

Phase I: Isolation and Moralism, 1787–1918

Young America was isolated by geography, by the primitive state of world transportation and communication, by revolutionary hostility from England, and by language and culture from France. The affairs of Europe were avoidable and young America concentrated on its domestic development.

President Washington's Farewell Advice

President Washington's farewell address moved "our detached and distant situation" from geographic necessity to strategic advantage:

> Why forego the advantages of so peculiar a situation? Why quit our own to stand upon foreign ground? Why, by interweaving our destiny with that of any part of Europe, entangle our peace and prosperity in the toils of European Ambition, Rivalship, Interest, Humour or Caprice. (Washington [1796] 1948)

Lest young America be tempted out of isolation, Washington warned the eight-year-old nation about bigger nations:

> The Great rule of conduct for us . . . is in extending our commercial relations to have with them as little *political* [emphasis added] connection as possible. So far as we have already formed engagements let them be fulfilled, with perfect good faith. Here let us stop. (Washington [1796] 1948)

Washington's approach to international relations was sceptically pragmatic: avoid outsiders except to facilitate the trade that helps us.

But Washington not only warned against treaties and alliances, he warned against relational feelings of friendship and hostility:

> . . . nothing is more essential than that permanent, inveterate antipathies against particular Nations and passionate attachments for others should be excluded; and that in place of them just and amicable feelings towards all should be cultivated. The Nation, which indulges in towards another an habitual hatred, or an habitual fondness, is in some degree a slave. It is a slave to its animosity or to its affection, either of which is sufficient to lead it astray from its duty and its interest. (Washington [1796] 1948)

Washington advocated a disengaged relational style to maximize our self-interests within a calculating power-based interpretive framework.

The farewell address can be read as a father-to-country chat about relationships. Solitude permits personal growth. The youngster is warned to stay out of other people's affairs and to put self-interest above either friendship or enmity. The youngster should be known and liked by everyone but bound to no one. Washington's advice may sound cold to modern ears, but it embodied a dominant theme of his day and legitimized it forevermore.

International relations in Washington's day were governed by the *balance of power principle.* The principle, evident in the Constitution's elaborate scheme of checks and balances, held that world order could only be maintained if the power of nations could be held in delicate balance, because wars were caused by power imbalances. Washington's warning against animosity and friendship sought to insulate America from European calculations.

Monroe's Doctrine of Hemispheric Neighborhood

If Washington rationalized geographic isolation and prescribed a calculated withdrawal from international affairs, President James Monroe helped to parlay isolation into international influence. The transformation began with a brief passage in his 1823 state of the union address, buried between the postal budget and population growth:

> In the wars of the European powers in matters relating to themselves we have never taken any part, nor does it comport with our policy to do so. It is only when our rights are invaded or seriously menaced that we resent injuries or make preparation for our defense. With the movements in this hemisphere we are of necessity more immediately connected. . . . [We] declare that we should consider any attempt on their part to extend their [European] system to any portion of this hemisphere as dangerous to our peace and safety. (Monroe [1823] 1966)

"Let's mind our own business" had become "Since we're minding our own business, we will not allow you to bother our neighbors." Later historians and diplomats grasped the importance of Monroe's statement. Perhaps more importantly they saw that the European powers seemed to have accepted it. They elevated and elaborated Monroe's statement and enshrined it as the Monroe Doctrine.

Imperialism and Manifest Destiny

Actually, the Monroe Doctrine involved America in international relations while claiming to isolate us. It did this by expanding the scope of "our business" to include the interests of our neighbors and by stating the conditions under which we would engage in power relations with other nations.

Washington's farewell address had warned against foreign entanglements beyond those necessary to facilitate commerce, and Monroe's Doctrine had pledged to protect the freedom of the Western Hemisphere. But the rise of American commerce in the late nineteenth century invited rhetorical adjustment because much of that commerce relied on hemispheric neighbors for resources and markets.

Events came quickly. In 1893, Hawaiian sugar planters overthrew the queen and applied for territorial status. Then the war with Spain brought us Cuba and the Philippines. Finally, we encouraged Panama's revolt against Colombia to permit construction of the canal. Americans needed a rhetoric that framed these developments in terms of isolation, hemispheric welfare, and moralism; and imperialist rhetoric performed that function.

The first contention of imperialist rhetoric was something that George Washington would have approved; America was acting to protect its expanded economic interests, no more and no less. Second, imperialists argued that America should protect the hemisphere by protecting our neighbors from themselves. As Albert Beveridge argued in his famous "March of the Flag" speech:

> The rule of liberty that all just government derives its authority from the consent of the governed, applies only to those who are capable of self-government. We govern the Indians without their consent, we govern our territories without their consent, we govern our children without their consent. How do they know that our government would be without their consent? Would not the people of the Philippines prefer the just, humane, civilizing government of this Republic to the savage, bloody rule of pillage and extortion from which we have rescued them? (Beveridge [1898] 1989, 374)

America's ability to protect our hemispheric neighbors and, for that matter, other non-European nations stemmed from the imperialists' conviction that Americans were better in *kind* than were these other peoples (Bass and Cherwitz 1978).

The argument that Americans were naturally superior to other peoples permitted the third imperialist contention—a moral obligation to share our blessings with inferior peoples everywhere. Again, Beveridge framed the issue:

> It is a noble land that God has given us; . . . It is a mighty people that He has planted on this soil; . . . It is a glorious history that our God has bestowed upon His chosen people; . . . Have we no mission to perform, no duty to discharge to our fellow-man? God endowed us with gifts beyond our deserts (sic) and marked us as the people of His

peculiar favor, merely to rot in our own selfishness, as men and nations must, who take cowardice for their companion and self for their deity? (Beveridge [1898] 1989, 374)

Beveridge's depiction of the alternatives subsumed the immorality of conquest and exploitation within a transcendent morality of missionary assistance. Imperialist rhetoric depicted national restraint and our respect for the sovereignty of others as selfish and immoral. One's recourse to the imperialist mission was to argue either that America was not God's favored nation or that Americans were not superior in kind to less civilized peoples—arguments that were difficult for politicians to extend.

The key response to the imperialist rhetoric came from Democratic and Populist presidential candidate William Jennings Bryan. Using America's colonial heritage to address the issue of superiority from the colonials' perspective, Bryan lashed out at Republican imperialists who had denounced Filipino objections to foreign dominance:

> Let them condemn the speech of Patrick Henry . . . Let them censure Jefferson; of all the statesmen of history none have used words so offensive to those who would hold their fellows in political bondage. . . . Let them censure Washington, who declared that the colonists must choose between liberty and slavery. Or, if the statute of limitations has run against the sins of Henry and Jefferson and Washington, let them censure Lincoln, whose Gettysburg speech will be quoted in defense of popular government when the present advocates of force and conquest are forgotten. (Bryan [1900] 1989, 393)

Bryan's interpretation of the imperialism question asked Americans to choose between two national identities: that of a former colony that supports freedom from colonial oppression and that of a colonial power committing the very acts responsible for its own revolution. For that reason, he said, "We cannot repudiate the principle of self-government in the Philippines without weakening that principle here."

The debate over imperialism employed two divergent narratives. Imperialists supported their programmatic preferences with sacred myths about God's chosen people, a sense of mission, and sacred obligations; whereas anti-imperialist arguments proved the more practical over time, but they were overpowered in the short term by the compelling power of the imperialists' sacred myths (Bass and Cherwitz 1978).

The controversy found resolution in Theodore Roosevelt's corollary to the Monroe Doctrine. Roosevelt's mostly imperialist Republicans wanted to expand international commerce under the "march of the flag" but the anti-imperialists and Democrats had correctly identified the practical difficulties. Roosevelt noted the need to protect American interests overseas and the absence of any means for enforcing international law other than force. "Therefore," said Roosevelt:

> it follows that a self-respecting, just, and far-seeing nation should on the one hand endeavor . . . to provide substitutes for war, which tend to render nations . . . more responsive to the general sentiment of humane and civilized mankind; and on the other hand that it should be prepared, while scrupulously avoiding wrongdoing itself, to repel any wrong, and in exceptional cases to take action which in a more advanced stage of international relations would come under the head of the exercise of the international police. A great free people owes it to itself and to all mankind not to sink into helplessness before the powers of evil. (Goldsmith 1974, 2:1236–37)

The Roosevelt corollary combined the imperialist themes of moral superiority and international involvement with the anti-imperialist themes of national restraint and respect for sovereignty. In practice, the Roosevelt corollary to the Monroe Doctrine came to mean that developing nations could govern themselves so long as they did so in accordance with American interests; when they failed to do so, we could intervene as a sort of international police in support of morality, peaceful isolation, and hemispheric protection.

The Monroe Doctrine and its Roosevelt corollary still undergird American foreign policy rhetoric. Today, it effectively means that we can intervene in Europe, Asia, and Africa and that we will take umbrage, and possibly action, if other nations intervene in South or Central America. Beveridge's rhetoric echoed loudly through the 1978 Panama Canal arguments of Phillip Crane and the New Right and in President Reagan's depiction of America's mission as the world's "last best hope."

Phase II: Making the World Safe for Isolation, 1918–1947

World War I was fought for three years before the Germans sank the *Lusitania* and goaded America to fight. President Woodrow Wilson's idealistic rhetoric essentially urged Americans to fight to make the world safe for isolation. But the postwar paradise could not materialize without American help, and Wilson's idealistic rhetoric propelled him full speed into the peace negotiations.

Woodrow Wilson's League of Nations

Wilson personally influenced the postwar world order at the peace talks by reconceptualizing the world in American terms. Wilson had realized that the world could no longer allow American isolation. Since the balance of power principle itself had inspired the mutual defense treaties that had transformed the assassination of Archduke Ferdinand into World War I, an alternative approach seemed essential. The nations of the world would establish a League of Nations to resolve disputes short of war, and America would join it to preserve our isolation (a logical twist worthy of Monroe).

But the triumphant president returned to find an isolationist Republican Senate unwilling to ratify the treaty. Wilson refused to compromise, even with moderates, and whistle-stopped in vain to pressure his Senate opponents. Although most writers have attributed Wilson's defeat to his rigid idealism (Blum 1956; Link 1957), Jeffrey Tulis argues convincingly that Wilson's difficulties stemmed primarily from his novel use of rhetoric. The technical points that Wilson needed to clarify the treaty for senators bored the public, and his emotional public arguments made delicate judgments in the Senate more difficult. Simply, Wilson used two conflicting persuasive styles to persuade two distinct audiences, and the approach compounded his problem (Tulis 1987).

Most Americans believed that they had won "The war to end all wars," as President Wilson had described it; and they had tired of war, moralism, sacrifice and "the gap between Wilson's lofty rhetoric and the peace treaty he helped produce" (Green 1987, 87). America preferred to be left alone, but the world was unavoidable.

The Good Neighbor Gets Involved

The Great Depression demonstrated the interdependence of twentieth-century nations, and Franklin Roosevelt refined America's role in his first inaugural address. "In the field of world policy," said Roosevelt,

> I would dedicate this Nation to the policy of the good neighbor—the neighbor who resolutely respects himself and, because he does so, respects the rights of others—the neighbor who respects his obligations and respects the sanctity of his agreements in and with a world of neighbors. (Roosevelt [1933] 1938, 14)

In Roosevelt's hands isolation became less cautious.

The Spanish civil war, the Japanese invasion of Manchuria, the Italian invasion of Ethiopia, and Hitler's war with Great Britain and

France made isolation difficult during the 1930s. Nevertheless, isolationists had national hero Charles Lindbergh and the "America First" movement, and they controlled foreign policy.

But American interests were intertwined with those of Britain and France. On June 11, 1940, Prime Minister Winston Churchill telegraphed Roosevelt that "nothing is so important as for us to have 30 or 40 old destroyers you have already had reconditioned . . . [to] bridge over the gap of 6 months before our wartime new construction comes into play" (Goldsmith 1974, 2:1749). What should a "good neighbor" have said to Churchill's request? The neighbor metaphor had invited the very feelings of friendship and animosity that had worried President Washington.

Roosevelt extended his metaphor. When your neighbors' house is on fire, he reasoned, it is in your interest for them to put it out before it spreads to your house. It is not, however, in your interest to sell your hose to the neighbors: you want your hose returned in good condition after your shared danger has been extinguished. He further depicted the destroyers as old, unused hoses ready to be sold for scrap metal. In return, Great Britain would grant 99-year leases for air and naval bases that would expand our defense outposts.

Attorney General Robert H. Jackson's landmark legal review assured him that the commander in chief of the navy was fully empowered (1) to assign those destroyers but not ships under construction to a nation at war without violating international law regarding neutrality and (2) to accept options for military bases without congressional approval, so long as no commitments, supervision, or activation were required (Goldsmith 1974, 2:1760–70). Presidents since Franklin Roosevelt have increasingly claimed broad discretionary authority in foreign affairs.

Debate raged about Roosevelt's lend-lease decision. Although very few Americans wanted a Nazi Europe, support for the Allies began a series of steps leading inexorably to our participation in World War II. It is debatable whether American isolation ended before or after the destroyer deal, but it was gone by December of 1941 when the Japanese attack on Pearl Harbor and the Senate's declaration of war ended American isolation.

World War II as Rhetoric

President Roosevelt's depiction of the Japanese attack was crucial to the war effort because it framed American involvement in terms that warranted the isolationists' support. Roosevelt's narrative contrasted American sincerity with Japanese duplicity and preempted the "isolated incident" reaction with its depiction of continuing developments. Although he could have said that the Japanese had launched attacks against Malaya, Hong Kong, Guam, the Philippines, Wake Island, and Midway Island, Roosevelt conveyed the sense of relentless onslaught with parallel structure:

> Yesterday the Japanese Government also launched an attack against Malaya.
> Last night Japanese forces attacked Hong Kong.
> Last night Japanese forces attacked Guam.
> Last night Japanese forces attacked the Philippine Islands.
> Last night Japanese forces attacked Wake Island.
> And this morning Japanese forces attacked Midway Island. (Roosevelt, 1941, 24)

What would tomorrow bring, peaceful isolation?

Roosevelt's depiction of the attack framed two implicit goals. The first was retribution: "No matter how long it may take us to overcome this premeditated invasion, the American people in their righteous might will win through to absolute victory." The second blended cousin Theodore's corollary and Wilson's cry to make the world safe for democracy: "We will not only defend ourselves to the uttermost but will make it very certain that this form of treachery shall never again endanger us." (Roosevelt, 1941, 25)

With the precarious dam broken at Pearl Harbor, isolationists were rhetorically stranded on an island of principle amid the raging floodwaters of duplicity, attack, retribution, and obvious vulnerability. Although Roosevelt's critics pointed to the destroyers and his lend-lease policy, to a general lack of preparedness, to carelessness, and to his alleged desire to enter the war, their concerns paled in the face of national peril; and it was the isolationist rhetoric that went for scrap metal.

Upon the death of Roosevelt in April 1945, Harry Truman ascended to the presidency almost totally unprepared. It fell to him to decide whether to drop the atom bomb on Japan. Truman released a statement announcing the Hiroshima bombing that echoed with the themes of Roosevelt's war address. For example, Truman said:

> The Japanese began the war from the air at Pearl Harbor. They have been repaid many fold. And the end is not yet. . . . We are now prepared to obliterate more rapidly and completely every productive enterprise the Japanese have above ground in any city. We shall destroy their docks, their factories, and their communications. Let there be no mistake; we shall completely destroy Japan's power to make war. . . . If [Japanese leaders] do not now accept our terms they may expect a rain of ruin from the air, the like of which has never been seen on this earth. Behind this attack will follow sea and land forces in such

numbers and power as they have not yet seen and with the fighting skill of which they are already well aware. (Truman [1945] 1961, 197, 199)

Hiroshima was retaliation for Pearl Harbor both militarily and rhetorically. Both were surprise attacks intended to destroy a nation's ability to fight (Hikins 1983). Truman completed the themes, goals, and imagery of Roosevelt's call to arms as the A-bomb produced his absolute victory.

The demonstration of the American A-bomb's awesome power—unknown to Truman or anyone else until after he had penned his statement—would, theoretically, make the postwar world safe for an isolated America: "With this bomb we have now added a new and revolutionary increase in destruction to supplement the growing power of our armed forces" (Truman [1945] 1961, 199). But the postwar world had changed irrevocably.

Phase III: Cold War Rhetoric, 1947–1989

An America accustomed to either isolation or war required orientation toward the postwar world. From 1945 to 1947, America heard three competing foreign policy rhetorics, each individually unable to orient the nation.

Three Foreign Policy Rhetorics

John F. Cragan (1981) has explained three distinct foreign policy rhetorics that were eventually combined to form cold war rhetoric. If we conceive of the postwar world as a cube, then these three rhetorics are its height, width, and length.

The Rhetoric of Cooperation

The rhetoric of cooperation envisioned a world of good and peaceful nations subject to two kinds of war: wars caused by international outlaws like Hitler and wars caused by conflicting interests. With the outlaws removed from the scene, peace-loving nations could resolve their differences through international forums—a World Court or a United Nations—and through combined police power to prevent the rise of new outlaw states.

Because this rhetoric made sense to two important audiences, it encouraged an unlikely alliance. Wilsonian Democrats perceived that World War II had proven the need for a League of Nations, and Willkie Republicans blamed individual leaders like Hitler and Roosevelt for entangling us in war. Peaceful isolation could best be secured, they believed, by establishing an international peacekeeping force to police the world and thus deter adventurous leaders.

Unfortunately, one of the police turned out to be the most adventurous postwar nation. The Soviet Union absorbed the nations of Estonia, Latvia, and Lithuania and refused to withdraw from Berlin and East Germany. They could do so because their veto power in the United Nations Security Council effectively disarmed the international police force and because the world knew the impossibility of invading Russia.

The Rhetoric of Red Fascism

The rhetoric of red fascism explained Soviet expansion with the rhetoric used previously to explain German and Italian fascists. It stressed a totalitarian police state able to disregard its treaty obligations because of its ideological commitment to international expansion. The rhetoric and imagery were familiar to Americans and still aroused tremendous moral fervor. But if indeed the Soviets were the Nazis reincarnate, then American foreign policy would have to eliminate the Soviet system to make the world safe once again.

But Americans were tired of war, if not warlike rhetoric, and war with Russia posed tremendous strategic problems. And yet, if the Soviets were indeed just like the Nazis, how could their threat to world peace be ignored? The red fascist rhetoric contributed mightily to Americans' diagnosis of international tensions, but it advanced no workable prescription.

The Rhetoric of Power Politics

The familiar balance of power rhetoric depicted Soviet expansion as a powerful nation filling a power vacuum. It rejected the cooperationist and red fascist notions of moral and immoral nations and suggested, instead, a world of amoral self-interested nations seeking to minimize their risks. The Soviets had taken advantage of the chaos to establish a buffer against future invasions.

Power politics was the province of an elite eastern, Ivy League diplomatic corps. Like their foreign counterparts, these urbane strategists could discuss dispassionately national interests and formulate practical alliances. Careful diplomacy occurs behind closed doors between coolheaded diplomats who know one another and their power resources. But many Americans had begun to view these elite diplomats with suspicion. Veterans and their families had fought and sacrificed to rid the world of people like Hitler, and they were suspicious of closed-door diplomacy by many of the people who had failed to prevent World War II and Soviet expansion.

The Truman Doctrine: Containment

The three rhetorics were merged into one on March 12, 1947, when Truman asked Congress for aid to Greece and Turkey. His new approach, labeled the Truman Doctrine, blended elements of all three rhetorics into a policy of containing communist influence.

The cooperationist ideal served as Truman's "paradise lost," as in his depiction of Greece as an "industrious, peace loving nation [that] has suffered invasion, four years of cruel enemy occupation, and bitter internal strife" (Truman, [1947] 1963). The peaceful Greek paradise had been lost because of red fascism, as his address merged nazis and communists into one abstract "cruel enemy . . . way of life":

> At the present moment in world history nearly every nation must choose between alternative ways of life. . . . One way of life is based upon the will of the majority, and is distinguished by free institutions, representative government, free elections, guarantees of individual liberty, freedom of speech and religion, and freedom from political oppression. *The second way of life is based upon the will of a minority forcibly imposed upon the majority. It relies upon terror and oppression, a controlled press and radio, fixed elections, and the suppression of personal freedoms.* (Truman [1947] 1963, emphasis added)

Truman's second way of life subsumes both communists and nazis.

Whereas the peaceful paradise had been threatened by red fascists, it had been protected by the U.S. But in the face of treacherous red fascism, the cooperationist solution *alone* would prove inadequate, said Truman:

> We shall not realize our objectives, however, unless we are willing to help free peoples to maintain their free institutions and their national integrity against aggressive movements that seek to impose upon them totalitarian regimes. This is no more than a frank recognition that totalitarian regimes imposed upon free peoples, by direct or indirect aggression undermine the foundations of international peace and hence the security of the United States. (Truman [1947] 1963, 178)

Truman's solution was not the red fascist's annihilation of Russia but a strengthening of the balance of power. The three principles that would become known as the Truman Doctrine sought to restore a favorable balance of economic, military, and strategic power in Greece, Turkey, and beyond:

> I believe that it must be the policy of the United States to support free peoples who are resisting attempted subjugation by armed minorities or by outside pressures.

> I believe that we must assist free peoples to work out their own destinies in their own way.
> I believe that our help should be primarily through economic and financial aid which is essential to economic stability and orderly political processes. Truman [1947] 1963, 178–9)

The red fascist threat to cooperationist peace was to be *contained* within a favorable balance of power, even if presidents would need to say, "The extension of aid by this country does not mean that the United States condones everything that the Greek [or later Korean, Vietnamese, Iranian, or Philippine] Government has done or will do." (Truman 1947, 177) The policy would be to support noncommunist governments under siege, whatever their failings, to avoid a power vacuum into which communism could rush, whether through armed aggression, internal subversion, or even free elections.

The Truman Doctrine speech marked the beginning of cold war rhetoric. Truman embarked on a balance of power policy clothed in the rhetorics of cooperation and red fascism. Danger would be countered with the open hand of the United Nations and the closed fist of economic and military aid for friendly, if imperfect, governments.

The MacArthur Challenge

The Truman Doctrine contained the spread of communist influence with economic aid and a patchwork quilt of mutual defense pacts like the North Atlantic Treaty Organization and the Southeast Asia Treaty Organization, which made an armed attack on one member an armed attack on all the others. The intent of these pacts was not to secure Belgian or Thai protection for America, but to prevent power miscalculations by the Soviets. President Truman, therefore, assigned Americans under General Douglas MacArthur to a United Nations "police action" in Korea in order to repel the North Korean aggression and restore the preinvasion boundary.

It was perhaps unavoidable that industrial strength personalities like Truman and MacArthur would clash over containment. MacArthur was a general who liked to attack, Truman was a politician who calculated risks, and they were half a world apart fighting a war. MacArthur openly criticized the administration's policy of containment, charged Truman with imposing unprecedented restrictions on a commander, defied Truman's ban on interviews, provoked unwanted Chinese involvement in the war, and issued a virtual ultimatum to the Chinese that made peace more elusive (Duffy 1988). Predictably, the president dismissed the general.

Although insubordination was the obvious problem, Truman emphasized MacArthur's inability to support the nation's foreign policy.

MacArthur received a hero's welcome and addressed a joint session of Congress, and his supporters called for Truman's impeachment. Some suggest that Truman should have stressed MacArthur's defiance to bolster his own credibility (Ryan 1987). But MacArthur's insubordination stemmed from his inability to understand the factors that made containment the only viable foreign policy. The larger issue was public acceptance of containment. As one critic observed, "Truman, unlike MacArthur, seemed more concerned with defending a policy and a principle, than with defending himself" (Duffy 1988, 93–94). MacArthur prophetically told Congress that "old soldiers never die, they just fade away," but the issue of limited warfare would not fade. The red fascist notion that the enemy must be vanquished, rather than merely contained, as well as anger about MacArthur's dismissal boiled beneath the surface of American foreign policy making during the 1950s and thereafter.

The Truman Doctrine frames American foreign policy still. It was evident in our foreign policy toward Afghanistan, Berlin, Cambodia, China, Cuba, the Dominican Republic, El Salvador, Grenada, Iran, Iraq, Lebanon, Libya, the Philippines, Taiwan, and Vietnam, to name only a few memorable cases. But within the cold war rhetoric heard since 1947, we can discern several distinct phases that deserve mention.

Superpower Confrontation, 1953–1962

Dwight Eisenhower, once an aide to MacArthur, ran for president on a Republican platform that pledged to "revive the contagious, liberating influences which are inherent in freedom" and to end "the negative, futile and immoral policy of 'containment'." But military experience caused Eisenhower to adjust his stance from the "retaliatory striking power" advocated by many Republicans to one of aiding "only by peaceful means, the right to live in freedom" because "The one—the only—way to win World War III is to prevent it" (Divine 1981, 14–16). The red fascist rhetors had suffered a major setback.

The Eisenhower administration expanded Truman's two ways of life into a moral crusade. Generals and coaches often depict conflicts as moral crusades to justify, to motivate, and then to excuse brutal acts that would otherwise be neither committed nor endured. Eisenhower's moralistic twist permitted Americans to adopt the communists' techniques to beat them at their own game—things like espionage, propaganda, armaments, and covert support of armed uprisings.

Eisenhower's rhetoric combined themes familiar to several communities by infusing Truman's framework with the imperialists' themes of superiority, morality, and mission. The moral themes undercut debate but constrained the administration's ability to negotiate and compromise (Wander 1984).

Nevertheless, Eisenhower's turn from liberation to containment infuriated many red fascist rhetors. Senator Joseph McCarthy charged that communists had infiltrated the American foreign policy apparatus, and his hearings terrorized Washington for several years until the Senate censured him. One of his supporters inferred that communists had taken over the Senate and founded the John Birch Society to recapture America from communist influence.

John Kennedy was very much the cold warrior for most of his administration. From his inaugural vow—"Let every nation know, whether it wishes us well or ill, that we shall pay any price, bear any burden, meet any hardship, support any friend, oppose any foe to assure the survival and the success of liberty" ([1963] 1964a)—to his remarks near the Berlin Wall—"There are some who say in Europe and elsewhere we can work with the Communists. Let them come to Berlin!" ([1963] 1964b)—Kennedy was committed to the Truman-Eisenhower policy.

But Kennedy inherited an Eisenhower-CIA plan to support a refugee invasion of Cuba at the Bay of Pigs, and its failure embarrassed the president and sent Premier Castro looking for protection from America. The Soviet missiles sent ostensibly to protect Cuba triggered the 1962 missile crisis, in which America and the Soviet Union moved to the brink of nuclear war over the balance of nuclear power.

Third World Brushfires, 1962–1972

In the Cuban Missile Crisis, Kennedy and Khrushchev both saw the need for a diplomatic safety net that could prevent nuclear confrontations. Kennedy, therefore, revised American policy in his American University commencement address ([1963] 1964a). He redefined "peace" from Truman's and Eisenhower's paradise lost to a practical objective, obtainable neither through conquest nor through nuclear balancing but by negotiating a series of concrete agreements (Wander 1984).

The pursuit of agreements required Kennedy to downplay ideological differences in favor of shared practical interests and to thaw the cold war by denouncing "unnecessary irritants and purely rhetorical hostility" (Windt 1987). Kennedy argued that total war was an irrational policy alternative, that nuclear arms constituted neither an efficient nor an effective deterrent, and that peace rather than war had to be "the necessary rational end of rational men." Under the old, now irrational assumptions, peace had seemed attainable through the stockpiling of nuclear arms. But the missile crisis had demonstrated that the Truman-Eisenhower solution had become the central problem: Superpower confrontations had become too likely, too explosive, and too difficult to resolve. Lest his audience reject his analysis as peculiar, Kennedy discussed the problems remaining between America and Russia and affirmed support for our allies—even more notably in his Berlin speech two weeks later (Kennedy, [1963] 1946).

The two governments quickly instituted the hot line, toned their moral denunciations down to pre-Eisenhower levels, and negotiated self-interested treaties banning above-ground nuclear testing and restricting the spread of nuclear weaponry. Conflict had begun to shift from superpower confrontations to developing Third World nations. Kennedy pursued this policy by preventing a power vacuum in South Vietnam. Although several credible accounts suggest that he planned to withdraw those troops after the 1964 election, Kennedy nevertheless used American troops to support a weak, corrupt, noncommunist government to avoid a power vacuum.

Kennedy's 1963 foreign policy evidenced all three rhetorical themes. The American University speech seems a return to the worldview of cooperation and trust, the Berlin Wall speech seems a return to MacArthur era red fascist rhetoric, and the commitment of American military assistance to South Vietnam seems a continuation of the containment policy. But taken collectively, these speeches suggest a revision of American policy within an ongoing rhetoric. Kennedy, and later Johnson, downplayed the moralistic two-ways-of-life theme so that he could work toward the technical management of practical problems (Wander 1984).

President Johnson exhorted Americans to dedicate themselves to the fulfillment of Kennedy's goals, and America cheered. But which of Kennedy's three foreign policy themes would he follow? Each had a constituency, and the new president needed to forge a consensus behind one of them. Johnson exploited a skirmish in the Gulf of Tonkin to legitimize a "spontaneous retaliation" planned months in advance (Johnson 1964; Cherwitz 1978). The Tonkin retaliation, coming as it did during August of the 1964 presidential campaign, completely preempted the appeal of Barry Goldwater's call for a tougher policy in Vietnam.

Because Johnson's early Vietnam rhetoric relied on the key symbols of "peacemaker," "enemy," and "savior," rather than on developed and documented arguments, it hampered public understanding of the war (Logue and Patton 1982). But lack of understanding and the use of compelling symbols can combine to evoke general support, and it worked just that way for Johnson. His personal commitment poured more and more resources—people, money, national prestige, and presidential credibility—into the poorly understood war. By 1968, Americans had begun to tire of a duty that had dragged on for too long, but the North Vietnamese and Vietcong continued to pursue what they perceived as a holy crusade (Turner 1985).

Had Johnson chosen to frame his Vietnam policy with tightly reasoned discourse, he might have confined criticism to reasoned discourse. But Johnson's early decision to circumvent the admittedly tricky rational approach created a divisive rhetorical situation. Because he had framed the war as a necessary symbolization of American values and character, criticisms of the war were widely construed as attacks on America.

Eventually, domestic conflict over this undeclared war led to a regime-level conflict over basic American values. Vietnam-era rhetoric brimmed with the core values of morality, peace, and patriotism (Smith and Smith 1985). Supporters of the war and antiwar demonstrators agreed that the Vietnam War was about the values of morality, peace, and patriotism; but they construed these three values in such different ways that two distinct cultures had emerged by 1968: "mainstream" America and a "counterculture." The net result was that the Vietnam War weakened rather than strengthened the balance of power because the war, and the domestic division it eventually engendered, expended more of our resources than it cost our adversaries.

Largely because President Johnson had earlier tied the Tonkin retaliation to his personal credibility and because he justified the war with symbols rather than information, he contributed significantly to a political climate composed of a failing war effort, declining personal credibility, and increasing disagreement over the meaning of America's cherished symbols and values. Under Johnson's care, the small transfusion to keep South Vietnam alive increased until the donor nation hemorrhaged severely, and the patient could not be saved.

Meanwhile, America was torn between Johnson's war on poverty and his war in Vietnam: which should get the whole-hearted effort implied by the war metaphor? His rhetoric exhorted Americans to wage war against both poverty and the Vietcong, confusing the public's sense of priorities (Zarefsky 1986; Turner 1985).

Americans drove Lyndon Johnson from the White House in 1968 largely because (1) he had failed to provide a coherent and compelling framework through which diverse Americans could reconcile and support his Vietnam and poverty wars, (2) the framework he had employed had contributed to deep cracks in the societal consensus, and (3) Johnson's rhetoric had emphasized his personal association with the Vietnam issue while associating domestic progress with the Kennedy legacy, thereby enhancing the stature of his primary opponent on the Vietnam question—Senator Robert Kennedy. Because this chapter concerns the relationship between foreign policy and social consensus, we must consider the dynamics of the 1968 presidential election.

By 1968, America was in shambles; the war was faring badly, and mainstream Americans were beset by black militants, by segregationists angered by what they perceived as federal interference in state governance, and by countercultures that advocated drugs and sexual freedom and opposed the war, established institutions, and power in general. First Johnson withdrew from the presidential race; five days later Reverend Martin Luther King, Jr., was killed; then Democratic front-runner Robert Kennedy was killed, and then the Democratic community turned on itself when the Chicago police of party kingpin Richard Daly clashed violently with antiwar demonstrators during the party's convention. Democrat Hubert Humphrey, Republican Richard Nixon, and Independent George Wallace each tried to find the arguments that would create a satisfactory national consensus.

Because Richard Nixon had always protected himself by playing his adversaries against one another, he was the candidate best suited to the electoral task of 1968. He exploited widespread public fears of Wallace, black militants, hippies, and demonstrators; and he used the Vietnam question to evoke support from conflicting communities. Central to his approach was the argument that national security prevented public presentation of his secret plan to end the war. Many who had disliked Johnson's restraint construed Nixon's ambiguous statements as a plan to escalate the war, and many who had opposed the war altogether construed them as a plan to withdraw from Vietnam. Nixon won the election with only 43 percent of the popular vote; which is to say that 57% of the Americans who voted in November 1968 opposed Nixon, and the 43 percent who voted for him consisted of some citizens who expected escalation and others who expected withdrawal. Nixon's presidential prospects were less than rosy.

Nixon kept his plan secret for almost a year, by which time the prospects of a 1972 Kennedy challenge had crashed at Chappaquiddick. Nixon's November 3, 1969, address announced "vietnamization" of the war, denounced radicals, and thanked the "great silent majority" of supporters. The new policy balanced bombings with negotiations, commitment with staged withdrawals, Kissinger's deft negotiations with Agnew's harsh denunciations, and antiwar demonstrators with the great silent majority (Nixon 1969).

The November address increased Nixon's approval-to-disapproval margin by a dramatic 21 percent to a level that he would never exceed. He had begun to forge a consensus where Johnson had failed; public approval of the president had moved in one year from -1 percent to +48 percent as the war dragged on (King and Ragsdale 1988, 299–302). How had Nixon done it?

The Nixon administration *affirmed* mainstream interpretations of American culture, treated cooperation and ambivalence as support, and transformed, where possible, Johnson's symbolic stances into rational policy arguments. They also *subverted* the legitimacy of opposing groups, especially those violently or even outspokenly critical of the mainstream interpretations. The Nixon-Agnew rhetoric had nurtured consensus in opposition to "troublemakers" (King and Anderson 1971). In short, Nixon's polarizing rhetoric used the war that had toppled Johnson to forge his consensus; Nixon's approval averaged 56.4 percent during the war, afterward it averaged 34.1 percent.

Détente, 1972–1980

As the Cuban Missile Crisis had steered Kennedy away from superpower confrontations, the Vietnam experience steered Henry Kissinger and his advisees—Presidents Nixon and Ford—away from Third World quagmires. Kissinger was a scholarly expert on power politics, and he guided America toward direct, but nonconfrontational relations with the Soviet Union by introducing China as a third factor. The Kissinger-Nixon-Ford policy played China and Russia against each other, much as Nixon had played Reagan and Rockefeller Republicans against one another to win the nomination. It took a lifelong red fascist rhetor like Nixon to establish relations with China and Russia without being branded as "soft" or "pink." Precisely because liberals called for a more cooperative policy and conservatives thought Kissinger too trusting, Kissinger, Nixon, and Ford could balance their critics against one another while pursuing détente. Ford defeated Ronald Reagan in the primaries and came within 57 electoral votes, and less than 2 percent of the popular vote, of beating Jimmy Carter. Although he was defeated largely on domestic issues, Kissinger's diplomacy came to an end.

President Carter lamented our cold, pragmatic support of ruthless leaders and restored moralism to American policy. He called for human rights and demanded that our allies prove themselves worthy of our support. But where the Eisenhower administration had portrayed an America embroiled in a cataclysmic struggle against evil, Carter urged us to enact that goodness. Carter's moral rhetoric indirectly encouraged the rise of conservative, moral voices like the Moral Majority and the Religious Roundtable. His human rights initiatives worried power politicians, who feared for our imperfect allies; and his rhetoric of kindness worried opponents of red fascism, who feared that he underestimated the communist menace. These critical communities found one another in the emerging New Right movement that challenged Carter on three fronts.

The New Right first challenged the proposed Panama Canal treaties of 1978. Negotiations to revise the arrangement between the U.S. and Panama had been supported by Presidents Johnson, Nixon, and Ford; but ratification came during Carter's term. He voiced arguments originally heard from the Nixon and Ford administrations and won the ratification vote. But the New Right stressed the vulnerability of a trusting America and warned that the treaties would enable Panama to hold America hostage. The New Right used the treaty vote to target, and to win, several congressional seats in November 1978.

A year later, Islamic fundamentalists stormed our embassy in Tehran and took the personnel hostage because we had granted asylum to their deposed shah. Red fascist and power politics rhetors saw in the hostages confirmation of their predictions about Panama, although there was no sign of communist influence and Kissinger had supported asylum for the shah. Carter urged delicate diplomacy but surprised his supporters with a military rescue mission that played the trump card without freeing the hostages. Events seemed to affirm the New Right's narrative, but where were the Russians?

When the Soviets, aware of our Iranian distraction, invaded Afghanistan in December 1979, the rhetorics of red fascism and power politics joined in opposition to Carter's policy. Carter did begin to act strategically, but his major responses were a grain embargo and a boycott of the Olympic Games, which infringed on America's economic and propaganda opportunities and avoided direct retaliation against the Russians. A rhetorically adroit president might have bolstered public confidence in our policy by attributing blame to the power politicians' miscalculations and to the animosity produced by our support of corrupt regimes. Not entirely unlike Johnson, Jimmy

Carter was defeated because he could advance no compelling, coherent foreign policy narrative to frame unfolding world events.

Standing Tall and Sitting Down, 1981–1989

A favorable balance of power cannot be sustained by a divided nation. President Reagan seems to have understood more fully than had Johnson and Nixon that real national unity cannot be achieved by attacking domestic adversaries. Reagan's first-term foreign policy addresses uncorked a barrel of vintage red fascist rhetoric and identified no domestic adversaries (Smith 1987). He used Afghanistan to intensify the red fascist themes downplayed since 1963, and he transformed Carter's moralism into a born-again moral condemnation of the Soviet Union as an "evil empire."

Reagan's red fascism relied less on developed arguments than on vivid characterizations of the Soviet Union. Robert Ivie has identified eight classes of metaphor used by Reagan to decivilize Russia for his first-term audiences (1984). The Soviets were depicted as a *natural menace* with images of darkness, shadow, and storms; as untamed *animals* that preyed on others; as *primitives* who were barbarous bullies; as unfeeling *machines* that were instruments of destruction and war machines; as cruel *criminals* who lied and cheated; as *mentally disturbed people* with deep fears and hostilities; as *fanatics* and *ideologues* consumed by their Marxist-Leninist religion; and as a *satanic and profane nation*, an evil, godless neighbor exercising arbitrary power. Ivie argues that Reagan's metaphors structured political reality for most Americans even in the absence of verification.

But when a Soviet fighter plane shot down a Korean passenger plane, killing hundreds of civilians in September 1983, Reagan had rhetorical verification. He exploited the tragedy by condemning the Soviets in inflammatory language, calling it a "crime against humanity" with "absolutely no justification, either legal or moral," and contrasting Soviet savagery with the behavior of civilized nations like ours. Soviet explanations were dismissed as "confused," whereas our evidence was "incontrovertible." The first half of the address was vintage red fascist rhetoric.

But the President's responses to this crime against humanity were unusually meek: he renewed a ban on Soviet flights to America, he called for resolutions of condemnation, he announced that his secretary of state would not meet with the Soviets unless they provided information and reparations, and he called for the passage of his defense budget (Reagan 1983a). Reagan's conservative supporters were outraged and called for a harsh retaliation, while his more moderate critics were relieved that he had not taken more drastic action (Ingold 1987).

Reagan used the KAL 007 incident to affirm his decivilizing metaphors and to reiterate his red fascist imagery. By invoking mild sanctions, he invited pressure toward the hard-line policies that he himself wanted to pursue and rendered potential critics as apologists for the Soviets. Subsequent investigations clarified many elements of the "confused" Soviet narrative and controverted some of our incontrovertible facts (Young and Launer 1988).

Also during 1983, Reagan stationed marines in Lebanon to fill a power vacuum and invaded the tiny Caribbean nation of Grenada. The terrorist truck-bombing of the Beirut barracks symbolized the frustrations of containment; and the easy victory in Grenada fulfilled the central fantasy of red fascist rhetoric, as American soldiers overwhelmed communists, liberated the locals, found arms and other evidence of a military presence, drove communist influence out of the area, and rebuilt a healthy "postwar" Grenada. Three decades later, General MacArthur's policy had been enacted.

By emphasizing scenic factors in his Beirut narrative and Americans as agents of change in his Grenada narrative, President Reagan distanced America from disaster and associated us with victory (Birdsell 1987). His narrative suggested that the spirit of red fascism that had caused the KAL disaster had inspired the terrorists who killed the marines and had sought expansion into the Western Hemisphere. The liberation of Grenada had driven that influence out of the Caribbean, serving as both a rescue and a retaliation. Most Americans reveled in the thrill of the Grenada mismatch, even though the administration had contributed to the communist coup by rejecting the overtures of a less radical leader. If America could stand tall in Grenada, America could stand tall anywhere else.

Red fascist rhetoric dominated Reagan's first-term rhetoric. He sought peace not through delicate balance but through superior strength—a direct repudiation of power politics. The evil empire imagery contributed to congressional approval of increased defense spending (Ingold 1987).

Reagan's red fascist rhetoric worked for a variety of reasons that soon changed. A string of ailing Soviet leaders had made clear and decisive responses to Reagan unusual, until the rise of Mikhail Gorbachev, a younger, progressive, more flexible leader. Second, Reagan had used a familiar narrative in which the U.S. was both moral and potent at a time when Americans hungered to see themselves as both. But because Reagan satisfied that hunger, our appetite changed toward normalized relations with Russia and arms limitation. Third, Reagan had attributed America's problems to external devils, thereby fostering domestic unification. But the Soviets stopped acting devilishly after the KAL disaster, and Gorbachev's policies of *perestroika* and *glasnost* undermined Reagan's depictions.

Reagan envisioned a Strategic Defense Initiative, known also as SDI or Star Wars, that would render all nuclear arms useless. Although its advocates claimed that SDI would bring military superiority and the ability to keep peace, power politicians warned that the potential for superiority could provoke hostile Soviet action to prevent a power shift. By lacing his SDI speeches with critiques of the principle of nuclear deterrence, Reagan spoke to people who perceived nuclear weapons as the preeminent danger. Increasingly, the evil empire came to consist of Middle Eastern terrorists and Central American communists, while Gorbachev came to symbolize reasonable, civilized leadership. This culminated in the arms reduction treaty of 1987 and in joint American and Soviet efforts to combat terrorism.

While negotiating arms reductions with Gorbachev, Reagan argued strenuously for aid to the Nicaraguan Contras. Congressional support swung back and forth on each vote, perhaps because supporters were split between the goals of overthrowing Ortega and containing his influence, a split aggravated by Reagan's movement toward Gorbachev. But in another sense, Reagan was able both to depict Gorbachev as an increasingly civilized negotiator and to preserve domestic unity largely because he transferred the evil empire imagery from Russia to Nicaragua, Libya, and Iran. The resulting White House frustration led to the Iran-Contra scandal that undermined aid for the Contras and hostage negotiations as well as public and Senate perceptions of Reagan's foreign policy competence.

Ronald Reagan served two rhetorically different terms; he stood tall during the first term and sat down to negotiate during the second. But there were other differences as well. His depiction of the Soviet Union as an evil empire evolved into a warmly personal working relationship with Gorbachev. His vow never to deal with terrorists evolved into the futile Iranian arms deal. His commitment to save American hostages evolved into a continuing Middle Eastern hostage problem. Refusal to negotiate with the Soviet Union evolved into a historic arms reduction treaty. And his clear, moral, and decisive rhetoric evolved into a confusing rhetoric that excused our attack on an Iranian passenger plane and failed to (1) win continuing support for Contra aid, (2) justify the Iran-Contra operation, and (3) topple a Panamanian dictator indicted for drug smuggling.

Conclusions

The early chapters of this book explained how individuals make sense of their environments, how they base their social groups on their interpretations, and how they attempt to define and order the world for those who fail to understand things their way. More recent chapters explored the institutionalized processes through which Americans attempt to shape America's choices. This chapter traced the evolutionary character, the interpretations, and the reinterpretations of American goals, values, and visions guiding our conduct in the world.

Our dominant national goal in foreign policy has always been isolation—to be left alone in peace. More badger than eagle, we have often been roused from isolation to fight fiercely for a cause that we perceived as sufficiently moral. But those periodic forays inevitably made isolation impossible.

After tracing our foreign policy rhetorically, it should be evident that the continuing principles, justifications, and visions are heard from various advocates and parties over time. It is less productive to discuss "liberal" and "conservative" policies than to study the process through which our presidents forged foreign policy consensus by interweaving arguments and policies from a coalition of interpretive communities.

Because both American isolation and the elimination of communism have been practical impossibilities since World War II, America has pursued a policy of containing communist influence that has dressed containment in a variety of rhetorical garments, depending on prevailing public needs. We have heard containment presented as practical politics, as a moral crusade, as a strategy of peace, as an international obligation, as a grand opportunity, and as a challenge to freedom. In each case, presidential statements ground administration depictions of our national security interests in past statements of principle and in terms of prevailing public goals, symbols, ideology, and visions in order to win public acceptance.

References

Bass, Jeff D., and Richard Cherwitz. "Imperial Mission and Manifest Destiny," *Southern Speech Communication Journal* 43 (Spring 1978): 213–32.

Beveridge, Albert. "The March of the Flag." In *American Voices: Significant Speeches in American History, 1600–1945,* edited by James Andrews and David Zarefsky, 374–8. New York: Longman, 1989.

Birdsell, David S. "Ronald Reagan on Lebanon and Grenada: Flexibility and Interpretation in the Application of Kenneth Burke's Pentad." *Quarterly Journal of Speech* 73 (August 1987): 267–79.

Blum, John Morton. *Woodrow Wilson and the Politics of Morality*. Boston: Little, Brown, 1956.

Bryan, William Jennings. "Imperialism." In *American Voices: Significant Speeches in American History, 1600–1945*, edited by James Andrews and David Zarefsky, 390–404. New York: Longman, 1989.

Cherwitz, Richard A. "Lyndon Johnson and the 'Crisis' of Tonkin Gulf: A President's Justification of War." *Western Journal of Speech Communication* 42 (Spring (1978): 93–104.

Cragan, John F. "The Origins and Nature of the Cold War Rhetorical Vision." In *Applied Communication: A Dramatistic Perspective*, edited by John F. Cragan and Donald Shields, 47–77. Prospect Heights, IL: Waveland Press, 1981.

Divine, Robert A. *Eisenhower and the Cold War*. New York: Oxford University Press, 1981.

Duffy, Bernard. "President Harry S. Truman and General Douglas MacArthur: A Study of Rhetorical Confrontation." In *Oratorical Encounters: Selected Studies and Sources of Twentieth-Century Political Accusations and Apologies*, edited by Halford Ross Ryan, 79–98. Westport, CT: Greenwood, 1988.

Goldsmith, William N. *The Growth of Presidential Power: A Documented History*. 3 vols. New York: Chelsea House, 1974.

Green, David E. *Shaping Political Consciousness: The Language of Politics in America from McKinley to Reagan*. Ithaca, NY: Cornell University Press, 1987.

Hikins, James W. "The Rhetoric of 'Unconditional Surrender' and the Decision to Drop the Atomic Bomb. *Quarterly Journal of Speech* 69 (November (1983): 379–400.

Ingold, Beth A. J. "Ideology, Rhetoric and the Shooting Down of KAL 007." In *Essays in Presidential Rhetoric*, 2d ed., edited by Theodore O. Windt and Beth Ingold, 415–28. Dubuque, IA: Kendall-Hunt, 1987.

Ivie, Robert L. "Speaking 'Common Sense' about the Soviet Threat: Reagan's Rhetorical Stance." *Western Journal of Speech Communication* 48 (Winter 1984): 39–50.

Johnson, Lyndon B. Radio and television report to the American people following renewed aggression in the Gulf of Tonkin, August 4, 1964. In *Public Papers of the President: Lyndon B. Johnson, 1964*, 927–28. Washington, D.C.: Government Printing Office, 1964.

Kennedy, John F. Commencement address at American University in Washington, June 10, 1963. In *Public Papers of the President: John F. Kennedy, 1963*, 459–65. Washington, D.C.: Government Printing Office, 1964.

———. Remarks at the Rudolph Wilde Platz, Berlin, June 26, 1963. In *Public Papers of the President: John R. Kennedy, 1963*, 524–25. Washington, D.C.: Government Printing Office, 1964.

King, Andrew A., and Floyd Douglas Anderson. "Nixon, Agnew, and the 'Silent Majority': A Case Study in the Rhetoric of Polarization." *Western Journal of Speech Communication* 35 (Fall 1971): 243–55.

King, Gary, and Lyn Ragsdale. *The Elusive Executive: Discovering Statistical Patterns in the Presidency.* Washington, D.C.: CQ Press, 1988.

Link, Arthur S. *Wilson the Diplomatist: A Look at His Major Foreign Policies.* Chicago: Quadrangle Books, 1957.

Logue, Cal M., and John H. Patton. "From Ambiguity to Dogma: The Rhetorical Symbols of Lyndon B. Johnson on Vietnam." *Southern Speech Communication Journal* 47 (Spring 1982): 310–29.

Monroe, James. Seventh annual message, December 2, 1823. In *State of the Union Messages of the Presidents*, edited by Fred L. Israel, 202–13. New York: Chelsea House, 1966.

Nixon, Richard M. Address to the nation on the war in Vietnam, November 3, 1969. In *Public Papers of the Presidents: Richard M. Nixon, 1969*, 901–9. Washington, D.C.: Government Printing Office, 1971.

Reagan, Ronald. Address to the nation on the Soviet attack on a Korean civilian airline, September 5, 1983. In *Public Papers of the President: Ronald Reagan, 1983*, vol. 2, 1227–30. Washington, D.C.: Government Printing Office, 1983a.

———. Address to the nation on events in Lebanon and Grenada, October 27, 1983. In *Public Papers of the Presidents: Ronald Reagan, 1983*, vol. 2, 1517–22. Washington, D.C.: Government Printing Office, 1983b.

Roosevelt, Franklin D. Inaugural address, March 4, 1933. In *The Public Papers and Addresses of Franklin D. Roosevelt, 1933*, Compiled by Samuel I. Rosenman. New York: Random House, 1938.

———. "December 7, 1941—A Date Which Will Live In Infamy—Address to congress Asking That a State of War Be Declared Between the United States and Japan, December 8, 1941." In *The Public Papers and Addresses of Franklin D. Roosevelt, 1941*. Compiled by Samuel I. Rosenman. New York: Harper and Brothers, (1941) 1950.

Ryan, Halford Ross. "Harry S. Truman: A Misdirected Defense for MacArthur's Dismissal." In *American Rhetoric from Roosevelt to Reagan*, 2nd ed., 92–101. Prospect Heights, IL: Waveland Press, 1987.

Smith, Craig Allen, and Kathy B. Smith. "Presidential Values and Public Priorities: Recurrent Patterns in Addresses to the Nation, 1963–1984." *Presidential Studies Quarterly* 15 (Fall 1985): 743–53.

———. "Mistereagan's Neighborhood: Rhetoric and National Unity." *Southern Speech Communication Journal* 52 (Spring 1987): 219–39.

Truman, Harry S. Statement by the President announcing the use of the A-bomb at Hiroshima, August 6, 1945. In *Public Papers of the Presidents: Harry S. Truman, 1945*, 197–200. Washington, D.C.: Government Printing Office, 1961.

———. Special message to Congress on Greece and Turkey: The Truman doctrine, March 12, 1947. In *Public Papers of the Presidents: Harry S. Truman, 1947*, 176–80. Washington, D.C.: Government Printing Office, 1963.

Tulis, Jeffrey. *The Rhetorical Presidency.* Princeton, NJ: Princeton University Press, 1987.

Turner, Kathleen J. *Lyndon Johnson's Dual War: Vietnam and the Press.* Chicago: University of Chicago Press, 1985.

Wander, Philip. "The Rhetoric of American Foreign Policy." *Quarterly Journal of Speech* 70 (November 1984): 339–61.

Washington, George. Farewell address, September 19, 1796. In *Basic Writings of George Washington*, edited by Saxe Commins. New York: Random House, 1948.

Windt, Theodore O. "Seeking Detente with Superpowers: John F. Kennedy at American University." In *Essays in Presidential Rhetoric*, 2nd ed., edited by Theodore O. Windt and Beth Ingold, 135–48. Dubuque, IA: Kendall-Hunt, 1987.

Young, Marilyn J., and Michael K. Launer. "KAL 007 and the Superpowers: An International Argument." *Quarterly Journal of Speech* 74 (August 1988): 271–95.

Zarefsky, David. *President Johnson's War on Poverty: Rhetoric and History.* University of Alabama Press, Montgomery, AL: 1986.

Chapter 11
POLITICAL MOVEMENTS AND SOCIAL CHANGE

Not all political communication occurs through legitimate channels. People frustrated by the response of institutionalized authorities to their grievances sometimes challenge the legitimacy of the political system itself. This chapter will examine movements as political phenomena dependent entirely on their symbolic manipulations. Our concern will not be with riots, spontaneous outbursts of hostility, or one-time protests but rather with large-scale, ongoing grass-root groundswells that influence thought and behavior. Although some movements achieve their announced objectives, most indirectly influence a political system's operation by altering the climate of prevailing opinion.

Movements Defined

A *social movement* is "an organized, uninstitutionalized, and significantly large collectivity that emerges to bring about or to resist a program for change in societal norms and values, operates primarily through persuasive strategies, and encounters opposition in what becomes a moral struggle" (Stewart, Smith, and Denton 1989). Let us consider the implications of this definition.

First, movements are interpretive communities of individuals arising from the bottom up, unlike the *established order* (government, corporations, contemporary labor unions, universities, and churches) that emphasizes legitimate authority from the top down. Members of the established order periodically voice movement sentiments, but only rarely do they condone the movement's tactics. Neither the soapbox orator's speech nor John Cougar Mellenkamp's "Scarecrow" album is a social movement, but such messages contribute to the general sense of movement by defining grievances and social identities and by prescribing alternatives.

Movements have no legitimate authority, and they are countered by the established order, whose allocation of authority and resources they challenge. Since they cannot legislate, decree, tax, imprison, enforce, or address the nation on prime-time television, movement resources typically consist of people, organizations, and argument—all of which require communication. We shall later examine the essential functions performed by rhetoric.

Social movements are organized but uninstitutionalized. *Organization* refers here to a coordinated division of labor that recognizes functional needs and offers a sense of collective identity. A collectivity is organized if its adherents have a sense of identity and leadership, otherwise it is considered diffused. The Religious Right of the 1980s frequently spoke of the secular humanist movement and its threat to Christian America, but few of the alleged secular humanists had any sense of organization or leadership. Secular humanism may be a philosophy, a doctrine, or an ideology, but it cannot be considered a social movement without organization.

Institutionalization, on the other hand, refers to legitimate and continuing influence on systemic behavior, usually through a law or charter that formally recognizes a role. Congress, the stock exchange, and the Catholic Church are all institutionalized organizations, as tax collector, attorney general, and president are institutionalized roles. The New Deal's National Industrial Recovery Act and the reorganization of the new Chrysler Corporation institutionalized organized labor by formally sanctioning labor's role in corporate management. Institutions influence our lives regardless of their temporary occupants because they provide the structural girders of societal organization.

Organization and institutionalization are not synonymous. Crowds are unorganized but uninstitutionalized; political parties and legislatures are institutionalized organizations; "we the people," the public, and voters are institutionalized but unorganized collectivities; movements are organized but uninstitutionalized collectivities. When an organized community is granted a legitimate, continuing voice in decision making, it becomes part of the established order and ceases to be a movement. Institutionalization alters a collectivity's resources and constraints and, therefore, its rhetorical situation.

This definition of movements resists the common temptation to differentiate between movements and countermovements for a variety of reasons, all related to the role of perspective in human affairs. Every movement seeks *both* to bring about some changes and to resist other changes. They may seek to change behavior and protect existing values, to change values and rationalize preserved behavior, to extend the benefits of citizenship to some communities at the expense of others, or to preserve the rights and privileges of some communities from the encroachment of others. The movement-countermovement distinction implies that two uninstitutionalized organizations fight each other, when in actuality both jockey for position to influence the society and its established order. It matters little to the established order whether a movement wants leftward or rightward change, since they are a nuisance and embarrassment in either case.

The most clearly embattled contemporary movements are the pro-choice and pro-life forces, whose frustrations stem largely from the established order's general avoidance of the fray. The wishbone model presented earlier suggests that the established order is usually unwilling to take decisive stands on hotly contested issues. Which is "movement" and which is "countermovement" is a matter of perspective, but both are movements.

Movements direct their primary efforts toward changes in norms and/or values rather than simple behavior. It takes a variety of people with overlapping, intense interests to create and sustain a movement, and those intense interests rarely overlap at the behavioral level. But at the level of norms and values, people talk about an abstract right to engage in a disvalued behavior like drug use, abortion, profanity, street preaching, or striking. Pro-choice forces argue that women should be allowed to choose abortion—not that abortions are desirable—even as right-to-life forces argue that one's right to choose pales in comparison to the fetus's right to live. Abortion is a behavioral decision that dramatizes the divergence between the value systems of two interpretive communities.

To qualify as a movement, a community must satisfy *all* aspects of the definition; it must be an organized, uninstitutionalized, and significantly large collectivity that emerges to bring about or to resist a program for change in societal norms and values, operates primarily through persuasive strategies, and encounters opposition in what becomes a moral struggle. One distinguished scholar has discussed the Johnson administration's war on poverty as an *establishment movement* (Zarefsky 1977), but that approach blurs otherwise distinctive rhetorical situations facing the disenfranchised grass-roots poor and the legitimate, tax-supported social bureaucracy. Conversely, protests, trends, fads, riots, and prophets are not unimportant; but they should not be confused with ongoing movements.

Causes of Movements

Why do movements arise at some times rather than others? Basically, movements arise when many people come to experience a shared relative deprivation that exceeds the credibility of the established order.

Relative Deprivation

Sociologists long ago concluded that discontent cannot be inferred from objective measures like per capita income, occupation, or political status (Wilson 1973). Happiness and discontent, instead, are personal judgments of our perceived accomplishments and conditions relative to expectations that we perceive as reasonable. When life's rewards fall short of our expectations, we experience *relative deprivation.*

There are three types and three dimensions of relative deprivation. We can feel deprived of *wealth, prestige,* or *influence* whenever we perceive these qualities to fall short of our legitimate expectations. The seriousness of each felt deprivation varies along three dimensions: the *magnitude* of the discrepancy, the *intensity* with which it is felt, and its *pervasiveness* in the community (Runciman 1966). Students of a dissatisfied community could construct a wealth-prestige-influence by magnitude-intensity-pervasiveness grid to chart the members' expressed dissatisfactions and to identify the interpretive framework to which movement rhetoric might successfully appeal.

People are most likely to experience relative deprivation when something familiar is suddenly taken from them. Nineteenth-century employers who announced wage cuts on payday frustrated their workers' economic, prestige, and influence expectations at significant levels of magnitude, intensity, and pervasiveness. In the 1940s, America thanked women for their work in defense plants by depriving them of their newfound self-sufficiency to make room for returning veterans. American authorities today seem less likely to frustrate people's expectations quite so blatantly, partly because of past movements.

Today, relative deprivation stems most often from *stalled progress* and *rising expectations.* Felt deprivation increases when the rate of progress toward expectations is slowed. It is not uncommon for people with a grievance to charge that no "real" progress has been made. A speaker might claim that blacks are no better off today than in 1950—despite the desegregation of public facilities, the extension of voting rights, the protection of civil rights, and the delegitimization of discrimination—because they have accepted second-class participation in a racist society. Another speaker might claim that women are no better off today than in 1960—despite an altered national consciousness, more varied professional opportunities, and a narrowing of the income gap—because gender-based inequities still exist. In both cases, the rate of change slowed, and this stalled progress has accentuated the sense of deprivation.

Because our sense of deprivation increases when expectations increase faster than rewards, a second source of relative deprivation consists of rising expectations. Rhetors inflate expectations by legitimizing hopes and dreams, by contrasting an audience's circumstances with those of comparable groups, and by using recent changes to nurture new aspirations ("Our new wealth and prestige have yet to be reflected in political power."). Progress kindles hopes and dreams, making expectations even less attainable as today's fulfilled expectations become the assumptions from which we approach tomorrow. A moderate dose of relative deprivation provides motivation, but an intensely felt deprivation of significant magnitude pervading a population must be addressed by that population's legitimate authorities if they are to remain credible.

Institutional Credibility

Everyone experiences some disparity between expectations and "reality," and it is up to the established order to legitimize the distribution of expectations and resources. The distribution need not be enthusiastically embraced by everyone, it need only be tolerated.

The established order may respond to dissatisfaction by emphasizing gains and marginalizing disappointments, by depicting expectations as unrealistic dreams, or by enhancing the community's perception of progress. These choices are risky, because every decision to soothe one constituency carries the potential for ruffling another. Through it all, the established order must remain *credible* among its citizens.

Of course, the established order is able to do more than handle transactions of wealth, prestige, and influence. Through transformational leadership, it is possible to enhance citizen identification with the symbols, values, and heritage of the society. The Nixon administration's Vietnam rhetoric, for example, enabled white conservatives disaffected from the federal government over civil rights protests to follow their intense antidemonstration feelings into patriotic support of the government.

In short, the established order must rebuild its credibility among dissatisfied, as well as satisfied, citizens. The wishbone model suggests that the establishment will compromise only as necessary to keep the ship of state afloat. When the established order accentuates the sense of relative deprivation, it pushes moderates further out on the wishbone. A power-wielding order that repeatedly denies its dissatisfied people economic progress, prestige, and influence and that fails to convince them of its trustworthiness, expertise, or dynamism will find itself face-to-face with a growing movement to seize its power.

Disaffection

If movements grow around relative deprivation and if the established order survives on its institutional credibility, then citizens' comparison level of alternatives is a pivotal concern. We saw earlier that relationships endure until one or more parties perceives a preferable alternative. Thus, individuals support the established order, however passively or inadvertently, until an alternative becomes preferable—just as the colonials remained British subjects until excessive taxation without representation made the relationship unbearable.

An individual turns from the mainstream to a movement when *dissatisfaction* turns to *disaffection*. When, in Eric Hoffer's phrase, people become, "sick and tired of being sick and tired" their sense of deprivation exceeds their sense of commitment, and the movement is preferred despite its risks (Hoffer 1951).

Most people need some kind of symbolic catalyst or *trigger event* to move from dissatisfaction to disaffection. Millions of perceived injustices increase dissatisfaction, but our confidence and belief in the system are rarely shaken by personal experiences alone. Instead, cultural disaffection requires a cultural symbolic shock. The Boston Massacre, the Dred Scott decision, the Pullman Strike, the Birmingham demonstrations, the Kent State shootings, and the Panama Canal treaties all led hordes of dissatisfied Americans to say, "That's it, I can't put up with any more of this." At such points, those persons found the movement more credible than the established order.

The established order's task becomes one of retaining its legitimate authority while reestablishing its credibility among the disaffecteds. Franklin Roosevelt's administration faced the worst domestic crisis other than the Civil War. The economy was dead on inauguration day, and a variety of movements had seriously undermined the established order's legitimacy. The New Deals of 1933–36 were far-reaching efforts to win back as many disaffecteds as possible. Labor was granted the rights of unionization and collective bargaining, Huey Long's "share our wealth" people were enticed with a progressive income tax, Townsend's petitioners for public pensions were lured with Social Security, and the list went on (Brinkley 1982). Roosevelt convinced both the unemployed and the working poor that he was one of them by working knowledgeably and energetically to solve their mutual problems. His effort was so successful that when his two most popular radical supporters, Huey P. Long and Father Charles Coughlin, turned against him over his moderation, Roosevelt rolled to a landslide reelection despite a still unhealthy economy.

It is important to emphasize that the established order can compound its problems by using coercive power against a movement. Examples abound: the Romans and the early Christians, slaveholding states and the Underground Railroad, nineteenth-century industrialists and nonstriking union workers, the British Empire and Gandhi's passive resistors, and the Chicago police and the 1968 Democratic Convention protests. When the established order's credibility is on the ropes, the use of coercive power against its own citizens is carefully watched by all.

Studying Movement Communication Systemically

The general analytical question about movement communication should be this: "Which individuals, conceiving themselves to be what "people" in what environment, use what relational patterns and what adaptive strategies with what evolutionary results" (Stewart, Smith, and Denton 1989)? This framework highlights the adaptive, interdependent, evolutionary, interpretive nature of societal communities and emphasizes the role played by depiction and interpretation as people reinterpret their world. This presumes that conflict and change can be both productive and destructive and that change should be managed so as to maximize the positive benefits and to minimize damage. But conflict and change cannot be prevented simply by welding fluid political persons, ideas, arguments, and goals in place.

This question enables us to examine political movements without adopting the perspective of either the established order or the movements. The more familiar, stability-oriented alternative (What do these troublemakers want, and why do they not use accepted procedures?), like the change-oriented alternative (Why won't they listen to the people when they know we are right?), adopts an ideological perspective before examining the evidence. Our interpretive approach encourages objective consideration of the merits of both the movement and establishment positions.

Which Individuals?

"Which individuals?" directs our attention to the persons who comprise the social movement and the established order. Certainly, this must include biographical information about leaders. Autobiographies of Mohandas Gandhi, Malcolm X, and Big Bill Haywood give valuable self-report insights into their movements' development and direction, and reputable biographies provide contextual information as well.

But we also want demographic information about the individuals who did, and did not, join the movement. Which individuals were they, what did they want, and how did the movement provide it for them? Surveys can be especially helpful. Fred Grupp's survey of the secretive John Birch Society's membership revealed that they were younger, more prosperous, better educated and more Republican than the rest of the nation, and that they had come of age during the Great Depression and World War II in the small towns of less populous or fluctuating states (Grupp 1971). In short, Birchers had grown up well off in a changing world in which their federal government had contributed to changes that increasingly threatened their sense of stability. Moreover, two thirds of the Birchite college graduates had majored in natural sciences, engineering, agriculture, medicine, and commerce. These were fields that emphasized a linear, prescriptive way of thinking, which compounded their difficulty in interpreting the complex sociological, psychological, philosophical, and political changes about them. These experiential factors nurtured a pool of persons particularly susceptible to the Birch Society's cerebral argument that America was fast declining because our institutions had been taken over by the Kremlin.

Scrutinizing the characteristics of individual leaders and members will help to explain their abilities and susceptibilities. But as important as who they are is who they think they are.

What "People"?

By turning our attention from objective characteristics to subjective identities, we focus on how individuals envision themselves as members of a community. A particular collective identity may, but need not, square with the demographic characteristics.

Michael McGee reminds us that communist, nazi, and democratic orders have all been legitimized in the name of "the people," but who are "the people," and how are their interests ascertained? McGee argues that "peoples" arise around symbols, cultural myths, and images from the collective past rearranged into a new vision articulated by an emerging leader (McGee 1975). Persons collectivize around the vision, and it gains force until it reaches a point of dissociation and decay, perhaps to be rediscovered by a subsequent movement. The established order frequently adopts these symbols, myths, aspirations, and images. For example, Democrats nominated Populist candidate William Jennings Bryan for president in 1900 and incorporated several Populist party planks into their platform.

Since identification is best accomplished through narrative, movements tell many stories about the deprivations of persons resembling their audience. The revolutionaries told about the Stamp Act, the Boston Massacre, the Boston Tea Party, Nathan Hale, and the Declaration of Independence. Union organizers sang of hardships, strikes, employer treachery, and strength in numbers. Student protestors told of Berkeley, Columbia, the Chicago 7, Woodstock, and Kent State. When a narrative dramatizes how "people like us" rebelled against similar deprivations, the audience can identify with the collectivity and support action in its interest.

But the most likely to revolt are rarely the most deprived. Organizer Saul Alinsky divided society into haves, have-nots, and have-a-little-want-mores. *Haves* protect their wealth, status, and power. *Have-nots* want some of what they lack, but because they must struggle to survive, they are typically resigned and fatalistic. The *have-a-little-want-mores* are "social, economic and political schizoids" who try to benefit from changes without risking what they have (Alinsky 1971, 12–21). "Want mores" are, therefore, the pivotal constituency in movement activism. Movements consist, in Alinsky's view, of a few have-a-little-want-more leaders able to mobilize have-nots. Movements generally fail if the haves can establish the movement's threat to the rest of the want-mores.

But remember that many of the most seriously deprived in a society may identify with the established order. Indeed, many persons respond to relative deprivation by rationalizing it. If they trust the established order, they can interpret their deprivation as a noble sacrifice or as "taking turns." They can marginalize the deprivation as unimportant or peripheral. They can use the deprivation to remotivate themselves to "open new doors." And they can retell the narrative, using the deprivation as a springboard toward a promising future. Deprivation and identification are rhetorical and interpretive processes, not mechanical and objective descriptions.

What Environment?

Persons and peoples exist in a depicted/interpreted sociopolitical environment consisting of interpretive communities, institutions, exigencies, needs, symbols, and reasons—all of which require depiction and interpretation. Who is in charge? Are the rules fair and appropriate? What are the current social and economic conditions? Is there growing sentiment to change things?

Every movement faces a we/they environment, but who is which? Having defined its own "people," the movement's depiction of competing groups will vary. Some feminist groups welcome male participation, some reject it, and still others have no clear policy. Some radical labor groups wanted a fair share of profits, while others fought to end what they termed "wage slavery." Rich white men over 30 were particularly repugnant to student protestors of the 1960s, regardless of their own affluence, race, or gender, because they seemed to have benefitted from a variety of social and economic injustices. Implicitly, any person free of wealth, whiteness, machismo, or excess years might yet have been reached ("Hey, man, why do you want to be like "'them?'").

The established order, therefore, needs to establish a convincing depiction of the environment, its legitimacy, and its efficacy. Most of that burden is borne by its ongoing claim to legitimacy, which provides a large measure of public presumption on its behalf. But the established order becomes vulnerable when its narrative depiction of the environment cannot be reconciled with the experiences of its citizens. President Hoover's unbending opposition to emergency relief efforts during the Great Depression and his unblinking optimism about recovery inadequately explained the everyday experiences of half the society, whereas Roosevelt's depiction provided greater fidelity. By transforming the established government and economy from an impediment into a pathway to a brighter future, Roosevelt short-circuited a variety of vocal movements.

Institutions like the courts, Congress, and police are buoyed by consensus authority beliefs, even when they are challenged. Antiwar protestors characterized police officers as "pigs" and baited them to overreact. When the Supreme Court ruled segregation unconstitutional and expressed concern for the rights of the accused, some of the disaffected attacked the legitimacy of the judiciary in books like *Nine Men Against America.*

One frequently used environmental technique is the *conspiracy argument.* Conspiracy arguments have six general characteristics. First, they try to establish the impression that all of our adversaries are in cahoots against us. Isolated, often divergent, "theys" are merged into one enemy whose powers are exaggerated through the alleged secret planning. Second, these arguments presume that the environment is so well ordered that all disappointments derive from the conscious, coordinated efforts of the powerful covert conspirators. Third, conspiracy arguments presume that (1) "God is on our side" and, therefore, (2) anything short of total success proves that powerful, unscrupulous, destructive forces must have been at work. Fourth, the conspiracy is a Manichaean struggle of good versus evil, in which a group of amoral supermen undermine an entire way of life unless stopped by militant crusaders willing to fight to the finish (Hofstadter 1965).

A fifth characteristic of conspiracy arguments, (the good ones, anyway) is that they are self-protecting; to disprove the conspiracy argument is to admit that you, yourself, have been duped by the conspiracy. Because the John Birch Society's Robert Welch argued that it was impossible to underestimate the communist conspiracy, he defeated every "But they would never . . . " or "But they couldn't possibly . . . " with a "See, you underestimate them!"

Finally, conspiracy arguments tend to be unusually complex and heavily documented, as authors demonstrate meticulously the existence of pieces and paths of the conspiracy. But it is one thing to prove that two people had an opportunity to conspire, and quite another to prove that they actually did so; especially when we claim to presume innocence.

David Brion Davis suggests that Americans historically have been susceptible to conspiracy arguments for three reasons (1971). First, conspiracy arguments attribute our frustrations and setbacks to other peoples' deceitful scheming. Second, our distaste for social classes and special privilege harbors a suspicion that they exist, hidden from view. Finally, a society that prides itself on its egalitarianism best explains gross inequalities as evidence of illegitimate power. In Davis's view, these three cultural susceptibilities contribute to the steady parade of conspiracy appeals in American rhetoric.

Conspiracy arguments are important because they describe a world whose actual operations are at variance with appearances. They attribute responsibility for unwanted trends to powerful individuals working in concert, thereby inviting morally outraged retaliation. Legally, it is insufficient to argue, for example, that President Kennedy could only have been killed by a conspiracy. It would be legally necessary to identify the specific individuals and to prove that they actually worked together to commit the act. But it is *rhetorically* sufficient for movements to advance plausible narratives that contribute to a sense of public dissonance. This causes people to reinterpret their environment and to reconsider their interpretive systems and communities.

Movements that rely on conspiracy arguments create an intricate subculture. Adherence to the movement requires either a detailed familiarity with the people, events, and dangers associated with the alleged conspiracy, a willingness to disbelieve one's prior interpretation at the direction of the movement's leaders, or both. These movements provide an unusually strong sense of inclusion by providing inside information and moral support that can be shared only with a select few. Once involved in an anticonspiracy movement, one's options are limited, since defection will be construed as proof of conspiratorial espionage.

Whether movements rely on conspiracy arguments or not, they must beware of the established order's pronouncements. Remember that the established order controls legitimate definitions and procedures. A movement that accepts the established order's vocabulary, logic, motives, and beliefs accepts the environment that justifies the very institutions, norms, and values it hopes to change. Groups of women and blacks pressured publishers to expunge sexist and racist language conventions from our books lest such constructions perpetuate discrimination. But distinctions linger. Women's athletics have received just enough attention to create nicknames like "Lady Bulldogs" that presume that the *real* Bulldogs are male. Every policy announcement and concession by the established order is presented in an official narrative that affirms not only its beliefs, priorities, and logic but its legitimate power to depict and interpret as well. Movements accept these "givens" at their own peril.

What Relational Patterns?

How do the individuals in the movement interact to alter their environment? Most people think of soapbox orators, placard-waving demonstrators, and crowds of marching people confronting authorities; and, indeed, these are relational patterns. But they represent only a few of the possibilities.

Grass-roots movements begin in familiar settings. Quiet and tedious trades like cigar making encouraged conversation to pass the time, and conversation often turned to life-style, grievances, and experiences in other places and in other jobs. But the noise in textile and steel mills long precluded conversation during working hours and, thus, slowed unionization. Miners working with dynamite, brute strength, and constant danger were prepared to take violent action.

Campus demonstrations were most numerous in the springtime, when students knew one another and had time to gather outdoors before finals week. When most universities moved exams to early May, they undermined the potential for continuing demonstrations. The civil rights movement developed in black churches, where morality, intense participation, a sense of worth, and a sense of community were already well developed. Relational patterns are significant because the nature of the forum—whether workplace, church, outdoor campus, or cramped apartment—enhances the participants' interpretation of appropriate concerns and values.

Relational patterns are also important as the movement and establishment select their audiences. Rhetors need to influence an audience capable of resolving their exigencey, but that requires careful judgment. They might need to influence a handful of officials, or they might need to change widely held beliefs. Movements usually need to enlist the sympathy and support of unaffected and disinterested citizens if they are to convince the established order that it is out of step with "the will of the people."

The movement must therefore convince uncaring moderates that their interests lie with the movement. Two examples illustrate the volatility of these relational choices. Independent truckers during the late 1970s wanted to mobilize public opinion against shippers in order to bring about a favorable labor settlement. They tried to summon that pressure by clogging interstate highways with 35-miles-per-hour truck convoys. The public was indeed outraged, but not at the shippers. The truckers quickly settled their dispute on unfavorable terms. Their strategy had alienated hordes of disinterested moderates driving innocently to Grandma's for the weekend and, thereby, validated the employers' "unreasonable troublemakers" narrative.

Unemployed Pittsburgh steelworkers protested the Carnegie-Mellon Bank's investment in foreign steel production by renting safe deposit boxes for the safekeeping of dead fish. With the protestors absent from the scene and the fish ripening by the hour, customers of the posh bank held the management accountable for the stench. The protestors' central argument—that Carnegie-Mellon Bank was rigid and insensitive to the needs of the people it served—was dramatized by creating a situation in which monied customers experienced similar insensitivity. The bank eventually modified its policy.

Both protests dramatized worker complaints and brought previously uninvolved and disinterested citizens into the play. Because the truckers posed a direct and visible source of annoyance, they reaped public anger; but the bank itself was the direct and visible source of annoyance. Once involved and interested, the citizenry pressured those it held accountable. The truckers failed because they visibly antagonized the wrong audience, while the steelworkers succeeded by creating depositor-bank interaction.

Several movements have used small group meetings to identify concerns and common interests. These discussions tend to move through four distinct stages (Chesebro, Cragan, and McCullough 1973). The first stage is a *self-realization of a new identity* in which participants claim or admit a characteristic that is unjustly oppressed by the larger society. They then *develop a group identity through polarization* as the nature of the experienced deprivation and its source are agreed on, and expressions of "I" and "you" become "we" and "they." Third stage participants identify and reject the establishment values responsible for the deprivation and *establish new values for the group*. Finally, the group *relates to other revolutionary groups* by considering how established values, as well as the group's newly identified values, may oppress others. Some groups fragment in the face of their own inclination to oppress, while others find solidarity with people oppressed for other reasons.

What Adaptive Strategies?

Social movements are communities of individuals adapting with their environment. Remember that the adaptive process is symbiotic; we adapt to our environment and we adapt our environment to us. Wise movement strategies grow out of a realistic appraisal of individual, collective, institutional, and environmental resources and vulnerabilities. There are no uniformly effective strategies because no two movements are ever identical, no two situations are ever identical, and societies evolve based on previous movements and other changes.

Movement strategy, like electoral strategy, can be properly appraised only after demographics, perceptions, environments, and constraints have been identified. Too many observers pronounce a strategy wise or clever because it once worked for another movement on another day. There are two problems with that approach. First, it oversimplifies by ignoring the variables that influence success. Passive resistance worked in India and America largely because it was directed at the deep-seated Anglo and American pride in fairness and community. It is doubtful that passive resistance by Jews would have deterred Hitler's plan for genocide; and it is less than certain that it will induce South African whites—largely isolated from Anglo-American culture and accustomed to hardship and survival tactics—

to end apartheid. Secondly, persuasiveness is undermined when audiences detect or suspect strategizing. As in used-car sales, magazine sweepstakes, scripted telephone solicitations, and dating behavior, detected strategizing may be successful; but the sense of recognition and observation distances an audience from the immediate message and recalls prior incidents.

The movement's choice of strategies is ideally guided by the its need to accomplish five rhetorical functions (Stewart, Smith, and Denton 1989). If these functions are performed inadequately, the movement will fail. The movement must effectively *transform perceptions of history* by providing an alternative narrative of the past, present, and future. Second, the movement must effectively *transform perceptions of society* by providing an alternative characterization of social groups, forces, and institutions. Third, the movement must channel dissonance and thought by *prescribing courses of action* for those who accept the narrative and characterization. The movement must also offer and encourage mobilization for action, not only to bring about the desired change but to dramatize its narrative- characterization prescription and to establish its viability in the public eye. Fifth, strategic choices must provide a basis for *sustaining the movement* lest supporters lose interest or commitment after a particular demonstration or campaign.

As long as there is a movement, the functions are performed; and as long as the functions are performed, there is a movement. Functional behaviors are the life signs of movements. Stop the historical and societal transformations and the movement is disoriented; stop prescribing and mobilizing and the movement is lethargic or handicapped; stop sustaining and the movement is comatose. Students of movement rhetoric can compare various movements' performance of these five rhetorical functions.

Movements manage their resources relative to those of the established order, and they must be careful to maximize rather than to deplete those resources. They need to anticipate the institutional response and to work to produce a preferred instrumental reaction. Second, movements can perform these functions either strategically or casually; just as you can either monitor your diet for calories, cholesterol, and sodium or wolf down whatever sounds good at the moment. Movements that act and react without strategically considering their alternatives take unnecessarily grave risks.

John Waite Bowers and Donovan Ochs have catalogued the general strategies of agitation and control (1971). The strategy of *petition* entails the movement's presentation to established authorities of a formal demand signed by many people. Sometimes it works. But by denying a petition, the establishment denies change within the legitimate system and pushes the dissatisfied toward disaffection. Through the accumulation of signatures, the task orientation, the painless method of signifying support, and the symbolic formal presentation to leaders, petition performs all five functions. But petitions grant the legitimacy of established authority by requesting that it accede to their petition, and establishments usually refuse, sometimes roughly.

Promulgation is the preparation and dissemination of the movement's diagnosis, prognosis, and prescription for societal improvement. Soapbox orators, pamphlets, slogans, songs, plays, placards, buttons, teach-ins, and parades all attract attention and articulate the theme, often using conspiracy argument to account for the failure of petition. Sometimes, promulgation can modify pressures on the wishbone just enough to bring about compliance with a second petition before widespread antagonisms develop; and sometimes promulgators antagonize law enforcement personnel.

Polarization is the movement's effort to break with the established order by creating its own culture and jargon. The goal is to make it difficult for persons sympathetic to the movement's deprivation to maintain their allegiance to the established order. The movement develops a highly differentiated construct system of god and devil terms that compel individuals to take sides. The counterculture of the 1960s and the Black Power movement used this strategy to advantage.

Polarization is often dramatized through *nonviolent resistance*, which is public noncooperation for the purpose of advancing a cause. Many forms of passive resistance are nonverbal and subtle. The counterculture movement of the 1960s resisted established norms by enacting their prescription to "Do your own thing" with long hair, beards, beads, drugs, tie-dyed T-shirts, psychedelic posters, and acid rock. The liberation phase of the women's movement resisted established norms with pantsuits, slacks, harsh language, cohabitation, and an avoidance of bras and cosmetics. Individuals polarized from the established order can nonverbally make personal statements that require no direct confrontation with authorities.

It is also possible to resist laws and procedures nonviolently. Bowers and Ochs differentiate between nonviolent resistance that seeks no response and the strategy of escalation and confrontation, which invites overreaction. Some antiwar protestors refused to pay income taxes on the grounds that their money would be used to finance war. This nonpayment differed from normal tax evasion because it was (1) publicly announced and (2) designed to advance a cause rather than personal fortune—some contributed an equivalent amount to the movement—and (3) the protestors presented their cases in court and accepted punishment. However, conflict was not assured, since the IRS prosecutes a finite number of tax evasion cases and the government could have chosen to avoid publicizing opposition to the war.

Escalation and confrontation occurs when a movement engages in an activity that cannot be ignored by legitimate authorities. Autoworkers sat down in a plant to simultaneously stop work and prevent the introduction of strikebreakers. Management could not leave the valuable plant in the hands of angry workers, but the siege and assault that followed contributed to the union's argument that corporations owned the government. Civil rights demonstrators would enter segregated facilities and then passively resist invitations to leave, compelling police to remove them. But the white establishment's use of police dogs, electric cattle prods, clubs, and generally rough treatment shocked the rest of the nation where integration was not criminal. Escalation and confrontation is a strategy designed to disorient moderates by validating movement depictions of institutional injustice.

When escalation and confrontation fail, some movements turn to a combination strategy misleadingly called by Bowers and Ochs *guerilla and Gandhi.* This strategy couples violent acts by some parties with nonviolent acts by others to create a contrast that enhances the appeal of moderates. Only rarely does this approach come from unified leadership. Instead, it occurs as factions develop over the need for direct action. While the American Federation of Labor struck for better wages and working conditions, the Industrial Workers of the World resorted to bombings and assassinations. While Martin Luther King, Jr. led nonviolent protests, Black Panthers carried arms and other militants rioted. This distinction highlights again the necessity of differentiating between movements and the diverse organizations of which they are comprised.

With few exceptions, American institutions have been more responsive to nonviolent protests when violent protests rendered the moderates comparatively attractive. But in many other cases, the actions of the violent fringe discredited moderates and seriously damaged the movement. It is a delicate "carrot and stick" strategy that almost always turns out badly for the stick wielders. Nevertheless, our institutions have often found carrots tastier when stick wielders were nearby.

An all-out *guerrilla* strategy consists of terrorism, sabotage, and destruction intended to hamper the continuance of established practices. The destruction of plant machinery and mines, the bombing of abortion clinics, the destruction of draft records, the assassination of authorities, and brutalizations by Ku Klux Klan and Nazi agents exemplify this strategy. These acts differ from strategic acts of *revolution* because they are individual acts rather than part of a concerted plan to overthrow the established order through force and violence. Guerrilla acts leave the basic institutional structure intact, revolutionary acts do not.

The establishment's first response is usually *avoidance*, in the hope that an isolated incident by a handful of unsophisticated malcontents will blow over. Authorities can route the complaint through a labyrinth designed to bury it in red tape, engage in counterpersuasion, or simply pretend not to notice it. If their estimation of the movement is correct, they can put the controversy to rest. But if they underestimate the movement's sophistication or the appeal of its narrative, then their avoidance enables the movement to gather strength.

A second common institutional response is *suppression*—an overt effort to stop the movement in its tracks. Government can *harass* movement members in a variety of ways: by auditing their taxes, by mocking their "funny" clothes, by arguing with petitioners, or by heckling speakers. They can explicitly *deny* the movement's demands, but that confirms the movement's existence and significance; or they can deny its means to organize or protest by requiring parade permits and imposing curfews or other restrictions. They may *banish* movement leaders, as when Attorney General A. Mitchell Palmer's 1920 "Red Raids" rounded up suspected Bolsheviks for deportation. Or they may *purge* the movement from society by declaring war on it, as Great Britain has done with the Irish Republican Army.

Suppression may be necessary and advisable when guerrilla and revolutionary acts needlessly endanger innocent people, and these tactics may work when there are but a handful of extremists. But we have already seen that suppression plays into the hands of a movement's escalation and confrontation strategy by creating martyrs and rallying points. The Romans could not suppress Christianity; the British could suppress neither American nor Indian independence movements; and segregationists could not suppress civil rights. But the temptation is nevertheless strong. It is worth repeating that suppression is sometimes necessary and advisable, but precisely when it is necessary and advisable is a difficult question that demands every citizen's careful thought. Suppression simply to preserve one's self-interest can be both immoral and counterproductive.

The established order's third strategic option entails an *adjustment* of its norms, values, or behavior. It might accept the movement's less controversial demands, such as a wage increase without granting the right to unionize; or it might make a procedural change without granting the substantive demand, such as accepting student input without changing university policy.

The established order will sometimes co-opt the movement by taking over its personnel, appointing a student to the dean's task force, or advocating its issues, as when the Johnson administration pressed to reform voting rights. Imagine the dilemma had the president appointed Martin Luther King, Jr., as a special assistant secretary of health, education and welfare for racial justice! Bureaucratic flypaper would have precluded his effectiveness, but the administration could have directed attention to his appointment as an indication of its sincerity while (1) radicals disavowed King for selling out to the system and (2) moderates searched for a new leader. But in refusing such an appointment King would have undermined his credibility with the have-a-little-want-mores.

Precisely because co-optation and adjustment are powerful responses to movement strategies, movements ask for considerably more than they want. Frequently, an adjustment by the establishment gives them precisely what they most wanted, although some supporters will be disappointed.

The establishment's final option is complete *capitulation* to the movement's demands. This is rare. Remember that the establishment is at the top of a wishbone pulled by opposing forces. If it capitulates to the movement it will betray the pressures of its opposing constituencies: those who dislike the movement's goals, those who dislike its means, those who simply like stability, and those who think the establishment has already yielded too much. Moreover, movements are so large, diverse, and uninstitutionalized that factions will disagree about the object of capitulation. A lame-duck official could conceivably say, "I will concede anything on which you agree *unanimously*" and then allow infighting among factions to fritter away the opportunity. Finally, capitulation is rare because it denies established authorities any opportunity to save face. They often see capitulation as both a personal defeat and a rejection of the established order's historical and societal narrative.

The student of political movement persuasion needs to identify the strategies used and the pattern or sequence in which they occur. One movement may tarry too long with avoided petitions, while another may invite banishment and purging with guerrilla acts that repel moderates. One movement may use a single strategy for a number of issues and audiences, while another may use a variety of strategies for a handful of issues and audiences. Those are rhetorical choices that merit critical scrutiny.

What Evolutionary Results?

As communities of people use communication to adapt to one another and to their environment, everything changes. It is therefore possible to identify evolutionary phases or stages in movement persuasion by isolating recurrent patterns.

Charles J. Stewart has suggested a five-stage life cycle of social movements based on the rhetorical functions dominant at each point (Stewart, Smith, and Denton, 1984). The life cycle begins during quiet times. But even when no exigence, audience, or collective identity attracts unusual attention, there are philosophers, poets, theologists and social critics thinking about life as it is, as it can be, and differences between the two. During this *genesis* stage, the exigence or deprivation is identified; but few people pay attention. The concerned few expect the established order to resolve the problem, and, indeed, they normally do. Even if the establishment continues to ignore the deprivation, little happens unless a significant segment of society perceives it as an exigence. Eventually some trigger incident—like Rosa Parks's refusal to sit in the back of a Montgomery bus—dramatizes the exigence, validates the percolating concern, and draws public attention to the deprivation.

Public attention ushers in the *social unrest* stage of the movement's life cycle. The quiet thinkers are replaced by agitators able to relate the exigence to the experiences and interpretive systems of potential adherents. Effective agitators draw on their audience's motives, beliefs, and need for narrative coherence and fidelity to create dissonance about the exigence and the credibility of the established order. The embryonic movement may proclaim its vision with a manifesto advancing its diagnosis of the social ill, its prognosis, and its prescription for action.

The thinkers' message is transformed as it is embraced by still more people, and the excitement of fantasy chaining itself nurtures a sense of collective identity. Movement adherents petition and promulgate, while authorities avoid or suppress.

Social unrest sometimes evolves into *enthusiastic mobilization* by movements and the establishment. During this stage, people aroused by the agitators begin to discover common interests and directions. But immigrant workers speaking a variety of languages, young people pocketed on university campuses, and affluent housewives scattered across the nation do not coalesce magically into movements. Pulling these people together and directing their efforts is a complicated task requiring creativity and organizational skills. The agitators who had replaced the thinkers are themselves replaced by organizers.

The establishment must now take the movement seriously and either suppress it or adapt to it. Suppression will either set the movement back or lead to escalation; while adaptation will either satisfy their demands or whet their appetite. Once matters have gone this far, we typically see a series of exchanges between the movement's nonviolent, confrontational, and guerrilla acts and the establishment's suppressive and adaptive responses. This is the most visible and familiar stage of movement activity.

The fourth stage of the movement life cycle is a *maintenance period.* The movement-establishment clashes take a serious toll on the movement, and some of its leaders and many of its members will be tempted to leave the movement. They become tired of the fines, jail terms, and loss of employment. They become tired of the indirect hardships of commitment, like ill health, broken friendships and marriages, and the absence of leisure time. Some find other causes to pursue; some leave because their particular objective or moment has passed; and some leave simply because the novelty has gone.

The final defeat of the Equal Rights Amendment hurt the woman's movement deeply, not so much because the amendment was not enacted (it had served as a potent rhetorical vehicle for changing national norms) but because so many adherents saw ERA as the movement's sole objective. Movements need back-burner issues to sustain interest and enthusiasm during dry spells.

A movement must maintain its vitality if it wants to preserve its gains. We have all read about this scenario many times: (1) workers demand a raise but management refuses them, so (2) the workers vote to unionize and management responds with a nice raise, so (3) the workers shrewdly reject the union, and (4) management cancels the raise.

Because authorities wield their greatest strength during quiet times, they should resist the temptation to land a knockout punch. President Nixon's staged troop withdrawal's had begun to defang the antiwar movement in early 1970 until his decision to protect the withdrawal by invading Cambodia triggered demonstrations and student strikes across the country. Establishments can avoid creating new triggering incidents that could foster a new wave of mobilization by letting the movement slip from view, by adjusting to its more compelling points, or by co-opting the elements that appeal to persuadable constituencies.

The fifth stage of the life cycle is *termination*, in which the movement ceases to be a movement. The movement may lose its adherents, its organization, or its program for change or it may itself become part of the established order like the League of Women Voters or the AFL-CIO. The movement and its leaders, martyrs, incidents, symbols, and arguments become part of the larger culture to be rediscovered by future philosophers, poets, and social critics who ponder life as it might have been.

Conclusions

A movement is not necessarily a bad thing, but it is symptomatic of relational problems. A movement suggests that an established order permitted a keenly felt grievance to fester. Most of us, most of the time, find most movements and demonstrations irritating—trouble-making misfits making a big fuss about nothing. They arise around a sharp sense of relative deprivation and an established order unable to maintain its credibility.

No society can thrive if its political order changes hands with every controversy. But the Framers predicated the American constitutional system on the social contract between government and the governed, and they guaranteed the rights of peaceful assembly, free speech, and a free press as means of enforcing that contract. All Americans are today grateful to those who protested against British imperialism, slavery, child labor, and racial segregation; and most appreciate the efforts of those who protested for collective bargaining, Social Security, and every American's right to vote. Had those protestors yielded to legitimate authority in their day, we would still live in slave-holding British colonies governed by white males over 21. Sometimes extrasystemic protest is both permissable and necessary. But when?

Students of movement persuasion need to consider a variety of factors before drawing their conclusions. The admittedly cumbersome question "Which individuals, conceiving themselves to be what 'people' in what environment, use what relational patterns and what adaptive strategies with what evolutionary results" frames those factors developmentally.

References

Alinsky, Saul. *Rules for Radicals: A Pragmatic Primer for Realistic Radicals.* New York: Random House, 1971.

Bowers, John Waite, and Donovan J. Ochs. *The Rhetoric of Agitation and Control.* Reading, MA: Addison-Wesley, 1971.

Brinkley, Alan. *Voices of Protest: Huey Long, Father Coughlin, and the Great Depression.* New York: Alfred A. Knopf, 1982.

Chesebro, James W., John F. Cragan, and Patricia McCullough. "The Small Group Technique of the Radical Revolutionary: A Synthetic Study of Consciousness Raising. *Speech Monographs* 40 (June 1973): 136–46.

Davis, David Brion. *The Fear of Conspiracy.* Ithaca, NY: Cornell University Press, 1971.

Grupp, Fred W. "Personal Satisfaction Derived from Membership in the John Birch Society." *Western Political Quarterly 24 (March 1971): 79–83.*

Hoffer, Eric. *The True Believer.* New York: Mentor, 1951.

Hofstadter, Richard. *"The Paranoid Style in American Politics" and Other Essays.* New York: Alfred A. Knopf, 1965.

McGee, Michal C. "In Search of 'The People,': A Rhetorical Alternative. *Quarterly Journal of Speech* 61 (October 1975): 235–49.

Runciman, Walter. *Relative Deprivation and Social Justice.* Berkeley: University of California Press, 1966.

Stewart, Charles J., Craig Allen Smith, and Robert E. Denton, Jr. *Persuasion and Social Movements.* Prospect Heights, IL: Waveland Press, 1984.

Wilson, John. *Introduction to Social Movements.* New York: Basic Books, 1973.

Zarefsky, David. "President Johnson's War on Poverty: The Rhetoric of Three 'Establishment' Movements." *Communication Monographs* 44 (November 1977): 245–54.

CONCLUSIONS

"One cannot effectively study leadership in the American democracy," writes political scientist James David Barber, "without searching out how public discourse works" (1988, xi). At the risk of sounding ungrateful for this vote of interdisciplinary confidence, an even stronger statement is in order.

This book has argued that one cannot effectively understand the ebb and flow of political life in America without understanding human communication. Without communication, there are no individual or social identities, no alliances, no laws, no movements, no elections, no deliberation, no adjudication, no ceremonies, no information. In short, without communication there is no community. It is possible to study policies and institutional structures without considering the interpretive dynamics of persons and groups in search of understanding. But why would we want to?

Our view of politics began not with the institution or philosophies but with individual symbol-using *homo sapiens*, each of whom experienced needs and found ways to satisfy them. Among those means were labeling and reasoning, which led inexorably to a tendency to prefer some means and satisfactions over others. Through functional interdependence, the needs became sources of community power, shared symbols became language, reasons became shared rhetorical visions, and preferences became ideologies. Individuals interpreted the world in uniquely personal ways that affected, and were affected by, an interpretive community.

It is people, individually and collectively striving to make the world into an understandable place, who create and use both political and communication processes. Barber alludes to understanding "how public [and presumably private] discourse works," much as Kenneth Burke referred to humans as "symbol-using" creatures. As Burke is often construed to mean "*Symbol*-using", Barber will probably be construed to mean that we need to understand "how *public discourse* works."

The proper focus should be on people as symbol-*using* creatures for whom public and private political discourse *works*. Our underlying human needs influence how we will use political communication, and it is the assessment of our needs that shapes the politically oriented talk that we hear; and the satisfaction of those needs creates the needs we will attempt to satisfy tomorrow. The lack of coherence and fidelity during the Carter years led to the crystal clarity and homespun fidelity of the Reagan years, which contributed to the dumbing-down of the electorate for the 1988 campaign.

In pursuit of this need satisfaction, we have evolved a set of political institutions and practices that work for us, sometimes quite well. Each institution and practice has evolved a unique rule-governed communication system, such that political communication functions in peculiar ways in different arenas, nurturing peculiar interpretive communities. Journalists, candidates, legislators, presidents, judges, diplomats, agitators, and researchers all approach political communication in functionally different, but equally, important ways.

This book has attempted to set forth a communicative view of American politics. We have not considered communication as an intervening variable in government, nor have we jumped from underlying needs to political behavior, nor have we emphasized political speeches and commercials. What we have tried to emphasize is the quest by individual citizens for political understanding and the means they have devised for creating it. As we have so often heard, "Politics is talk." And because things get done through politics, and politics get done through communication, we can profitably study politics as communication.

Reference

Barber, James David. *Politics by Humans: Research on American Leadership.* Durham, NC: Duke University Press, 1988.

Appendix
METHODS FOR STUDYING POLITICAL COMMUNICATION

Every study of political communication employs a research method that influences its evidence and conclusions. One author might speculate about the appeal of a speech; while another might survey audience reaction; and a third might compare drafts of the speech. These approaches are not confined to academic research. When journalists explain election returns, for example, some rely on reporter expertise; others study exit polls; and still others interview strategists. This appendix will clarify the nature of systematic research and explain some of the techniques.

Scholars have long debated the comparative virtues of various research methods. One school thinks that everyone should learn one technique and use it effectively; another argues that different questions demand different methods (Pearce, Cronen, and Harris 1982). People who learn only one method deny themselves the opportunity to tackle a variety of questions, while people who cherish that freedom relinquish some measure of methodological expertise. In either case, the study of communication requires a variety of methods and able people to apply them.

Students of political communication need to understand the fundamentals of rhetorical criticism, content analysis, survey techniques, experimentation, and historical research, whether they actually use them or not. Anyone who relies exclusively on one type of information will miss too much to be considered a good candidate, advisor, scholar, or reporter. Practitioners and general readers, too, need to assess the information they receive from advisors, news reports, and friends. Let us discuss the research process and then explain five basic research methods.

Characteristics of Good Research

Good research is systematic, impartial, thorough, and significant. *Systematic research* is planned and conducted thoughtfully. Skilled researchers know what to study and why, and they avoid interesting material that is marginally relevant. Survey researchers study previous research before formulating their questions, and historians know whose files to examine before traveling to an archive.

Impartial research strives for fairness. In political communication, impartiality means separating your political and intellectual interests. Impartial political research is insightful rather than ideological, perceptive rather than partisan. This is especially important for the practitioner, since biased research distorts conclusions and strategy.

Thorough research follows all leads and considers all possibilities, relying on primary rather than secondary sources. This concern sometimes tempts researchers toward thorough studies of narrow subjects. But *significant research* changes the way readers think about the subject. *Theoretical significance* concerns the conception of communication, while *topical significance* concerns thinking about the event. Research that spurs further research and discussion is called *heuristic.*

Professor Franklin Knower is reputed to have told his research students that any project worth doing cannot be done well, and that any project that can be done well is not worth doing. The escape from this discouraging state of affairs, known as Knower's Ratio, is to undertake the most significant research project that can be done well.

The Research Process

Every research project should be pursued systematically, beginning with a general question and a bibliography. Use encyclopedias, textbooks, newspapers, magazines, and general circulation books for initial orientation and background. Your working bibliography should include well-documented books by credible experts, articles in academic journals like *The Quarterly Journal of Speech* and *Presidential Studies Quarterly,* and government or research institute studies.

The second step is to read the bibliographic entries. You cheat only yourself by reading your good materials carelessly. Be sure that you understand the author's position and its proof. Try to find a point on which the experts' interpretations of their evidence disagree, and refine your research question accordingly.

Third, decide what kind of information you will need to answer your research question and the method most able to produce that information. Do you need data on public reaction or background from a speechwriter? Do you need reflective consideration of message subtleties or a quantitative profile of a set of messages?

Fourth, apply the research method to your question and design a study to answer the research question. Follow the general guidelines in this appendix to select a method and consult one of the many excellent books available for further assistance.

Fifth, execute the study and assess the research question in light of the results. How does the original dispute look in light of your study? Conclude by explaining the new point.

Sixth, write your report. The reader should be able to tell from your study exactly how and why you studied, and concluded, what you did. If not, your report is insufficiently systematic. Most studies can be written with subdivisions for *problem, method, results* and *discussion,* and *conclusions,* although historical and critical studies rarely use these labels. As you write, bear in mind the adage that there is no such thing as "good writing," there is only "good rewriting." Prepare a working draft of your report, and then edit it for excess verbiage, awkward constructions, potential misunderstandings, cliches, and inadequate support. Then edit the revision. Keep revising until your deadline arrives.

This research process is fundamentally the same regardless of method, but the choice of method affects the data collection and analysis. Bowers and Courtright suggest three helpful maxims for researchers (1984):

1. It always takes longer than you think.
2. Anticipate the unanticipated.
3. Do not trust others to do it if you can do it yourself.

Qualitative Research Methods

Qualitative research methods emphasize judgment over measurement and are used to study subtle or illusive phenomena. Although a few qualitative researchers argue that appearances mislead, most simply like to offer their considered judgments without being bound by rigid procedures and tests.

Qualitative research does not use statistics and, frankly, that tempts many novice researchers. It may be easy to undertake qualitative research, but it is especially difficult to do it well. Historians and critics have the burden of proving their arguments without universal yardsticks for verification. That means that they must argue carefully and cautiously, anticipate counterarguments and alternative explanations, and thoroughly document their conclusions. It is wise to consider the responsibilities of qualitative research before undertaking it.

Historical Research

Primary materials are not difficult to obtain. U.S. Government Depository Libraries contain *The Congressional Record, The Weekly Compilation of Presidential Documents, The Department of State Bulletin,* and many other government publications. Special collections in Washington include the Smithsonian Institution National Museum of American History's Political History Division, as well as the Library of Congress. Presidential libraries containing White House central files and personal files include Hoover's in West Branch, Iowa; Franklin Roosevelt's in Hyde Park, New York; Truman's in Independence, Missouri; Eisenhower's in Abilene, Kansas; Kennedy's in Boston; Johnson's at the University of Texas in Austin; Ford's at the University of Michigan in Ann Arbor, and Carter's in Atlanta. The University of Oklahoma has a vast collection of political campaign commercials, Purdue University houses the video archives of the congressional television service C-SPAN, and Vanderbilt University has been videotaping and archiving network news broadcasts for about 20 years. Also of potential interest are New York University's Tamiment Institute Library of radical and socialist causes and Wayne State University's Walter P. Reuther Library of Labor and Urban Affairs, which includes the archives of the United Autoworkers Union. Check your campus library and nearby for special opportunities. Many of these libraries and the National Endowment for the Humanities offer grants to underwrite travel costs for graduate research and, sometimes, for undergraduate projects.

The first step in historical research is to delineate your subject. This means defining the event, the participants, and the period. For example, rather than studying Watergate, focus on the development of the Plumbers Unit, the reasons for the Watergate break-in, press coverage of Watergate, White House strategy planning, development of the impeachment momentum, the developing pressures toward resignation, the granting of the Nixon pardon, or some other aspect of the topic.

Second, identify the primary materials to be studied. These may include transcripts of speeches or hearings, audio or video tapes, personal files and memoranda, government documents, personal memoirs, interviews, or news reports. Normally, the more versions you have the better. A transcript of New York Governor Nelson

Rockefeller's 1964 speech urging the Republican party to condemn the extremism of Communists, Socialists, Klansmen and John Birchers is helpful. But a tape of the address reveals that the convention literally booed Rockefeller off the platform to make way for nominee Goldwater's "extremism is no vice" response. Likewise, minutes of a discussion can usefully balance the participants' accounts.

Third, differentiate public from private sources. Public sources are usually phrased so as to impress an audience, whereas private sources are more task oriented. Anyone's memoirs understandably put the best possible face on failures, but they reveal the figure's preferred version of history and, therefore, permit comparisons with both other memoirs and the private files.

Fourth, take clear notes on index cards about the primary materials. Each card should contain all the bibliographic material needed to identify the source. The most efficient way to do this is to immediately create a citation card for each source (author, title, volume, place of publication, publisher, date of publication, private or public source, library or archive, call number, and library location). Then give each citation card a code (like A–Z). As you write, take your notes; then you can simply jot "A p. 275" or "Z p. 17." Be sure that you put only one point or quotation per card so that they can be rearranged without difficulty. Put some kind of keyword or heading on each card to contextualize it (like "defense of legality" or "Richard III's appearance").

The fifth step is to sort your cards by topics rather than sources. This allows you to peruse related accounts of the same point and to note the differences between private and public accounts. A table will often work better than an outline, as when Watergate events can be sorted out by participants' memoirs.

Sixth, reconstruct the domino chain of historical events by moving through your file and interpreting the available evidence. This will lead to observations like, "all participants wanted 'to do what was right' but they could only agree on 'what would work.'" This reconstructed chain should show points of differentiation and convergence, fill in unknown details, and correct mistakes.

Finally, the conclusion should demonstrate both the changed historical development and its implications. The critical questions concern the spill-over effects of the rewritten history.

Do not rewrite history lightly. The sheer amount of documentation and interpretation required to support a significant historical point is necessarily great. Knower's Ratio strikes again: If you can briskly revise a historical point it probably is insignificant, and if the point is significant you will be unable to convince many people. The key is to balance your project by arguing the most important point that you can support satisfactorily.

Historical research is necessary and important. Rhetorical critics need it to assess the context for addresses and to follow the changes as speeches are drafted and revised. Content analysts need it to assemble innovative samples of messages. But historical research must not be confused with journalism or storytelling. Journalism reports on events from the perspective of a day, or perhaps a month, without a theoretical base. Storytelling recounts interesting, but all too often pointless, anecdotes or quips. Historical research takes a broader time perspective and interprets the stories.

Rhetorical Criticism

Rhetorical criticism illuminates and appraises a persuasive effort. "That was a good speech," "Boy, did he ever blow it," and "Well, Dan, the president didn't really say anything new" constitute only rhetorical commentary. Such commentaries may be worth hearing, but they are not systematic criticism. Criticism is highly personal and depends on the critic's ability to persuade readers. Although rhetorical critics have considerable freedom to improvise, they must be systematic.

Karlyn Kohrs Campbell outlined three yellow-pad steps that generate the kind of evidence needed to write most critical essays (1972). Her steps deserve our attention because they differ from those you would follow instinctively.

First, undertake a *descriptive analysis* of the message(s). The basic task is to describe the tone of the message with specific references to words and phrases. Descriptive analyses look for the message's tone, topic orientation, structure, logic, and strategy. Identify both the apparent purpose and the stated purpose of the message; when they differ, you may be on to something.

Consider also the supporting materials. Does the rhetor use testimony (whose?), statistics (from what source?), analogies (with what?), anecdotes (about what?), or illustrations (of what?). The description of the message should relate the kinds of supporting material used to the purpose and structure of the message.

Describe the self-image, or persona, created by the speaker: is she complex or simple, straightforward or evasive, open-minded or closed-minded, haughty or plain, robust or bland, energetic or calm? Especially when speech writers are involved, the persona may not match what you know of the speaker.

Explicit or implicit references to the audience suggest whether the speaker is approaching an existing or emerging audience, whether they seem united or divided on the subject and the speaker, and whether the audience has any power to modify the exigence. You will later compare these clues to your view of the audience. The best way to hone your descriptive abilities is through practice. After carefully describing the messages, the critic turns to step two.

The second step is a *historical-contextual analysis* of the rhetorical situation. Biographical information about the speaker is important, as is information about the development of the exigence that provoked the speech and the speaker-audience relationship. Consult sociological profiles of the audiences. These data are helpful when appraising the rhetor's adaptation to the audience's interpretive system. The Gallup, Harris, and Roper polls can usually be consulted, as can abstracting services like *Sociological Abstracts* and *Psychological Abstracts.*

Historical-contextual analyses should consider competing arguments and political forces. It is difficult in politics to find either the first word on an issue or the last. Any subject worth studying will have been discussed by other speakers worth hearing.

Analyze the supporting materials identified during step one. Are statistics accurate and valid? Is testimony authoritative and complete? Are analogies and metaphors reasonable? What sorts of available information were not used?

In the third, or *interpretative analysis,* step you adopt a theoretical framework. Draw on the descriptive and contextual analyses to select a critical method that illuminates the rhetorical effort. You can develop a new system or use established theory. The important point is that you must have a coherent framework for analyzing the rhetor's choices.

Campbell suggests choosing a critical system by answering four questions. First, what characteristics of the message should be highlighted? Second, does the speaker suggest a standard for evaluating the work? Third, which critical system will permit emphasis of the features emerging from questions one and two? And finally, which critical systems would be most supportive and most hostile to the speaker's choices? The answers facilitate selection of an appropriate theoretical framework. Three basic critical systems are described by Campbell.

Traditional rationalism, or *neo-Aristotelian criticism,* applies the principles of classical rhetoric to particular messages. It focuses on rational argument and the speaker's adaptation of arguments and evidence to the audience and occasion, the arrangement or structure of the parts of the message, and the appropriateness of the language. It emphasizes truth and the linear development of logical arguments. It is suitable for analyzing discourse that tries to prove a logical proposition, and it is well suited to policy addresses by political leaders. But its emphasis on classical principles gives this method an elitist bias, which makes it more appropriate for polite discourse than movement rhetoric; neither Malcolm X's ghetto-based radicalism nor the Ku Klux Klan's resistance rhetoric epitomizes Aristotle's teachings. Moreover, its emphasis on truth makes it appropriate for validating arguments within a rhetorical vision, but inappropriate for most addresses that try to change the dominant vision.

Traditional rationalism has been in general disfavor since the 1960s because it seems increasingly out of touch with the ways that real people persuade one another. But when used appropriately, traditional rationalism tells us about the appropriateness of a rational message and its choices.

Psychological criticism looks for the message effects. Effects studies are tricky because few social events have only one cause. Avoid the temptation to draw simple conclusions. Whereas neo-Aristotelian criticism appraises the message but avoids explanation of its effects, psychological criticism discusses effects in relation to the internal workings of the message. Effects studies are important for relating significant messages to their historical context, but they are quite difficult to substantiate.

Dramatistic criticism emphasizes symbolic interactionist principles. A purely dramatistic approach explores the speaker's use of language to depict the act, scene, agent, agency and purpose and to change the patterns of identification. This central role of depiction makes it appropriate for the study of protests and other rhetorical efforts to establish a new logical vision. This critical system gives more attention to symbolic patterns, cultural usage, situational truths, ethics, and rhetorical genres than do the other methods; but it does not help the critic understand the message's structure or effects.

Whichever critical system is used, the fourth step is the preparation of a *critical essay* that sheds new light on the rhetorical effort. Judgments of the message should be supported with direct quotations and examples, as well as outside information where appropriate. The introduction and conclusion should clearly explain the theoretical and practical significance of the research.

Quantitative Research Methods

Quantitative research methods assess the probability of differences between observed and expected behaviors, using four basic kinds of data. Either/or categories, like Democrats and Republicans, create *nominal data*, while *ordinal data* indicate rank order. *Interval data* specify equal steps between ranks, and *ratio data* have both equal intervals and an absolute zero point. Nominal, ordinal, interval, and ratio data provide increasingly more information and, therefore, permit increasingly close study and greater precision (Bowers and Courtright 1984). Election surveys may include the following items: "Do you support Candidate A, B, or C?" (nominal); "Rank the candidates in order of your preference" (ordinal); "Is your feeling about Candidate A very positive, generally positive, no opinion, generally negative, very negative?" (interval); or "Rate Candidate A on a 1–10 scale" (ratio). The ratio design permits comparisons that the nominal study does not. Your library has several books that explain the basic statistical tests, and you need not major in computer science to understand them.

The computer printout reports the value of your chosen statistical tests and the *probability values* (*p*). The *p* value represents the number of times per hundred that your results could occur by chance. Therefore, *p* < .01 *means that your result would occur less than once in a hundred times by chance; while p* < .51 means it could happen about half the time; and *p* < .99 means it could happen almost any time. Researchers require that the probability value be smaller than .05 to claim statistical significance.

Quantitative essays should proceed in clearly delineated sections. The first section needs to *explain your research question* in light of pertinent theory and research. The method section should so clearly, completely, and precisely *explain the procedures and tests* that a total stranger could read it and conduct the study. The third section should *present and discuss the statistical results*, complete with appropriate tables, to answer the overall research question. And the conclusions should *tie the results to the basic theoretical material* from the introduction.

Experimentation

Experimentation is a controlled test of cause and effect. Experimenters in the natural sciences deal with atoms, molecules, and particles that are interchangeable (if you've met one hydrogen atom, you've met them all). But people are complex, and that complicates the life of a social scientist. Some political communication questions demand controlled tests. For instance, a campaign advisor might assess candidate image strategies by having representative voters complete a questionnaire before and after viewing campaign commercials.

Experimental research relies on two or more factors that change, called *variables*. The *independent*, or predictor, variable is anything expected to cause a change in the *dependent*, or criterion, variable. Sophisticated experiments use multiple variables. The fundamental experimental research question is, what change in the independent variable is associated with what change in the dependent variable? *Correlational studies* test for the general association between variables like partisanship and voter turnout, but they are unconcerned with causality. *Causal studies* test whether a change in the independent variable is both necessary and sufficient to change the dependent variables. *Regression studies* work backwards to determine which independent variables most efficiently predict known changes in the dependent variables. All experimental designs are variations on these three themes.

The first step in experimentation is to state the fundamental question as an *hypothesis*: an increase in A will be associated with an increase in B; A will cause B, or B is caused by A. An hypothesis is substantiated by available theory and research studies, including those that discount the proposed relationship; it is not a guess.

Second, *operationalize* each variable either by specifying its conditions—"frequent voters" vote 70 percent of the time and "regular voters" over 50 percent of the time—or by specifying its measure— Bush supporters are those who so answer the questionnaire. Considerable care should be given to operationalization. "Highly credible sources," for example, are too often more credible to the experimenter than to the subjects. Avoid personal or arbitrary procedures, like "I know it when I see it," and operationalizations that others will surely challenge, like "Intellectuals are those who have completed grade 9."

Third, *design a study to test your operationalized hypothesis* in a controlled setting. A *pretest/posttest* design (1) measures the dependent variable, (2) exposes subjects to the operationalized predictor variable, and (3) remeasures the dependent variable. A posttest-only design (1) presents the predictor variable and (2) measures the criterion variable. This preserves natural reactions to the predictor but precludes information about the respondents' predispositions.

The design must provide control. An experiment might randomly assign respondents to four news groups (ABC, CBS, NBC, and none) to test the effects of the network watched on political information or attitudes. The control group would minimize the chance that nonnetwork information could account for audience changes. Some researchers control their questionnaires by asking the important questions in multiple ways, while others sanitize the experimental situation to remove extraneous variables. The statistical tests to be used are selected during the design stage, because the design must produce the appropriate data (nominal, ordinal, interval, or ratio) to conduct those tests.

The fourth step is to *secure respondents*. Great strides have been made in the protection of people from psychologically damaging experimental treatments. Most universities require advance approval of research involving human subjects. This clearance protects respondents from questions that are legally incriminating and from physically or psychologically harmful procedures and ensures their privacy and anonymity. Such clearance should pose no serious problem. Check with your professors before experimenting!

Respondents should represent the population you wish to study. This means that most political studies ideally involve more than college students.

Fifth, *administer the experiment* so that all treatments are identical. Typed or taped instructions, similar rooms and seating arrangements, and careful monitoring of distractions are important. Be wary of clever respondents who try to provide what they perceive you to want.

The sixth step is to *analyze the responses*. If the study has been designed carefully, this will be easy, but if you waited until this point to select a statistical test, you will have problems that may require consultation. The statistical tests will lead to the questions of probability and significance. Do not report results that exceed the .05 probability threshold.

The seventh step is to *assess your hypothesis* in light of your statistical results. This means answering the original research question: Was the change in the independent variable associated significantly with the predicted change in the dependent variable? Your data permit you to argue either that your careful study supported the connection or that it did not.

The final step is to *explore your study for "loose boards."* Look for operational errors, design problems, analytical errors, and alternative explanations. Try mightily to find your own oversights and to present alternative explanations that merit further study. Lastly, suggest possibilities for future research.

Experimental research is the most tightly controlled method and the most able to discuss causality. But this very control creates an artificiality that may undercut your efforts: you may have a very tightly controlled study of an unrealistic phenomenon

Survey Research

It is more efficient to seek opinions than to wait for them. *Survey research* is a systematic technique for asking questions and scrutinizing the answers (Hoinville and Jowell 1977). Familiar as we all are with opinion polls results, most people misunderstand the method.

First, *identify the population of respondents* whose opinions you wish to chart. This is critical. Since you probably need not generalize your results to all humans, ask yourself which people matter to this study and which do not. To map reactions to the 1986 tax reform, for example, you would need to reflect all tax brackets; to predict elections, you would need to study eligible and probable voters. You will eventually question a representative sample of the identified population.

Second, *decide how many respondents* you need to generalize to your population. Create a sample large enough to provide people in all the categories that interest you. When some interesting group is underrepresented in a reasonably random sample, *stratify* your sample by specifying the number of respondents per group and locating them. This enables you to weight their responses to approximate the population. Few serious surveys produce less than 100 completed questionnaires, although you might survey your class for practice.

Third, *locate potential respondents*. For television news watchers, for example, you might randomly call telephone numbers during the news shows. Sitting people are more responsive than moving people, since your questions serve as diversions rather than obstacles. For *representative* college students, try registration lines and cafeterias rather than libraries or pool rooms.

Fourth, *decide how to distribute your questionnaire* to your sample. Least productive are mailed surveys which cost about 50 cents each and produce at best a 30 percent response rate. With a 30 percent ratio rate you would need to mail 500 questionnaires to get 150 responses. Thus, the cost of these usable questionnaires would amount to $250 in postage alone. If your project requires mailed questionnaires, you might investigate possible funding from interested student groups. Personally distributed questionnaires are more efficient because you and your friends wait for the completed questionnaire and pay nothing for postage; you could pay several friends for less than the $250. Shopping malls, street corners, campus crossroads, post offices, and grocery stores provide reasonably good cross-sections of America, but check to avoid violating any ordinances or procedures. If a purely campus survey is appropriate, see if a professor can distribute questionnaires in class. Let the professor choose the time and adjust to it: teaching the class takes priority over questionnaires!

Fifth, *formulate your questions.* You are now able to adapt your language and phrasing to your sample, setting, and distribution needs. List everything you might want to know about the respondents and your subject. Then, transform each item into three or four different questions, since there are several ways to ask any question ("Do you plan to vote?" "Do you vote always, usually, sometimes, rarely, never?" or "When did you last vote?").

Closed-ended questions permit direct comparisons but restrict answers. Open-ended questions allow respondents to elaborate their positions but complicate direct comparisons. Edit to eliminate long and confusing questions, unfamiliar language or expressions, and tricky, leading, or biased questions. Murphy's Law implies that if respondents can misunderstand a question, they will. Beat them to it by trying to misunderstand, and fix the questions. Select the fewest number of questions appropriate to your respondents and phrase them in clear language and devise a format that can cover your needs.

Sixth, *structure the questionnaire.* Begin with the most answerable questions. Since demographic questions can arouse defensiveness, it is best to save age, gender, party, education, income, and the like for last. Instead, start by asking for general information about your topic, such as "Have you heard that there is a vacancy on the Supreme Court?" or "Have you been following the Iran-Contra hearings daily, every few days, weekly, hardly at all, never, what hearings?" This technique establishes a relationship between interviewer and interviewee and qualifies your respondents. For example, in 1978, few opponents of the Panama Canal "giveaway" treaties could correctly answer Gallup's factual questions, but they were, nevertheless, confident and convinced voters. By moving from closed-ended opinion questions to truly open-ended questions you can lead respondents from information to structured choices and then to conversation before seeking personal information.

Seventh, *distribute and collect the questionnaires.* Printed questionnaires should be neat, legible, and at least *look* easy to complete. Telephone questionnaires should be presented slowly, audibly, and politely, since many people will suspect a sales pitch. Always be friendly and accommodating, even when respondents are not. Keep track of the dates, times, and locations of distribution for subsequent reference.

Eighth, *tabulate and analyze your results.* This can be accomplished with a computer spreadsheet program that allows you to quickly enter responses into a data base. The data base can be quickly and easily transformed to analyze your results. Without a computer, you can use a master copy of the questionnaire to tabulate the number and percentage of responses to each answer, and you can even keep separate lists for each group of respondents.

Surveys are useful for systematically sampling the expressed opinions of a variety of people. They are better than guessing what people think or want, and systematic questioning permits the comparison of answers over time. But surveys are nevertheless self-report data, subject to socially acceptable, "half-baked," and self-serving answers that mislead.

Because surveys estimate the population's opinions from a representative sample, they entail a margin of error. Most published polls have a plus/minus 5-percent margin, so that "Jones 48 percent, Wilson 43 percent" actually means "Jones 43–53 percent, Wilson 38–48 percent." To increase precision, ask more people. But always interpret survey results within the margin of error.

Content Analysis

Content analysis is a method for finding patterns in the observable features of a broad sample of messages (Hofstetter 1981; Holsti 1969; Krippendorff 1980). It is more systematic than rhetorical criticism because it uses exacting statistical tests, but it is less sensitive than criticism to subtle nuances. Essentially, content analysis is like straightening a closet; you find some boxes, label them, and sort selected items into them.

First, *select the sample of messages* to be studied. The research question defines the universe of messages: network newscasts about the economy, social movement slogans, or gubernatorial campaign commercials. But as Knower's Ratio suggests, it is impractical to study so many messages. Therefore, select a representative sample of such messages. A systematic approach ensures a representative sample, so that your conclusions can be generalized to the universe.

Second, *develop a set of categories*. These categories will be the boxes into which you sort message features. You may wish to use established typologies like an inventory of cultural values or types of supporting materials, or you may wish to devise your own set. In either case, the categories must be justified and explained. Include an "other" category, which can be scrutinized for additional categories later.

The third step is to *define the coding units*. If the categories serve as closet boxes, the coding units are the items to be sorted. This is trickier than it might seem. Some research questions require you to categorize whole speeches; some look for arguments or themes within speeches; and others consider individual words. You must make, and justify, the choice. You must also decide whether to count items more than once: Was President Reagan's "Lebanon and Grenada" speech about the Middle East or Central America?

Fourth, *find every instance of the coding unit and assign each to its appropriate category.* This is a simple filtering process. Sometimes you can color code by highlighting the coding units with colored markers. For whole speeches, you might file the transcripts. Several people familiar with your technique should simultaneously code the same materials so that you can directly compare their decisions. Their consistency, called *intercoder reliability,* should be reported (Holsti 1969).

Fifth, *statistically test the data* generated in step four and assess the results. What do the tests and *p* values say about the research question? Do the data square with the theory? What specific verbalizations illustrate your findings?

Content analysis is useful when you want to find patterns in a large body of messages. Do Democratic and Republican campaign commercials use similar or different themes? Do protest songs from different eras or movements address similar or different concerns? Do presidential addresses reflect personal, partisan, temporal, or cultural values? These questions can best be answered through content analysis, because the statistical analysis of representative samples permits direct and controlled comparisons of observed and expected patterns.

Like rhetorical criticism, content analysis enables us to study naturally occurring messages. It is more systematic than criticism but requires more judgments than does experimentation. It can identify patterns in a sample of messages, but it cannot tell you why those patterns occurred.

Conclusions

Any study employs a method, and the chosen method affects the evidence and conclusions. This is important to researchers and to students of research, but in a larger sense it is important to anyone who wishes to be a careful consumer of political information.

Any research project that you undertake should satisfy the four criteria of good research, follow the general steps of the fundamental research process, and competently use an accepted research method appropriate to your research question. It is also important to remember that research is necessarily inconclusive, since many minds employing multiple methods produce conflicting conclusions. Thrive on it! When people challenge your research it means they find it sufficiently provocative to digest. If you can answer their questions, do so by polishing your essay. If you cannot directly answer their challenge, design and conduct a new study. But remember, you cannot convince everyone.

References

Bowers, John Waite, and John A. Courtright. *Communication Research Methods.* Glenview, IL: Scott, Foresman, 1984.

Campbell, Karlyn Kohrs. *Critiques of Contemporary Rhetoric.* Belmont, CA: Wadsworth, 1972.

Hoinville, Gerald, Roger Jowell, and associates. *Survey Research Practice.* London: Heinemann, 1977.

Hofstetter, C. Richard. "Content Analysis." In *The Handbook of Political Communication,* edited by Dan Nimmo and Keith Sanders, 529–60. Beverly Hills: Sage, 1981.

Holsti, Ole R. *Content Analysis for the Social Sciences and Humanities.* Reading, MA: Addison-Wesley, 1969.

Krippendorff, Klaus. *Content Analysis: An Introduction to its Methodology.* Beverly Hills, Sage, 1980.

Mohrmann, Gerald P., Charles J. Stewart, and Donovan Ochs, eds. *Explorations in Rhetorical Criticism.* University Park: Pennsylvania State University Press, 1973.

Pearce, W. Barnett, Vernon E. Cronen, and Linda M. Harris. "Methodological Considerations in Building Human Communication Theory." In *Human Communication Theory: Comparative Essays,* edited by Frank X. Dance, 1–41. New York: Harper and Row, 1982.

Williams, Frederick. *Reasoning with Statistics,* 2d ed. Atlanta: Holt, Rinehart and Winston, 1979.

Wimmer, Roger D., and Joseph R. Dominick. *Mass Media Research: An Introduction,* 2d ed. Belmont, CA: Wadsworth, 1987.

INDEX

level

Private   Motivating)   Symbolizing)   Preferencing)   reasoning)

public
(relationships)
community   power   language   ideology   logic
(fantasy theme)

↓

Politics
(communities
struggle for
power)